WHITMAN

An Interpretation in Narrative

WHITMAN

Portrait Bust in Clay by Edmond T. Quinn
Courtesy of the Sculptor

WHITMAN

An Interpretation in Narrative

BY EMORY HOLLOWAY

Illustrated with portraits and facsimiles
of Whitman's letters and diaries

With New, Second Preface by the Author

BIBLO and TANNEN
NEW YORK
1969

Printed in U.S.A. by
NOBLE OFFSET PRINTERS, INC.
NEW YORK 3, N. Y.

TO

E. B. H.

*Who has shown this book more kindness
than it deserves.*

AVE ATQUE VALE

An individual is as superb as a nation when he has the qualities that make a superb nation.

WALT WHITMAN, IN 1855.

You want to know in a word the sum total of my life philosophy as I have tried to live it and as I have tried to put it in my book. I will tell you. It is only the closest student who would find it in my works. . . . The sum total of my view of life has always been to humbly accept and thank God for whatever inspiration toward good may come in this rough world of ours and, as far as may be, to cut loose from and put the bad behind always and always.

WALT WHITMAN, IN 1891.

PREFACE

Each year Walt Whitman looms larger on the literary horizon of America. In 1915 he received ten votes for the Hall of Fame; in 1920, twenty; in 1925, forty-four, or almost a majority of the electors. In the last-named year was started the first movement to erect a statue to the poet, in New York City. At the same time the New York Public Library opened in its Main Exhibition Room a great display of Whitmaniana. Forty cases were crammed with Whitman editions, manuscripts, photographs, works of art, personalia, and criticism. Oil paintings, busts, plaques, medals, and etchings added testimony that the "good gray poet's" striking individuality had caught the eye of the artist as well as that of the reader and the maker of books. The exhibition was one to impress even the casual observer with the fact that, for better or worse, here was a man who had left his mark upon time. The translations from his writings alone numbered some twenty-five volumes, marking his influence as it has spread, from France, Germany, Italy, and Denmark, to South America and Japan. But the sixty volumes of biography and criticism showed that, like many a prophet and innovator, he has been the storm center of controversies, some of which bear only accidental relations to the man himself. And though his genius is today generally recognized by the intelligent, many opinions obtain as to his personal character, his philosophic teachings, his artistic importance. Thoreau, Moncure Conway, Dr. Richard Maurice Bucke, and John Burroughs found in Whitman something of the demi-god. Stevenson and John Addington Symonds discovered in him a sadly needed tonic for the anæmia of too much civilization. Many modern poets, sculptors, and painters found in him an inspiring crusader of art. Emerson, the first to praise him, at once greeted him "at the beginning of a great career." Yet there have been those who could describe him as neither poet nor philosopher, while others have sought to show that his life was immoral and his mentality abnormal.

Such a life cannot be neglected, though to the biographer it may seem to bristle with contradictions. Here certainly is no subject to be simplified by a theory, no ideal to be emphasized by discreet silence. He himself would not have it so.

> Do I contradict myself?
> Very well, then, I contradict myself,
> I am large, I contain multitudes.

We may find, indeed, that the contradiction is more fundamental than he realized, that it was often the undisciplined emotionalism of the child rather than the complex cerebration of the normal adult; but even so, youth is immortal and knows itself to be, and if in Whitman's form there be not always that perfection which makes art of so long life, there is a compensating vitality which provokes in the reader something more than ordinary æsthetic pleasure, or literary dislike. In another sense, the "multitudes" which he includes are the hosts of humanity in the America of the Nineteenth Century. Being in a curious sense a composite of our several cultures, a blend, as the future American must be, of more than one race, Whitman reminds every man a little of himself; yet no class in America seems to perceive in him the American. Perhaps he makes too concrete our crudity, our inexperience, our brag. And, possibly the more readily for that very reason, he is accepted by other countries as typical of us all. In any case, he is a literary figure almost unique in his strange blending of oriental and occidental influences, his absorbing of a country as yet ununified in its temper and its ambition, his equal relish for the classical and the romantic, his realism and his mystic idealism, his childish naïveté and his profound and far-seeing faith. But if this phenomenon be a matter of interest, there is inspiration in the demonstration his life gives of the opportunity enjoyed by a man with no advantages other

than his character and his talent, to rise in a democracy to a position of honor and influence.

So much new light has been thrown upon the life and writings
of Whitman since the last biography was published that a new
telling of his story seems appropriate. Perhaps there will always be a new one as age after age interprets him after its will
or need. And doubtless the personal equation of the writer enters into the present story also. But at least I have attempted
to paint a faithful picture of the man, wherever possible in his
own words. Nothing has been included merely for its intrinsic
interest, nothing excluded because it lacked such interest. If the
book be readable it must be because it provokes the reader to traverse with sympathy, though not without caution, the life events
of this great but human poet. Yet I have abbreviated the narrative by picking it up only where it has character, and where the
abundance of records makes it possible, without invention, to tell
an imaginative story. And I have refrained from employing
the man as a mere pedestal for his book, or from telling the story
of that book's now world-wide influence except insofar as it affected his personal life. So greatly has his fame spread since
his death in 1892 that not to make this distinction would mar
the symmetry of my plan. Indeed, the story of the book deserves a volume of its own, though I myself have no intention
of attempting to write it.

I have had two main purposes in writing this book. First, I
have tried, through thirteen years of study and research, to find
the necessary facts and the proper point of view for such a picture of Whitman as would remove him from the field of fruitless
controversy, that all that is noble in his poetry and in his example might begin to function in a larger realm than academic and
artistic circles. Second, I have tried to present that picture in a
manner acceptable to the general reader who, for whatever reason, as yet knows nothing of Whitman, rather than for the
scholar already versed in Whitman literature. The latter will
accordingly find, as in any new Whitman biography he must,
things he has seen before, though perhaps here displayed in a

new light. I have not delayed the narrative to cite evidence or authority, even when fuller knowledge has caused me to alter some of my previously published conclusions about Whitman. Most of that evidence can be found in my two volumes, "The Uncollected Poetry and Prose of Walt Whitman." Here it will be sufficient to add that in this study I have included nothing which is not, as I believe, provable fact or a logical deduction from such facts.

In addition to all those who lent assistance in my earlier Whitman publications, I wish to thank Messrs. Doubleday, Page and Company for permission to reprint the poem on pp. 314–15, of which they hold the copyright; Professor Bliss Perry and Messrs. Houghton, Mifflin and Company for permission to quote from a manuscript in the former's most helpful biography; Mr. Louis I. Haber and the New York *Evening Post* for permission to use the letter given on pp. 200–5; and the owners of the various pictures and manuscripts used as illustrations, whose names will be found in the List of Illustrations.

E. H.

Brooklyn, January 1, 1926

SECOND PREFACE

The opportunity to reissue this study forty-three years after its first appearance is gratifying to me, not only for the obvious reasons but also because it provides my first opportunity to correct certain errata and happens to conincide with the sesquicentennial of the poet's birth. I had hoped that my first Whitman volumes would appear during his centennial year, 1919, but they were delayed by World War I. This biography was written when that conflict was fresh in mind. Research since that period has greatly enlarged our knowledge of the poet's life and multiplied the interpretations of this factual information.

When, fifteen years ago, I retired from teaching I found leisure to rewrite this book, enlarging the text and supplying much detailed documentation in the hope of rendering it useful to the serious student as well as to the general reader for whom it had originally been intended. The result was two large volumes which proved so expensive to publish that, after a few years of frustration, I despaired of tempting a publisher. Thereupon I extracted and reshaped what I considered the most important of the new contributions and published them in a more manageable volume, *Free and Lonesome Heart*. In it I was primarily concerned with the problem of Whitman's emotional development. Then the two-volume manuscript biography was bound and presented to the New York Public Library, where it can be seen in the Berg Collection. Since it is there available to any student who may be interested in it, I am content to see the original text reappear with its limitations intact, as they must be in any photographic reproduction.

There would be no demand now for a new edition had not Whitman's *Leaves of Grass* demonstrated a viability only a few could foresee at the time of his death in 1892. In 1950 an entire volume was published tracing his influence in America since his death and other studies have examined his growing reputation elsewhere. A large number of editions and translations of his poetry have been designed to suit every taste and every purse. The attention he has won in the scholarly world is perhaps most strikingly attested by the *Collected Writings* currently being published by the New York University Press. To date seven large and handsome volumes have appeared, two more are expected by the sesquicentennial date, with perhaps four or five to follow within a year or two. No other American poet can boast a more scholarly or imposing monument. Last season some 14,000 visitors signed the register at the Whitman Birthplace, coming from forty-four states and a great many foreign countries. Today Le Monde salutes him as he saluted it over a century ago.

There are a number of reasons for such perennial appeal, such persistent topical appositeness. Most of those who respond favorably to the challenge he presents are impressed by the largeness of his view and his warm humanitarianism; yet each reacts in his own way, so that a stereotypic or orthodox image of Whitman is not easily formed, such as often removes a book from the company of contemporary authors and assigns it to a critical pigeonhole. This poet stimulates each reader to become as self-reliant and as self-contented in the presence of other men and of nature as is the poet himself. Such an appeal encounters few barriers of time or place. The "Song of the Open Road," commemorated in Jo Davidson's heroic statue, not only captures the American spirit of freedom but is typical of the poet's purpose and method. He indicates direction not destination, offers encouragement not discipline, a brave example not vicarious experience. No reader is diminished by reading Whitman, for to read him on one's knees is to misapprehend both the man and his poetic purpose. The great companions, the great thinkers, the great friends of mankind interfere neither with each other nor with the tenderfoot essaying a first adventure on the Open Road. Whitman would see "the littleness of man made great."

> The mechanics take him for a mechanic,
> And the soldiers suppose him to be a
> soldier, and the sailors that he has
> follow'd the sea,

And the authors take him for an author,
    and the artists for an artist,
And the laborers perceive that he could
    labor with them and love them,
No matter what the work is, that he is
    the one to follow it or has follow'd it,
No matter what the nation, that he might
    find his brothers and sisters there.

Another explanation of Whitman's enduring power lies in his paradoxical blending of conservative and radical themes and attitudes. Critics at certain periods have emphasized one side of his thought, at other times another; but neither is the true Whitman. Is Nature conservative or progressive? For Nature is his muse. It is easy to prepare a brief for either of these interpretations of his message. He advocated and exemplified change—in education, in literary and other arts, in politics, in ethics, in religion, in human relations. Yet he did not desire changes so sudden and violent that people, with their built-in time clocks and ingrained habits, could not keep abreast of them. For instance, in Reconstruction days he did not approve of giving the recently emancipated and ignorant Negroes the vote. On this issue he quarreled with his Abolitionist friend O'Connor; not that he opposed educating the ex-slave and admitting him to a franchise then denied to all women, but he thought an uneducated and uninformed electorate no sure guarantee of the democratic process as envisaged by the founding fathers. "Powerful, uneducated persons" he had always championed, for his beloved mother was one of them; but their power must come, not from uniting with others in noisy and manipulated groups, but from individual integrity and self-reliance. During Whitman's lifetime the feeling was strong that the future was America's special province, and only a philosophy which makes provision for constant change could serve such a dream. This is why the poet, though himself the product of a particular time and place, continues to have relevance and to provide inspiration. Even in non-democratic countries like Russia he has long been circulated, a translation for younger readers being now in preparation. (The orthodox communist critics naturally emphasize his celebration of "humanity moving in vast masses" rather than his "simple, separate person.")

In his first edition the poet affirmed:

> My foothold is tenon'd and mortis'd in granite
> And I know the amplitude of time.

The passage may have personal reference but more significantly it is the Cosmic Ego that speaks. The lines agree with his more explicit statements on human evolution and Hegelian philosophy. The life of which this son of the nineteenth century was a minute part he viewed in terms of its long foreground and its indeterminate future. The "granite" on which he finds so firm a base is not only the obvious present with its stable institutions, its social mores and mental attitudes, but also the immutable laws which are forever promoting change. He feels his feet securely planted on an unchanging past, on lessons gleaned by thoughtful men from human history, from astronomy, from geology—ideas which alter little except in their application. By taking such a long view of human amelioration, while abandoning the temporary and partial reforms which had engaged the energies of his youth, he, like his symbolical pioneers, marches in step with movements he cannot even clearly define. In this way he speaks for the future as well as the present and feels that he can take his due rewards hundreds, even thousands, of years hence, as prophets and creative innovators have always done. "The prescient poet," he says, "sees the solid and beautiful forms of the future where there are now no solid forms." His poetry, like his Brooklyn ferry, links generation with generation.

To state the matter more broadly, I should credit Whitman's impact upon an ever larger number of readers to what may be called his sphericity, his roundedness, his stable center of gravity. Whichever way he turns he never loses his equilibrium. There are so many sides to his personality, his thought, his sympathy, that each helps to modulate and counterbalance the others. A native of the countryside, he was equally at home in the city; born of middle class parents, he learned to walk on equal terms with transcendental literati, Tammany politicians, Brooklyn poets, artists, preachers and day laborers as later with the soldiers of both Civil War armies; he had scant formal schooling, yet Arnold Bennett called him one of the world's great teachers; trained as a realistic if sometimes sentimental journalist, he wrote much mystical verse; if he dreamed of the future, his standards of value derived largely from tradition; fascinated by science, he nevertheless looked upon his poetic mission as essentially religious—that of ennobling the spirit of modern man. He combined the child's capacity for wonder with a wisdom to be garnered only from experience, observation and contemplation. "His love above all love has leisure and expanse—he leaves room ahead of himself," as he declared in his first preface. Embracing in unusual measure the natures of both woman and man, he could attract both as few writers have done. He was not a universal genius like Leonardo da Vinci but he came near to being a universal man. Even his optimism was less the flower of his constitution or the product of a received faith than it was his reaction to a pessimism he knew well how to document.

> Roaming in thought over the Universe,
> I saw the little that is Good steadily
> hastening toward immortality,
> And the vast all that is call'd Evil I
> saw hastening to become lost and dead.

He taught himself to live with the evil as well as the good he found in himself, avowing that he would be the poet of both. A many-sided paradox himself in a paradoxical land and age, he never surrendered his "identity"; "When shows break up, what but One's-Self is sure?"

Such confident individualism is particularly relevant to contemporary America. When Whitman said of the great poet that by his "steady faith" he withholds a time that is "straying toward infidelity and confections and persiflage," he was thinking more of bewildered individuals than of men in groups. A few million people had undertaken to conquer a vast and all but uninhabited continent through their individual initiative, courage and self-reliance; but their descendants found that land so thickly populated and so little dependent on small farms for their food supply that three out of four families moved into already crowded cities. Naturally there was a problem of adjustment. How can a race of independent and individualistic laborers or small business men accommodate themselves to urban ghettoes, rabbit warrens of high rise apartments and suffocating systems of transportation without losing more or less of their sense of personal identity? And if division of labor is to mean the division of the laborer as well, then indeed "the world is too much with us." When the city dweller begins to feel that he is only a fraction of massed humanity engaged in cooperative labors and cooperative thinking, he is tempted to doubt his personal importance if not his unique existence. To all such Whitman offers his assurance: "An individual is as superb as a nation when he has the qualities that make a superb nation." Of course it is only through cooperation in peace or war that the great tasks of the modern world are to be performed; yet Whitman is a wholesome reminder that no chain is stronger than its individual links.

Finally, when Whitman freed his verse from traditional patterns of rhyme, meter and stanza, he made it flexible and therefore adaptable to many kinds of content; and he did this without losing his power to express emotion and to provoke thought and imagination. This too was a step toward the future, however one rates its effect on later experimentation in the myriad forms of modern verse. He said that the great poet should be the "august master of beauty." It would be exaggeration to claim that in this respect all or even most of his poems evidence such greatness; nevertheless many of his poems do exhibit such mastery, and to have left these "original examples" is not the least of his passports to posterity.

E. H.

Brooklyn, Spring, 1969

ERRATA

CONTENTS

CONTENTS

ILLUSTRATIONS

The medallion on the side of the cover is reproduced from the Alexander Finta medal designed for the Authors Club Memorial Fund, and is used with the permission of the sculptor and the Club.

BOOK I

A JOURNALIST IN BROOKLYN

WHEN, in January, 1846, the Brooklyn *Daily Eagle* lost by death its editor, the fact was of some consequence to the paper but of much more to its new pilot, Walter Whitman. For though, at the age of twenty-seven, he had given no promise of genius, yet he was destined to go far; and it was as editor of the *Eagle* that he began to think of himself in connection with the unique rôle he was to play in the history of his country. To him it appeared, it is true, only as a welcome opportunity to realize his life ambition as a journalist. Leaving at the age of twelve a school in which he was learning little, he soon had gravitated to the local printing offices, first as devil and then as compositor, but always with his eye upon the editorial sanctum. At twenty, after teaching a few country schools on his native Long Island, he had started a weekly newspaper at Huntington. But his fondness for basking in the sunlight or for floating languidly in the waters of the bay had occasioned such an irregular delivery of his papers that before the end of the year a more conventional and dependable editor had come to take his place. Since that time he had been trying his hand at many things—dabbling in politics, teaching school, writing sentimental prose and verse for the magazines, devoting a dime melodrama to the Washingtonian crusade against intemperance, working as compositor or editor on now forgotten newspapers in New York. At the moment he was writing a little each week for the Brooklyn *Star,* whose lack of enterprise he despised, and for this he was being paid four or five dollars a week.

If in his record there was little save party regularity to recommend him to the Democratic bosses who controlled the *Eagle,* started a few years before as a campaign sheet, there was still less in his training or his social position in the community. His almost complete lack of schooling betrayed him into many slips in his grammar and confirmed him in many obtrusive mannerisms. He had known no discipline except that of the printing office; and while many men of letters have come from that school with sharp eyes and awakened sympathies, it is, after all, a training in which interest counts more than accuracy, feeling more than form. In a sense, the city itself had been his chief teacher, for he went everywhere, enjoying the romance of a young world with undiscriminating enthusiasm. He also read widely, but without much plan. At home he found no library, for his parents were not educated either.

Walter Whitman, senior, was a carpenter, though when Walt was born, he had been living on an excellent farm inherited from more successful ancestors. He was a reliable workman and an honest man; but as he was not shrewd in business, his large family often knew the pinch of poverty, and still oftener lived in the shadow of a mortgage. Of course such a parent could impart to his children no more sense of mastery than he had himself, which was small indeed. They grew up according to their varying natures, acquiring some family affection but very little sense of family solidarity. In a day when religion was itself a discipline in respectability, the Whitman home knew no family worship. No wonder that for an imaginative boy the city would have to serve both as school and as home.

From his father Walt inherited English traits, the line running back to an early New England Puritan, which made him peculiarly responsive to the transcendental and reformatory sentimentality characteristic of his day. Equally important to him was the counterpoise which he owed to the healthy this-worldliness of his devoted Dutch mother. She was the heart of the family, and to her Walt was most strongly attached. But the Whitmans, though honest and respectable, were nobodies in the community when it came to lending prestige to their son, or to his new paper.

Yet in Whitman himself there was a large friendliness, a sanity

of outlook, an inflexible determination, that invited trust.
Physically he was above the average. His six feet of height,
his two hundred pounds of weight, his large but shapely hands,
his deep rich voice, and his untrimmed beard gave him the appearance of an athlete. Yet when he disrobed for his daily
swim at Gray's Salt Water Baths, at the foot of Fulton Street,
he disclosed skin as pink as a baby's, as tender as a woman's.
And in his mental make-up there was to appear the same persistent paradox. With courage and vigor such as the 1840's associated only with masculine minds, he yet had a sentimentality, a
tenderness, as commonly associated with feminine hearts. One
is not surprised to find in him, therefore, a strange blending of
politics and religion. His first tutor in the printing craft was an
old man who had many stories to tell of Revolutionary heroes.
By chance Whitman himself had been kissed, as a lad of six, by
Lafayette, on the occasion of the latter's visit to Brooklyn in
1825. In religion he took more after his mother's family, who
were Quakers, though he had attended regular Sunday schools
and Methodist revivals. Never a member of the church, he
nevertheless encouraged others to go to church—especially the
churches which retained a measure of primitive democratic simplicity. Pride and formalism he detested with the self-
righteousness of the social inferior. As we shall see, this blending of religion and patriotism ultimately gave direction and form
to his mission in life.

An editor with such qualities and antecedents was a risk for
a party paper, beyond doubt. But the *Eagle* had little to lose.
In its few years of existence it had developed but a small cir-
culation. Its office force consisted of only five or six persons,
including the proprietor, Isaac Van Anden, and the devil, Will
Sutton. The first and the last of its four pages were devoted to
advertising and legal notices, as was part of the third page. On
the second page editorials and news stories jostled each other,
as did communications and "the latest intelligence from Europe"
—later, that is, by twenty-seven days than it was in London.
This page was a mental transcript of the mind of the man who

must be editor, reporter, dramatic critic and book-reviewer all in one.

The work was congenial to Whitman, the pay good, and the future anything he could make it. Before long the paper began to take on new life. More space was given to reading matter, excerpts were liberally reprinted from the books the editor was reading, for the pious a column of "Sabbath reading" was run on Saturdays, and the paper was gradually made the organ, not so much of a party—except when an election impended—as of a personality. Van Anden, though sometimes irritated by his editor's irregular hours, exerted himself to make the most of the new order of things. One day, when new type had been bought for the *Eagle*, Whitman, taking his readers into his confidence, wrote an editorial to urge trial subscriptions, and incidentally to describe the relation he wished to establish with his public.

"There is a curious kind of sympathy (haven't you ever thought of it before?) that arises in the mind of the newspaper conductor with the public he serves. He gets to love them. Daily communion creates a sort of brotherhood and sisterhood between the two parties. As for us, we like this. We like it better than the more 'dignified' part of editorial labors—the grave political disquisition, the contests of faction, and so on. And we want as many readers of the *Brooklyn Eagle*—even unto the half of Long Island—as possible, that we may increase the number of these friends. For are not those who listen to us friends?—Perhaps no office requires a greater union of rare qualities than that of a *true editor*. No wonder, then, that so few come under that flattering title! No wonder that we are all derelict, in some particular! In general information, an editor should be complete, particularly with that relating to his own country. He should have a fluent style: elaborate finish we do not think requisite in daily writing. His articles had far better be earnest and terse than polished; they should ever smack of being uttered on the spur of the moment, like political

WALTER WHITMAN, SENIOR   LOUISA VAN VELSOR WHITMAN

WHITMAN'S PARENTS

oratory.. . . . An editor needs, withal, a sharp eye, to discrimi-
nate the good from the immense mass of unreal stuff floating
on all sides of him—and always bearing the counterfeit present-
ment of the real. . . .

"With all and any drawbacks, however, much good can always
be done, with such a potent influence as a well circulated newspaper.   To wield that influence, is a great responsibility.   There
are numerous noble reforms that have yet to be pressed upon
the world.   People are to be schooled, in opposition perhaps
to their long established ways of thought.—In Politics, too, the
field of improvement is wide enough yet; the harvest is large,
and waiting to be reaped—and each paper, however humble, may
do good in the ranks.   Nor is it a mere monotonous writer after
old fashions that can achieve the good we speak of. . . ."

Editing a paper was thus a form of democratic statesman-
ship.   With Whitman patriotism was a sort of religion, and he
conceived of it as essentially a new religion.   It had glamour,
it inspired, it involved responsibilities; in a word, it made life
at once serious and romantic.   In this he shared a feeling common in his day.   The young country was so loosely held together, was so hetereogenous in its varied provincialisms, was
so conscious of the experimental nature of its government, that
it felt a natural need to stress the more what unifying memories
and ideals it had.   The Fourth of July, for instance, was more
than a patriotic gesture; it had the value of a sacrament.

For weeks Whitman had been urging a proper observance of
Independence Day.   When it arrived he found that rain had
sadly thinned the procession.   Yet he waded through the mud in
the ardor of an enthusiast, saying to all whom he recognized, "A
fine day!"   He could not afford to admit defeat at the hands of
the weather, for it was, in a way, his own show.   He had vol-
unteered to write an ode to be sung to the tune of "The Star
Spangled Banner," and he thought it not the worst of his efforts
so far.

O, God of Columbia!   O, Shield of the Free!
More grateful to you than the fames of old story,

Must the blood-bedewed soil, the red battle-ground, be
Where our fore-fathers championed America's glory!
Then how priceless the worth of the sanctified earth
We are standing on now. Lo! the slopes of its girth
Where the martyrs were buried: Nor prayers, tears, or stones
Mark their crumpled-in coffins, their white holy bones.

And shall not the years, as they sweep o'er and o'er,
Shall they not, even *here,* bring the children of ages—
To exult as their fathers exulted before,
In the freedom achieved by our ancestral sages?
And the prayer rise to heaven, with pure gratitude given,
And the sky by the thunder of cannon be riven?
Yea! Yea! let the answer responsively roll
The echo that starts from the patriot's soul.

Decidedly it was not a good song, even when judged by the conventional poetic standards of his day. Yet the emotion it attempted to give voice was genuine. For Whitman had personal links with Fort Greene, the spot he celebrated, and, largely through his efforts in the *Eagle,* it was a little later converted into a public park. His great-uncle had fallen in the Battle of Brooklyn, and Major Brush, a maternal ancestor, had perished in an English prison. Of the prison-ship martyrs, to whose uncared-for remains he alludes in the ode, he could speak temperately no more than could Philip Freneau. His uncles had been in camp near by during the last war with England. To Whitman it was sacred ground—if only because Washington had trod upon it.

The vociferous celebration of the Fourth of July emphasized the national tendency to glorify liberty, rather than equality or fraternity. Whitman had read his Rousseau and had some knowledge of the tyrannical conditions in Europe which made the *Contrat Social* so welcome a polemic. His patriotism began in his reverence for Revolutionary heroes—already becoming legendary saints in fiction, in drama, and in political oratory— heroes whose heroism consisted in the fact that they had, at cost to themselves, won for the colonists the right henceforth to do as they pleased. But what, specifically, did Whitman wish the young country freed *from?* For one thing, from class rule. And in this aspiration the young editor voiced not only the *Zeitgeist* but also a personal need. His political religion, like every religion that grows, sought to free the worshipper from his but half-realized limitations through his faith. No one could have found fault with the opinion of Benjamin Halleck, Whitman's schoolteacher, that the boy would never amount to anything. Without family prestige, without education, without regular habits or a systematic mind, with dogged determination to have his way rather than steadiness of purpose—how far could one hope to go in an aristocracy? But in a democracy he thought it must be different.

He being a "strict constructionist," the conception of government held by the young editor was Emerson's—that the best government is that which governs least. The government, he said, should "make no more laws than those useful for preventing a man or body of men from infringing on the rights of other men." Since the function of the federal government was to do this for the states, the Union must be preserved at all costs, lest in its dissolution sections of the country revert to aristocracy and injustice. When one day the New York *Sun,* expressing the sentiment of the South, declared, "Our government is a union of free states, and not a consolidation of states," Whitman was quick to feel the possibility of civil war. With uncommon courage for a Democratic paper, the *Eagle* took issue with its New York contemporary:

"The worst of such insidious articles as the *Sun's* is that they depress the idea of the sacredness of the bond of union of these states. That bond is the foundation of incomparably the highest political blessings enjoyed in the world! And the position of things at present demands that its sacredness should be recognized by every and all American citizens—however they may differ on points of doctrine or abstract rights."

Yet to maintain his party's position on the question of the

supremacy of local self-government he was willing to play hands off, so far as the national government was concerned, even in the matter of an institution so inimical to his theory of democratic equality as was slavery in the South. "With the present slave states," he counseled his readers, "no human being any where out from themselves has the least shadow of a right to interfere!" When, however, it came to the extension of slavery into the free lands of the West, he was more and more outspoken; that touched the national life both in principle and in fact.

It was not strange that the indeterminate West should have caught his imagination. In the days of his *Eagle* editorship America's main achievements had been performed in the spirit and by the methods of the pioneer, a spirit which had been recently stimulated by the opening up of the regions from the Mississippi to the Pacific. And Whitman was the prophet, as later he was to be the poet, of the pioneer.

> O you youths, Western youths,
> So impatient, full of action, full of manly pride and friendship,
> Plain I see you Western youths, see you tramping with the foremost,
> Pioneers! O Pioneers!
>
> Have the elder races halted?
> Do they droop and end their lesson, wearied there beyond the seas?
> We take up the task eternal, and the burden and the lesson,
> Pioneers! O Pioneers!

In this West without a past democracy might achieve a life suitable to its nature. When, two years later, the "mania for owning things" (as Whitman called it) lured thousands of adventurous or disgruntled Easterners to take ship or caravan for the California eldorado, he remained untempted, content to enjoy the newest national enterprise in his fancy alone. In the West he pictured the "average man" in his true glory.

"Radical, true, far-scoped, and thorough-going Democracy may expect . . . great things from the West!" he announced from his editorial tripod. "The hardy denizens of those regions, where common wants and the cheapness of the land level conventionalism, (that poison to the Democratic vitality,) begin at the roots of things—at first principles—and scorn the doctrines founded on mere precedent and imitation. . . . There is something refreshing even in the extremes, the faults, of Western character. Neither need the political or social fabric expect half as much harm from those untutored impulses, as from the staled and artificialized influence which enters too much into politics amid richer (not really richer, either) and older-settled sections."

Whitman was unable to see that, the world being settled and largely controlled from settled communities, mere pioneering can in itself neither test nor establish a social or governmental experiment. The old must be regenerated, not simply escaped in a spirit of youthful protest. Yet Whitman's instinctive faith in the West not only was typical of the youth of his generation, but was a prophetic symbol of our history. Probably he would not have stated it so, but the democratic form of government was adopted in America as the only possible solution—the solution by compromise—of the conflicts between various Colonial cultures and ambitions. It was then, even less than now, a melting pot, from which emerged "average Americans," nor did it really wish to be. It was rather a communal experiment in living together, successful in proportion as it safeguarded the integrity of each as well as the rights of all. But in what section was that ideal to be so well realized as in the great Western region, peopled by all sections yet detached from the cultural past of all? There, if anywhere, the paradox of American colonization, duplicated in the many paradoxes of Whitman's ancestry and character, might be resolved through an idealization whose crude expression was found in pioneering. Lincoln the liberator, the conciliator, came by no accident from that West.

Yet there would be inaccuracy in inferring that Whitman desired a return to nature only as an escape from the complexities and refinements of civilization. He wanted the natural *in* civilization; and nothing could seem natural to him which repressed man's wholesome emotions or retarded their growth. Government only meddled and muddled when it tried to make a people happy; they must do that for themselves. And this they could not do if too conscious of other laws than those of their own nature. For this reason Whitman, following Emerson rather than Longfellow, declared for a thoroughly indigenous art and literature.

This could be accomplished, he thought, without prejudice to our traditional hospitality toward the trade and the peoples of the Old World. The great tide of immigration from Germany and Ireland, if encouraged, not only would extend the blessings of the chosen nation to peoples less fortunate, but would have the practical advantage of settling our immense domain with the very class who would most appreciate those blessings and do most to perpetuate them. The narrow and selfish "Nativists," the "100 per cent Americans" of that day, like the "Know Nothings" and the "Ku Klux Klan" of later periods, were, in spirit, not Americans at all as he understood the term.

"On the shores of Europe are panting multitudes, who sicken with nakedness and starvation. They weep—they curse life— they die. Partly through the excess of population, and partly through the grossly partial nature of the laws and the distribution of property, half the aggregate number of the natives of the Old World live in squalor, want and misery. Some seasons famine stalks through whole provinces and thousands are struck down ere the new moon fills her crescent. Then emaciated corpses strew the fields, and the groans of pale children are heard on the wayside, and savage murders are committed to get the means of life for dying women and infants. Amid the cities, too, (those great cities which many of our people would like to emulate in grandeur,) Poverty stalks unchecked, dragging by the hand his brother, Crime. There is too much mankind and too little earth. . . .

"And then look here at America. Stretching between the Allegheny Mountains and the Pacific Ocean, are millions on millions of uncultivated acres of land—long rolling prairies—

interminable savannahs, where the fat earth is covered with
grass reaching to a height unknown in our less prolific north—
forests, amid whose boughs nothing but silence reigns, and the
birds are not shy through fear of human kind—rich openings by
the side of rivers—trees and verdure making from year to year
their heavy deposits on the remains of the trees and verdure that
decayed before them.   The mind becomes almost lost in tracing
in imagination those hidden and boundless tracts of our territory—

> Where rolls the Oregon and hears no sound
> Save its own dashing.

We perhaps wonder what can be the intention of the Creator in
leaving for so long a time such capacities for human existence
and comfort undeveloped.   We lose ourselves in the anticipation of what may be seen there in future times—the flourishing
cities, the happy family homes, the stately edifices of public improvement, the sights and sounds of national prosperity.

"How, then, can any man with a heart in his breast, begrudge
the coming of Europe's needy ones, to the plentiful storehouse
of the New World?"

But they were not to transplant in America the manners and
customs of their native lands.   They were to become Americans.
Nor were those manners and customs, reminiscent of feudalism
and aristocracy, any longer to be imported by our publishers and
imitative provincial writers.   Scott was great reading for a boy,
but after all Scott was a Bourbon, a Tory and a High-Church-
and-State man—a poor guide for the children of democracy.
Even Shakespeare, incomparable analyst of the human heart,
was later to come under this indictment, for his page had caught
its purple glamour from those who wore the purple, not from
the common man on whose unromantic shoulders rested the
throne of the king.   But Dickens, now beginning to rival the
earlier popularity of Scott, there was a man for us.   When,
four years before, the Washington *Globe* had attacked Dickens

as a vulgarian, the young Whitman, then a compositor on the "Brother Jonathan" reading the stories of Boz as fast as they were pirated in America, had chivalrously come to the defense of Dickens and the Dickensian literature.   And this in the name of Democracy.

"A 'democratic writer,' I take it, is one the tendency of whose pages is to destroy those old land-marks which pride and fashion have set up, making impassable distinctions between the brethren of the Great Family—to render in their deformity before us the tyranny of partial laws—to show us the partial workings of the thousand distortions engrafted by custom upon our notions of what justice is—to make us love our fellow-creatures, and own that although social distinctions place others far higher or far lower than we, yet are human beings alike, as links of the same chain; and one whose lines are imbued, from preface to finis, with that philosophy which teaches to pull down the high and bring up the low.   I consider Mr. Dickens to be a democratic writer."

Indeed the enthusiastic young American had been so caught by Dickens's theatric method of catering to the popular taste for sentimental extravagance that he never quite outgrew the tendency to mix propaganda with art.   This was painfully apparent in "Franklin Evans," the temperance novelette which he wrote in unsuccessful imitation of his English favorite.   One should not suppose, however, that Whitman's mind was closed to the literature of the Old World, any more than to classical writings, with which he was familiar.   "For the beautiful creations of the great intellects of Europe—for the sweetness of majesty of Shakespeare, Goethe, and some of the Italian poets—the fiery breath of Byron, the fascinating melancholy of Rousseau, the elegance and candor of Hume and Gibbon—and much more besides—we of the Western World, bring our tribute and respect. Presumptuous and vain would it be for us to decry their glorious merits."   Nevertheless every age and every nation must clothe itself in literature of its own, and it was high time, he felt, for American writers to begin the creation of native fashions.

Whitman's book reviews seldom praised mere sentimentality, but he enjoyed the gentler writers, Lamb and Isaak Walton. He admired their placidity, their way of taking literature as a personal conversation with individual readers. Clearness he demanded. Even Carlyle was not to be praised for his turgidity, but in spite of it. Miss Bremer's stories of domestic life were then finding hosts of readers among the subscribers to the then popular but effeminate American annuals. Avoiding the affected sentimentality of Bulwer and the verbosity of G. P. R. James, they were full of interest for the editor of the *Eagle*— "the best books the whole range of romance-writing can furnish," he declared. They glorified the potent mild virtues, charity, forbearance, love—especially the love of a good gentle mother, such as Whitman himself adored with a sort of mariolotry. And Ruskin, steeped though he was in the art and culture of the Old World, showed what might be accomplished when a man of the upper classes obeyed in his writings the code of intellectual chivalry, *noblesse oblige*. Relating art to life, esthetics to the moral groundwork of character, he looked forward to an age less stilted, insincere and superficial than his own, and Whitman could respond to such enthusiasm and high-toned sincerity. Hazlitt too belonged with the torch-bearers. For once, a history of the French Revolution went to the bottom of the matter and exposed that cataclysm for what it was. "A noble, grand work!" the *Eagle* exclaimed, "a democratic work! It is a wholesome book for the young fresh life of our republic. . . . We hear of the 'horrors' of the French Revolution: as if mere blotches on the skin, an unsightly eruption athwart the face of a man, were more horrible than the long, dreary deadness, the lethargy and decay, of the vital organs within—while the blood should stagnate, and the veins and million nerves were forbidden their power and function. . . . We too dread the horrors of the sword of violence—of bloodshed, and a maddened people. But we would rather this moment over every kingdom on the continent of Europe, that the *people* should rise and enact the same prodigious destructions as those of the French Revolution, could they thus root out the kingcraft and priestcraft which are annually dwindling down humanity there to a lower and lower average—an appalling prospect ahead, for any one who *thinks* ahead!" Prophetic words those, though uttered in an obscure American print; for within the year France would be in the throes of another revolution, and, following her example, Kossuth in Hungary, and Garibaldi in Italy, would voice the aspirations of their oppressed peoples for autonomy and democracy, while Germany and Austria would make similarly vigorous though short-lived efforts for freedom. Then the young democrat's heart would throb in that dawn, however false a dawn, to be alive.

Yes, Hazlitt had had the right attitude toward the French Revolution. And Carlyle had been right too in his masterly diagnosis of the hidden causes of that eruption. When Carlyle died, in 1881, Whitman declared that, "rugged, mountainous, volcanic, he was himself more a French revolution than any of his volumes." His keen mind had detected "what a fœtid gas-bag much of modern radicalism is; but then his great heart demanded reform, demanded change—often at terrible odds with his scornful brain." In time Whitman was to be enabled to escape the Carlylian despair through a "soul-sight of that divine clue and unseen thread which holds the whole congeries of things, all history, all time, and all events, however trivial, however momentous, like a leashed dog in the hand of a hunter." But meanwhile he might learn something from the Scotchman's honest satire and might discover the shortcomings of democracy as Carlyle had exposed those of feudalism. He might benefit also by study of Carlyle's individual, dynamic style. When he first encountered that style, in reviewing "Heroes and Hero Worship" for the *Eagle*, he was as unprepared as other readers for the galvanic shock it gave him. "No great writer achieves anything worthy of him," he asserted defensively, "by merely inventing a new *style*. Style in writing is much as dress in society; sensible people will conform to the prevailing mode, and it is not of infinite importance anyhow, and can always be so

varied as to fit one's peculiar way, convenience, or circumstance."
Yet even in dress Whitman was soon to be as unconventional as
Carlyle ever was in language. Once he got used to the Carlylese
style, Whitman found it "strangely agreeable" and, for one who
would stand out from the general run of writers to lift up his
voice in the "barbaric yawp" of prophecy, a method strangely
effective and dramatic.

Goethe was another great writer to whom the young Whitman
responded gladly. When the latter read the *Dichtung und
Warheit* in Parke Godwin's translation, he was amazed at the
discovery of what "a history of the soul and body's growth"
might be: "the simple easy truthful narrative of the existence and
experience of a man of genius,—how his mind unfolded in his
earliest years—the impressions things made upon him—how and
when the religious sentiment dawned upon him—what he thought
of God before he was inoculated with books' ideas—the development of his soul—when he first loved—the way circumstances
imbued his nature, and did him good, or worked him ill—with
all the long train of occurrences, adventures, mental processes,
exercises within, and trials without, which go to make up the
man—for *character* is the man, after all." What a road-map
that sentence is of the life he himself was to live, the book he
was to write. Such a hint as to how direct, intimate, personal,
and vital the autobiography of a poet might be was sufficient to
cause Goethe to remain through Whitman's life as "the supreme
example of personal identity."

When Whitman turned to American books, he found a number of authors to give him hope. Irving he accepted for his
charm of style and his sentiment. Longfellow he quoted most
often, whose simple lyrics of domestic sentiment, and whose
reverential translation of European culture Whitman luxuriated
in, like the child of his age that he was, while the Harvard
poet's tendency to celebrate American traditions was, he thought,
a step in the right direction. Melville's earlier romances he
found most readable, but he would have to wait four years more
for "Moby Dick" to blend in fiction, as he himself was to blend

in verse, mystic romance with accurate realism. Bryant he always ranked high, and liked personally. But Emerson, in the heroic aspirations of his free thought, taught him most of all.

Turning over the pages of the New York exchanges one day, Whitman noticed a highly spiced review of a performance by the Keans which, as he chanced to know, had for some reason not come off at all. At once his lance was levelled. "Most of the 'criticisms' in the metropolitan press," he told his readers, "are written *before the plays are played*—and paid for by the theater, or other parties. Of those which are not so paid for, the majority are the fruits of solicitation, favoritism, and so on. In the midst of all that stale and unwholesome utterance, the speaking of a single paragraph of unbiased truth falls like an alarming and terrible thing." He himself expected, and had long accepted, free tickets or passes to public performances which he attended in his capacity as editor; but he would have the donors know that his freedom of opinion was not to be bribed by such means. He loved the theater too well. "The drama of this country *can* be the mouthpiece of freedom, refinement, liberal philanthropy, beautiful love for all our brethren, polished manners and an elevated good taste. It can wield potent sway to destroy any attempts at despotism—it can attack and hold up to scorn bigotry, fashionable affectation, avarice, and all unmanly follies. Youth may be warned by its fictitious portraits of the evil of unbridled passions. Wives and husbands may see perhaps for the first time in their lives, a long needed lesson of the absurdity of contentious tempers, and of those small but painful disputes that embitter domestic life—contrasted with the pleasant excellence of a forbearing, forgiving and affectionate spirit. The son or daughter just entering the door of dissipation may get timely view of that inward rottenness which is concealed in such an outside of splendor. All—every age and every condition in life—may with profit visit a well regulated dramatic establishment, and go away better than when they came." But, he added, for this "the whole method of theatricals, as at pres-

ent pursued in New York, needs first to be overthrown." Its
weakness lay in its imitation, affectation, insincerity. Whitman
himself had acted sundry "second parts" in an amateur dramatic
company up on Broadway, and though he did not excell as an
actor he came to value highly the performer who could feel his
rôle. That was what gave Macready his power, even when
silent upon the stage. It was what he admired in Mrs. Siddons,
in Kean, and in Charlotte Cushman. So with Booth in "Richard" or "The Merchant of Venice," and Edwin Forrest in
Payne's "Brutus" at the Bowery. It was the Bowery's insistence
upon this sincerity in its actors that had led Whitman, some years
previous, to frequent it rather than the more select Park Theater opposite the Astor House on Broadway. Five or six years
before his connection with the *Eagle* the Bowery plays had become to the drama what the dime novel was to standard fiction—
cheap, vulgar, melodramatic. But in the days when Forrest
and Booth had played there, and "The Last Days of Pompeii,"
"Mazeppa," "The Lion Doomed" and Cooper's "Wept of the
Wish-ton-Wish" held the boards, it was full of American character, unrestrained by the growing ambition to ape the English.
What a cross-section of American life in the two thousand persons who crowded it from pit to gallery! He could recall and
describe it half a century later:

". . . the audience mainly of alert, well-dressed, full-blooded
young or middle aged men, the best average of American-born
mechanics—the emotional nature of the whole mass aroused
by the power and magnetism of as mighty mimes as ever trod
the stage—the whole crowded auditorium, and what seethed in
it, and flushed from its faces and eyes, to me as much a part of
the show as any—bursting forth in one of those long-kept-up
tempests of hand-clapping peculiar to the Bowery—no dainty
kid-glove business, but electric force and muscle from perhaps
2,000 full-sinewed men—(the inimitable and chromatic tempest
of one of those ovations to Edwin Forrest, welcoming him back
after an absence, comes up to me at this moment). . . .

"I can yet remember (for I always scanned an audience as

rigidly as a play) the faces of the leading authors, poets, editors, of those times—Fenimore Cooper, Bryant, Paulding, Irving, Charles King, Watson Webb, N. P. Willis, Hoffman, Halleck, Mumford, Morris, Leggett, L. G. Clark, R. A. Locke and others, occasionally peering from the first tier boxes; and even the great National Eminences, Presidents Adams, Jackson, Van Buren and Tyler, all made short visits there on their Eastern tours.

". . . Not but what there was more or less rankness in the crowd even then. For types of sectional New York those days —the streets east of the Bowery, that intersect Division, Grand, and up to Third Avenue—types that never found their Dickens, or Hogarth, or Balzac, and have passed away unportraitured— the young ship-builders, cartmen, butchers, firemen (the old-time 'soap-lock' or exaggerated 'Mose' or 'Sikesey,' of Chanfrau's plays), they, too, were always to be seen in these audiences, racy of the East River and the Dry Dock. Slang, wit, occasional shirt sleeves, and a picturesque freedom of looks and manners, with a rude good-nature and restless movement, were generally noticeable. Yet there never were audiences that paid a good actor or an interesting play the compliment of more sustained attention or quicker rapport."

But if the manager attempted bombast and fustian, he might expect to hear from these children of nature in the pit. Thinking of these great days in which the drama had spoken to the heart, Whitman was oppressed by the bills the theaters offered in 1846-1847. "Yankee" Hill was filling the house with his exaggerated burlesques of New England rustics at the Chatham. The Chambers street opera house was presenting high-class Italian music, but the Olympic was altogether popular, while at the Park one got only English managers, English actors, and English plays. Already a group of younger men, writers and artists, were voicing a demand for something native and natural. "After all," Whitman patriotically assured his public, "anything appealing to the national heart of the people, as to the peculiar and favored children of freedom,—as to a new race with a character separate from the kingdoms of other countries —would meet with a ready response, and strike at once the heart of all true men who love America, their native or chosen land." But a Moses was needed if this chosen people were to escape from their inferiority complex, a man of courage and genius and unselfish public spirit. Such a man did not instantly arise at the summons of the *Brooklyn Eagle;* but

The song is to the singer, and comes back most to him,
The teaching is to the teacher, and comes back most to him,
. . . .
The love is to the lover, and comes back most to him,
The gift is to the giver, and comes back most to him—it cannot fail,
The oration is to the orator, the acting is to the actor and actress not
  to the audience,
And no man understands any greatness or goodness but his own, or the
  indication of his own.

So the young editor's aspiration for a nobler drama for his country came back most to him, though in a form of art which was to bear the impress of many another aspiration as well. His desire for a new music, for example. From youth Whitman had heard good music. In "Franklin Evans" he had decried the use of sirens in saloons, as an unfair enticement to drink; but when he had learned to moderate his glass, he went freely and with enjoyment to hear the Cheneys and the Hutchinsons in Niblo's Garden and such places. He was pleased with their rustic simplicity, their freedom from dancing-school bows, hand-kissing, and the "patent-leather, curled-hair, 'japonicadom' style." He hoped that American singers might always sing without affectation the simple melodies of the heart. For his part, he would be uncomfortable in a civilization beset by so many complex fears, so many refined inhibitions, such a hot-house culture, that it must needs protect itself by a conventionalized art. It was, he thought, really unnecessary to admit the fact that America was as old as England in her life if not in her institutions; let her rather continue to claim the prerogatives and the privileges of youth.   And yet he knew that age or nationality has little to do with really great art; for the Italian opera, when sung by an Alboni, a Mario, a Badiali, or a Bettini, he always had words of gratitude and praise.   The impersonal technical perfection which reached its culmination in the popular coloratura singing of Jenny Lind, whom he heard at Castle Garden in 1850, was what left him cold, just as the writers of nineteenth century lyrics, singers who were in no sense "answerers," left him disgusted by their low ambition and their unheroic quest for beauty.

Our young editor must not be imagined, however, as always seriously employed with the politics and culture of his day.   He was not incapable of levity, of a sort.   He relished a pun as much as later columnists do.

"What do you think, Sir Reader, when we tell you that three ladies' slippers were 'pulled off' and bestowed upon us this morning?   We have 'em now—in a glass of water!"

When he did not feel disposed to write, he was as frank about it as Emerson was concerning his hatred of ritualistic prayers.

"The *Brooklyn Eagle* 'begs leave to state' that this is one of the dullest days it has ever experienced.   A flat turgidity seems to pervade everything.   Leaden clouds cover the heavens —the air is bitter and raw—there ain't any news—and *B. E.* is not i' the vein for knitting editorials, at all."

But on sunny days, summer or winter, he would go abroad, not only in quest of news, but to preserve the magnificent health which meant much more to Whitman than making money or even holding his job.   "Let us enjoy life a little," he would say to his readers.   "Has God made this beautiful earth—the sun to shine—all the sweet influences of nature to operate—and planted in man a wish for their delights—and all for nothing? Let us go forth awhile, and get better air in our lungs."   He was not much of an athlete—being, as he said, more a floater than a swimmer—but he enjoyed watching clerks and apprentices at a game of baseball.   For his own part, nothing pleased him

more than to climb up to the driver's box of one of Husted &
Kendall's East Brooklyn Omnibuses, to ride as far as they went,
and then to strike off afoot across fields and into the woods to
forget the din of Babel and to renew his sense of personal
identity with creation.   Sometimes William Cullen Bryant accompanied him, talking of his many European travels.

On other days Whitman would go in the opposite direction.
Reaching the door of the *Eagle* office, he would see, as often as
not, crowds of men and women rushing, then as now, lest they
miss a ferry-boat.   But Whitman never hurried.   "Posterity
surely cannot attach anything of the dignified or august," he
philosophized, "to a people who run after steamboats with hats
flying off, and skirts flying behind!   Think of any of the Roman
senators or the worthies of Greece, in such a predicament."   And
he *was* thinking of them, thinking that America's contribution to
history should be comparable to that of Greece and Rome.   He
tried to live in the philosophic spirit of Socrates, of Epictetus.
"We like the ancient and manly beard," he confessed, "the concomitant of the apostles, of the men of Rome, of Petrarch and
Tasso and Shakespeare."   Like Bryant, he could not bring himself to shave.   A little later he was to become indolent in sar-
torial matters, letting his beard grow into a bush, as if willing that, since he was a child of nature, nature should do as she
would with his personal appearance.   Possibly there was also
a desire to conceal the sensuous lips which so contradicted the
direct glance of his eye and the obstinate purposefulness of his
nose.   Or was it to be the badge of the commoner, like the
open-throated shirt he would soon be affecting?   There are
eminent scientists who deny sex to be fundamental in nature,
tracing sexual variation to a preponderance of masculine or
feminine cells in the individual.   In Whitman, if we may bor-
row a figure from science, there seemed to be, as he was to discover, no great preponderance of masculine cells.   Did the
beard serve as a silent, necessary assertion of his masculinity?

Whitman has meanwhile probably missed his ferry.   But he
will catch the next one, and he is content; to him the interest of

a journey never lay in getting somewhere. Though he had the freedom of the boat, and moved on terms of comradship among all who ran it, his favorite occupation was to stand at the side of the vessel, lost in poetic contemplation. He was about his Muse's business, though it would be another ten years before his mouth would be unstopped so that he could give musical utterance to the thoughts that filled him now.

Crowds of men and women attired in the usual costumes, how curious you are to me!
On the ferry-boats the hundreds and hundreds that cross, returning home, are more curious to me than you suppose,

And you that shall cross from shore to shore years hence are more to me, and more in my meditations, than you might suppose.
The impalpable sustenance of me from all things at all hours of the day,
The simple, compact, well-join'd scheme, myself disintegrated, every one disintegrated yet part of the scheme,
The similitudes of the past and those of the future,
The glories strung like beads on my smallest sights and hearings, on the walk in the street and the passage over the river,
The current rushing so swiftly and swimming with me far away,
The others that are to follow me, the ties between me and them,
The certainty of others, the life, love, sight, hearing of others.

Others will enter the gates of the ferry, and cross from shore to shore,
Others will watch the run of the flood-tide,
Others will see the shipping of Manhattan north and west, and the heights of Brooklyn to the south and east,
Others will see the islands large and small;
Fifty years hence, others will see them as they cross, the sun half an hour high,
A hundred years hence, or ever so many hundred years hence, others will see them,
Will enjoy the sunset, the pouring in of the flood-tide, the falling back of the ebb-tide.

It avails not, time nor place—distance avails not,
I am with you, men and women of a generation, or ever so many generations hence,

Just as you feel when you look on the river and the sky, so I felt,
Just as any of you is one of a living crowd, I was one of a crowd,
Just as you are refresh'd by the gladness of the river and the bright flow,
    I was refresh'd,
Just as you stand and lean on the rail, yet hurry with the swift current,
    I stood yet was hurried,
Just as you look on the numberless masts of ships and the thick-stemm'd
    pipes of steamboats, I look'd.

.   .   .   .

These and all else were to me the same as they are to you,
I loved well those cities, loved well the stately and rapid river,
The men and women I saw were all near to me,
Others the same—others who look back on me because I look'd forward
    to them,
(The time will come, though I stop here to-day and to-night.)

What is it then between us?
What is the count of the scores or hundreds of years between us?

Going ashore when the ferry touched at Fulton street, New York, Whitman had various opportunities for the sort of experiences he most enjoyed, and on various days he embraced them all. He might stroll up to Plumb's famous photograph gallery and spend hours looking at the daguerreotypes of the noted men and women of the day, seeking some hint of their lives in their faces, as on the streets he was continually doing. Or he might go to hear a concert by DeMayer at the Tabernacle, and be haunted by it for a month. He took great interest, also, in the Phrenological Cabinet, believing phrenology to be a real science. He was eager to welcome assistance from science, any science, in his effort to pierce the conventional surface of life that he might discover its inner spirit. When Fowler, the phrenologist, read the bumps on his head, Whitman was not displeased with the result. Was not the skill of the phrenologist attested by his affirmation of what Whitman knew to be facts, as when he rated very high the young man's caution, intuition, firmness, self-esteem, benevolence, destructiveness, and love of good living, and rated no less high those twin

expressions of the sex instinct, amativeness and adhesiveness?
Otherwise disposed, Whitman might stroll to the well shaded
Battery to watch the children at play, meditating meanwhile a
sentimental lyric upon the theme. One day, near Castle Garden,
he saw men in diving suits racing on the bottom of the river.
Sometimes he would get a Whitehall boatman to row him over
to Governors Island to have a look at the awkward young men
being whipped into shape as Stevenson's California Regiment,
later to play so large a part in the acquisition of that far territory for the government of Anglo-Saxons. Climbing the winding stairs in the turret of the old fort, he would then look out
upon a scene he loved.

"Far, far up stretched the rolling Hudson, with its elevated
banks dressed in green, and the white houses of Hoboken and
Jersey City—and the innumerable river craft coming and crossing and going on its capacious breast. To the south-west lay
the sleepy-looking hills of Staten Island, their sides dotted with
dwellings, and with not a flaw in the varied spread of their
gracefulness. On every side was the moving panorama of vessels, and flapping waves. There too was the great metropolis
to the north-east, its perpetual hum coming indistinctly to the
ear. Far above its loftiest roofs, towered the proud spire of
Old Trinity, and over the splendid verdure of the Battery trees,
rose the oval cupola of the Exchange; while a thick forest of
masts hid the shores of the right altogether from the eye. Nor
must we forget our own beautiful Brooklyn, with its saucy-
browed Heights jutting out on the river, and proffering their
claims for admiration to the sight of everybody in the neighborhood. And over those old battlements the ocean wind sweeps
incessantly—and it was a huge joy to breathe such stuff, after
coming from the streets, and slushed gutters of the city."

At times Whitman would flee from the city altogether, taking
train to the newly accessible eastern end of Long Island, always
dear to him from association with his boyhood wanderings and
the later rustications of his manhood. He shared with his age
a fondness for melancholy, and now and then he would take

the stage for Greenwood Cemetery, then miles out of town, and spend the late afternoon pondering on life and death, on fame and the vicissitudes of that genius which is to madness so near allied.

But he was not always so disposed to solitude, though he was always given to contemplation. One hot July day he was invited, as a member of the press, to join a party arranged by the contractors of the new City Hall, now Borough Hall. Some sixty men drove off in four large six-horse stages for Coney Island, to enjoy an outing and a clam-bake there. A dance on the hard sand, and then a splash and souse in the cool water. Here Whitman was thoroughly at home. In the form of ocean wave, the poet of nature might hug her to his bosom with more tangible satisfaction than the eye could know in caressing the sunset, or the cheek when bared to the salutation of the breeze. The clams were roasted in their own broth, Indian style, in beds covered with brush and chips. After the repast, good champagne was passed from lip to lip, and good fellowship with it. Toasts were drunk, Whitman taking to himself a share of credit for that which Congressman Henry Murphy proposed to the local press. But best of all was the return to Brooklyn in the cool of the evening. First activity, giving rein to the body and the social instincts; then the quiet meditations of the soul, that memories might be placed in amber. So, after his custom, the young poet climbed to the high seat beside the driver, his eyes upon the rising stars, his nostrils happy with the smell of new-mown hay.

But Whitman observed the life of Brooklyn which went on indoors as well. Like most self-educated men, he was always interested in schools. He had himself spent several years in the profession of teaching, and even as editor and later as poet he was always less a historian, less a critic, than a teacher. He argued for free seminaries. He urged that formal instruction be supplanted by a method addressed to the reason and the individual reactions of the pupil. Something in his nature compelled him to cry out against the use of the rod. In his own schoolroom he had forsworn it and established himself on a basis of friendly personal helpfulness to his students. He had once written a melodramatic story for the "Democratic Review" about a death from flogging, and had been pleased to see it reprinted again and again. With Horace Mann and Emerson and Thoreau, he took advanced ground in favor of moral suasion in the government of men, though he was not yet ready to deprive nations of the sword. In flogging he saw a certain human indignity; and its use in the navy he denounced as roundly as did Dana and Melville. Nor should such disciplinary methods be condoned even in the prison. He himself had seen what Sing Sing was like, and the Mount Auburn State Prison for Women. He knew some of the inmates, and he did not believe the prison made them better. The reformatory work of the kind-hearted Mrs. E. W. Farnham at the latter institution, similar to that of Mrs. Fry at Newgate or that of Thomas Mott Osborn at Sing Sing in recent years, he applauded. Whitman was as law-abiding as most men, and yet, feeling that real justice should look upon the responsible impulse rather than its accidental expression, he knew all men to be potential criminals.

You felons on trial in courts;
You convicts in prison-cells—you sentenced assassins, chain'd and hand-
    cuff'd with iron,
Who am I too that I am not on trial or in prison?
Me ruthless and devilish as any, that my wrists are not chain'd with iron,
    or my ankles with iron?

In all his life Whitman was in court but once, and that was rather a joke. While fishing in a pond near Babylon one day, not far from his father's farm, he was continually annoyed by a mischievous boy determined to have his fun, if not at the expense of the fish then at Whitman's. Finally exasperated, the latter coaxed the lad to row near in his boat, and then administered a sound thrashing with his rod. The culprit's father had Walt arrested, entrusting the prosecution of the case in the justice's court to General Nicholas Udall. Sure of himself, Whitman undertook his own defense. He admitted the thrashing, but excused it on the ground that he was defending the vested rights of fishermen. The jury, whose foreman was a hard-headed farmer with a Yorkshire brogue, returned almost immediately.

"Have you arrived at a verdict?" asked the justice.

"We 'ave, your Honor."

"What is the verdict?"

"We find 'e didn't 'it 'im 'alf 'ard enough!"

Despite the repeated protests on the part of the justice that the form of the verdict was irregular, that verdict stood.

As for capital punishment, Whitman could tolerate the idea no more than could Aldin Spooner, or Horace Greeley, or Bryant, or Whittier; and he skillfully argued the case, largely on sentimental grounds.

Toward other classes of unfortunates the editor of the *Eagle* was equally sympathetic. Working women, enslaved in the sweat-shops, and earning often as little as fifty cents a week, appealed not in vain to the championship of his pen. Nor did he neglect the institution of negro slavery, so inimical to his theories of liberty and equality. While he recognized the strength of the historical and constitutional arguments advanced by Calhoun, he nevertheless believed, like Washington and Jefferson, that even in the South human bondage would have to go. Of course the horrors of the "middle passage" should be stopped, even in the Brazilian trade, though it might take high-handed measures on the part of British and American men-of-war to do it. He published a very realistic description of these horrors as one of his first *Eagle* editorials, but he had little more to say on the subject till the very end of the year. Meanwhile he was watching with varying emotions the War with Mexico, begun in April, the result of which was to precipitate national questions concerning slavery which would test both him and the Union itself.

War often works the very mischief with a poet. It reveals

latent heroisms, it is true, it opens new vistas, it effectively dis-
·plays the national spirit against the lurid background of an
enemy's villainy, and it makes him peculiarly conscious of being
present at one of the birth-throes of history.   All this appeals
through his imagination to the patriotism, the aspiration, the
generosity of the poet heart.   But, being better equipped as
an advocate than as a judge, Whitman did not realize how
blindly partisan, how stupidly patriotic, how imperialistic the
war psychology was making him.   Greeley was but eight years
his senior, yet he was much more mature; and in using the New
York *Tribune,* a Whig organ, to rally a fearless opposition to
the selfish and partisan machinations of President Polk, he
might have steadied Whitman's own judgment—had the latter
been able to believe there was any democracy save in the Democratic Party.   James Russell Lowell, too, under the influence of
an Abolitionist wife, had no illusions as to the real purpose of
this "defensive" war into the heart of a weaker nation.   The
satirical wit of his hard-headed Hosea Biglow was making a
reputation for his creator.   But Whitman was as unlikely to
learn wisdom from an Abolitionist as from a Whig.

His faith in the "average man" had as yet no universal application.   It applied only to America, the America he knew,
where the average man was an Anglo-Saxon freeholder dwelling
in the holy land of democracy.   He felt some sympathy for the
Mexican people, but he was not hopeful concerning their future
unless they should come under the protecting wing of the American eagle.   Nor had he forgotten the Texan war of independence.   Wars of autonomy had always appealed to his love of
freedom, and his prejudice against the Mexicans had been
deepened by their gratuitous cruelties.   The month before the
Mexican War began, Whitman had chanced to read, in "Black-
woods," an excerpt translated from "A Campaign in Texas."
This was the autobiographical story of a young German, one
Von Ehrenberg, one of the three or four of Fannin's men to
escape from the massacre at Goliad.   The narrative impressed
him so strongly that he ran a column of extracts in the *Eagle,*

and years later he had no difficulty in retelling the experience
in the first person as one of the incidents in his imaginative history fit to be recorded side by side with episodes in his personal
life. The Mexican War, therefore, did not provoke in him
any great conflict of feeling, as, for instance, a civil war might do.

When General Taylor routed Arista at Resaca de la Palma,
Whitman exulted. He was sensitive to the long-lived American
superstition that might proves our right, and that an unbroken
record of successful wars must in some way be due to the approval of the democratic lord of hosts. He was in a mood to
declare war at once, without that delay which was being
counseled by Calhoun and the Abolitionists alike. With him
it was a war of revenge, at least at the beginning.

"Who has read the sickening story of those brutal wholesale
murders, so useless for any purpose except gratifying the
cowardly appetite of a nation of bravos, willing to shoot down
men by the hundred in cold blood—without panting for the day
when the prayer of that blood should be listened to—when the
vengeance of a retributive God should be meted out to those who
so ruthlessly and needlessly slaughtered His image?

"That day has arrived. . . . Let our arms now be carried
with a spirit which shall teach the world that, while we are not
forward for a quarrel, America knows how to crush, as well as
how to expand."

The hot young patriot did not see that America was crushing only to expand, and that editors like himself were unwit-
tingly playing the game of the adroit politician, James Polk.
Only the preceding year, while writing for the Brooklyn *Star*,
Whitman had expostulated eloquently against the jingoes who
were trying to bring on a war with England over the Oregon
boundary dispute, a situation in which there was almost an equal
casus belli, but less prejudice. Accepting every move of the
Democratic president without question—save when he demoted
the popular hero of Buena Vista for party reasons—Whitman
was arguing, a year before the war was won, that the annexation of a large part of Mexico was a foregone conclusion. He

salved his democratic conscience, so far as Mexican autonomy
was concerned, by believing that the Mexican people, at least
those living in Yucatan, were themselves eager for annexation.
In the presumptuous manner of a twentieth-century *Kultur*, he
argued:

"Nor is it the much condemned lust of power that makes the
heart respond to the idea of these new acquisitions. Such
greediness might very properly be the motive of widening a less
liberal form of government; but such greediness is not ours.
We pant to see our country and its rule far-reaching"—he could
imagine Canada and Alaska as parts of our future empire—
"only inasmuch as it will take off the shackles that prevent men
the even chance of being happy and good—as most governments are now constituted that the tendency is very much the
other way. We have no ambition for the mere physical
grandeur of this Republic. Such grandeur is idle and deceptive
enough. Or at least it is only desirable as an aid to reach the
truer good, the good of the whole people."

But the satisfactions afforded such a man as Whitman by the
indulgence of the belligerent spirit, even when it masqueraded
as an angel of light, were of necessity soon exhausted. Not
till the next year did the magnetic telegraph reach even as far
as New Orleans, so that the news of a campaign three weeks
away lost some of its glory in transmission. Moreover, the
Richard Harding Davis type of war correspondent was as yet
unknown, while the publicity director was the invention of later
statesmen and men of affairs. Then, too, Whitman embraced
in his nature many of the conflicting traditions of his country,
and pacifism was such a tradition, as Hosea Biglow's astound-
ing popularity was conclusively proving. When news arrived
that General Taylor had successfully stormed Monterey with
an army half the size of that defending the city, the *Eagle* expressed the hope that the government of the United States "will
bow sufficiently to that public opinion which over the whole
civilized world is arrayed against war, except on an extreme
contingency, as to leave no way untried to stop this contest

of ours with Mexico—and allow the United States to pursue its *peaceful* conquests—which are far grander and more blessed and more enduring than any conquests of force." But the war did not stop, and Whitman had to console himself with the belief that the figures of our losses had been exaggerated; that this was, as wars went, a relatively bloodless conflict; and that, in view of the fact that the population of the invaded country fraternized and traded with our soldiers, one could hardly call it a war at all. Of course he could not then know that in the peace negotiations the Mexican Government would present enormous claims for damages done to the property of this civilian population by these same fraternizing soldiers. But in due time the young sentimentalist would have an opportunity to learn at close range what a war really is. Then he would cry, "God damn all wars!"

By January, 1847, he had had enough. Declaring that he had upheld the President and the Army from the start in a just cause, he insisted, nevertheless, that "the time has arrived when all citizens should speak candidly and firmly on this subject of the Mexican War. Let it go no further! Enough has been done to revenge our offended honor. The Mexicans have been punished enough." But the martial imp would not retreat to his bottle at the command of a young man in Brooklyn, no, nor that of soldiers and diplomats; and the fall of 1847 found Whitman still asking, without hope of an answer, "When will the war be ended?" He then advised that an energetic push be made with a large army and have it done with. Not that he would accept peace at any price, the peace without victory being suggested by the aged Albert Gallatin. He would not annex the whole of Mexico, to be sure, but Americans should not forget that, after all, they were the conquerors and that the war had been expensive. Moreover, their manifest destiny pointed to the Southwest.

But that destiny was more troubled than the *Eagle* could have foreseen. In that distant land were being planted the seeds of civil war. Many hands were quick to prevent it—Webster and Greeley and Lincoln and Bryant and most of the Whigs and all of the Abolitionists. Nevertheless the seeds fell, and grew like dragons' teeth. By December, 1846, Whitman, perhaps with the Wilmot Proviso in mind but certainly not influenced by the example of any other editor, had come out courageously for free soil.

"If there are any States to be formed out of territory lately annexed, or to be annexed, by any means to the United States, let the Democratic members of Congress, (and Whigs too, if they like,) plant themselves quietly, without bluster, but fixedly and without compromise, on the requirement that *Slavery be prohibited in them forever.* We wish we could have a universal straightforward setting down of feet on this thing, in the Democratic Party. *We must.*"

Other papers throughout the North supported the Proviso, as did the state legislature and the lower house of Congress. But it was sent to the Senate only on the day of adjournment, and no final action was taken. During the recess of Congress the battle had to be fought out in the press. Whitman addressed his arguments to his own party and to the South, no less than to the free workingmen and taxpayers of the North, who, he averred, supplied four-fifths of the soldiers in the conquering armies in Mexico. He cited the words of Washington and Jefferson; he undertook to expose the sophistries of Calhoun; he drew a vivid picture of new states in which the pioneer stock from the democratic and individualistic North would meet the degrading and hopeless competition of slave labor. His most passionate plea, naturally, was addressed to the middle-class workingmen of the free states.

"And this it is which must induce the workingmen of the North, East, and West, to come up, to a man, in defense of their rights, their honor, and that heritage of getting bread by the sweat of the brow, which we must leave to our children. Let them utter forth, then, in tones as massive as becomes their stupendous cause, that their calling shall *not* be sunk to the

miserable level of what is little above brutishness—sunk to be
like owned goods, and driven cattle!—We call upon every
mechanic of the North, East, and West—upon the carpenter,
in his rolled-up sleeves, the mason with his trowel, the stone-
cutter with his brawny chest, the blacksmith with his sooty face,
the brown-fisted shipbuilder, whose clinking strokes rattle so
merrily in our dock yards—upon shoemakers, and cartmen, and
drivers, and paviers, and porters, and millwrights, and furriers,
and ropemakers, and butchers, and machinists, and tinmen, and
tailors and hatters, and coach and cabinet makers—upon the
honest sawyer and mortar-mixer too, whose sinews are their
own—and every hard-working man—to speak in a voice whose
reverberations shall tell to all quarters that the *workingmen* of
the free United States, and their business, are not willing to be
put on the level of negro slaves, in territory which, if got at all,
must be got by taxes sifted eventually through upon them and
by their hard work and blood.   But most of all we call upon
the *farmers,* the workers of the land—that prolific brood of
brown-faced fathers and sons who swarm over the free States,
and form the bulwark of our Republic, mightier than walls or
armies."

The Democratic state convention sidestepped the issue of
free soil, as Congress was to do, and the party went down to
defeat.   When the magnitude of the débacle was known, Whitman laid the blame squarely on those reactionaries who had
steered the convention in a cowardly course.   He had worked
in harmony with this organization for two years.   A year before he had been the local secretary.   But now Isaac Van
Anden, the present chairman and a Hunker, or slave-soil Democrat, was displeased with the tendency of his editor, if not precisely to bolt, at least to let the party bolt away from *him*.   And
when Whitman, in January, 1848, with a few lines exposed the
fallacy in the now famous letter of Senator Cass—who, with
his eye on the presidential nomination, had deserted the Wilmot
Proviso with the suggestion that in the new territory the principle of local self-government should apply—Whitman, the

Barnburner, was clearly out of place editing a newspaper owned by a Hunker conservative. No doubt the sudden termination of his growing usefulness came as a blow to the editor. Rumor had it that there was not only a "row" but some violence, in which the boot that had trod so many pavements in easy-going freedom was responsible for the precipitate descent of an unnamed politician down the editorial stairs. In any case, Walt had to go. He who had looked so far ahead for his country had not looked ahead for himself, and by the last of the month he was free to find another job. His first impulse, of course, was to fight. And the radical Democrats were with him. There was talk of a Free-soil paper to be started as their organ in Brooklyn, with Whitman at the helm, but nothing came of it at the time. However, the destiny that had undertaken the training of this national poet was preparing to teach him other lessons than that it is sweet and noble to die for one's country.

Whitman was not a man to mope over the loss of a position. As to his loss of income, he had preached that the desire for money was morbid. And as for the loss of his public, he had always found some new paper to edit. So he continued to enjoy his walks and his visits to the theater. One night as he was walking in the lobby of the Broadway, he met a Southern gentleman, evidently a man of means. This was a Mr. McClure, who was to start an independent paper in New Orleans in three weeks and was then in the North buying material and looking for an additional writer for his staff. He had doubtless read in the New York papers of Whitman's sacrifice for his principles, and rather liked the frank and self-reliant bearing of the young man. So they took a drink together, and in a few minutes had struck a bargain. Whitman was paid two hundred dollars for traveling expenses and was to receive good pay when he should begin work on the New Orleans *Crescent* the first of March. At last he would be able to see for himself the West of his dreams, and the South for which he had a natural affinity.

BOOK II

A CITY OF ROMANCE

HITMAN lost no time in starting south. On Friday, February 11, two days after his impromptu bargain with Mr. McClure, he was on his way by rail to Baltimore. With him went his brother Jefferson, who was just half his own age. He and Walt were better chums than any of the others. Jeff had some imagination, played well on the violin, and adored Walt. Mrs. Whitman doubtless loved these two of her sons best, and perhaps it was her wish that Jeff should go with his brother, if the latter must try his fortune in so foreign a clime as Louisiana. Should anything untoward happen to one, the other would then be present to look after him and to keep her advised.

Early on Saturday morning they changed at Baltimore to a railroad which, running west for a hundred and seventy miles, would convey them to Cumberland, nestling on the eastern side of the Allegheny mountains. They followed the watercourses, and marveled at cliffs and Alpine summits such as they had never seen before. Brooklyn, with its gentle and well-conned hills, was far behind them—already they were in the land of romance, the West. They stopped twenty minutes for lunch at quaint Harper's Ferry, with its houses squatting one above another on the hillside, its name as yet unlinked with the tragic career of John Brown. No sooner had the cars stopped than discordant bells sounded in the ears of the passengers as they were furiously assailed by runners for the rival hotels. When Whitman paid for the two dinners, he was happily surprised that it cost him but four bits. At Cumberland, railroad civilization ceased, giving way to the picturesque "Pennsylvania wagons." As Whitman noted in his diary:

"The town has a peculiar character, from its being the great rendezvous and landing place of the immense Pennsylvania wagons, and the drovers from hundreds of miles west. You may see Tartar-looking groups of these wagons, and their drivers, in the open grounds about,—the horses being loosed— and the whole having not a little the appearance of a caravan of the Steppes. Hundreds and hundreds of these enormous vehicles, with their arched roofs of white canvas, wend their way into Cumberland from all quarters, during a busy season, with goods to send on eastward, and to take goods brought by the railroad. They are in shape not a little like the 'Chinese junk,' whilom exhibited at New York—being built high at each end, and scooping down in the waist. With their teams of four and six horses, they carry an almost incalculable amount of 'freight'; and if one should accidentally get in the road-ruts before their formidable wheels, they would perform the work of a Juggernaut upon him in most effectual order. The drivers of these vehicles and the drovers of cattle, hogs, horses, &c., in this section of land, form a large slice of 'society.' "

They had arrived at sunset, and soon they, with seven other passengers, having had their baggage weighed, packed themselves into one of the four-horse stage coaches, which, with re-lays of horses every ten miles, would transport them in a night and a day of bone-breaking travel, to Wheeling, where they might take steamer for New Orleans. Stage-coach travel is conducive to the study of character, and Whitman made use of his first opportunity to compare the Americans he had known in New York with those from the pioneer West. A satirical person, he naïvely said, "could no doubt find an ample field for his powers in many of the manners and the ways of the West; and so can he, indeed, in the highest circles of fashion. But I fully believe that in a comparison of actual manliness and what the Yankees call 'gumption,' the well-to-do *citizens* (for I am not speaking so much of the country), particularly the young men, of New York, Philadelphia, Boston, Brooklyn, and so on, with all the advantages of compact neighborhood, schools, etc., are not up to the men of the West. Among the latter, probably, attention is more turned to the realities of life, and a habit formed of thinking for one's self; in the cities, frippery and artificial fashion are too much the ruling powers."

He was glad whenever the stage stopped, in the middle of the night, at a mountain inn. Jumping out upon the snow, he would enter the long, one-story house beneath the bare-armed trees. How weird the scene, as the flickering light from the mighty soft-coal fire fell upon the men who crowded about it, clad with such odd diversity of raiment! This, said Whitman, is good enough for a painter to work on—but he would have to forget imitation and do something in the American spirit to catch it.

"There were some ten or twelve great strapping drovers before the huge fire. The beams overhead were low and smoke-dried. I stepped to the further end of the long porch; the view from the door was grand, though vague, even in the moonlight. We had just descended a large and very steep hill, and just off on one side of us was a precipice of apparently hundreds of feet. The silence of the grave spread over this solemn scene; the mountains were covered in their white shrouds of snow— and the towering trees looked black and threatening; only the largest stars were visible, and they glittered with a tenfold brightness. One's heart, at such times, is irresistibly lifted to Him of whom these august appearances are but the least emanation. Faith! if I had an infidel to convert, I would take him on the mountains, of a clear and beautiful night, when the stars are shining."

With dawn came breakfast at Uniontown, beyond the Alleghenys; but another weary day of travel would have to be endured in the stage before its passengers might relax in the staterooms of the packet steamer *St. Cloud* moored to her wharf at Wheeling. The next morning Whitman was roused from his slumber only by the clanging of the bell at half past six. In making his toilet he missed the clear water of the Hudson. To while away the half-hour before breakfast, he strolled about the commodious steamer which would be his abode for almost two weeks. He was distinctly disappointed when he looked for the first time by daylight on the Ohio. It was muddy. "There is no romance in a mass of yellowish brown liquid," he said in disgust. He had evidently expected something idyllic, like the engravings in Godey's *Lady's Book.* However, he was in Rome and meant to accommodate himself to the custom of the country; soon he was washing in, and drinking, that same water. Already his body was having to take account of conditions strange to his Dutch upbringing, and he was rather surprised to discover that he could adjust himself with so little trouble. "What an india-rubber principle there is, after all, in humanity," commented the Puritan within him.

To Walt, long accustomed to the parsimony of New York boarding-houses, the bountiful meals which have always been a tradition on the river, seemed enormous in quantity and excellent in quality. When he had a chance to mail a letter home to his mother, Jeff wrote: "For breakfast we have: coffee, tea, ham and eggs, beefsteak, sausages, hot cakes, with plenty of good bread, sugar, etc. For dinner: roast beef, do. mutton, do. veal, boiled ham, roast turkey, do. goose, with pie and puddings, and for supper everything that is good to eat." But Walt was not a little annoyed that when he had eaten for five minutes he found every one else had bolted his meal and departed. It was the incessant activity of the American spirit that he had deplored on the Brooklyn ferry-boats cropping out here, and with no possible excuse. For there was nothing to do but to read cheap novels or to wait for a rare newspaper to be passed around, or to smoke and talk. The ladies in particular had a dull time of it, spending listless hours in silence. But for the Whitmans everything was new and romantic. The *St. Cloud* was never on schedule, for it could not be predicted how much freight would be taken on at each landing place. That depended on the clever little captain's luck in bargaining. But he took on enough to fill a New York liner, Walt knew that, and a conglomeration it was—hundreds of barrels of pork, lard and flour, bags of coffee, rolls of leather, groceries, dry goods, hardware, coops filled with live geese, turkeys, and fowls, which made the steamer sound like a barnyard. Live hogs, too, were driven aboard, and even a horse.

Most of the country was uninteresting, not yet having felt the ax and plow. But the human types at the stopping places were worth looking at, the numerous idlers—boys, old farmers and especially the tall, strapping, comely young men, of Whitman's own age. So much freight had to be taken on and discharged at Cincinnati that Whitman had time to stroll about the "Queen City," a bustling commercial town, fit to compare with New York, Philadelphia and New Orleans as an emporium of trade. But the landing was muddy and the streets uncleaned. As they approached the falls just below Louisville the captain had to decide whether to waste many miles by taking the canal around the "boiling place" on the Kentucky side or to shoot the rapids where the river drops twenty feet in three miles. With the characteristic hardihood of the pioneers, he determined to take the risk. The bottom was studded with immense rocks, and near the middle of the narrow channel there was barely room to pass between Scylla and Charybdis, and then only by a skillful turn of the wheel. As they passed, the pilot found that one wheel would not work, so that the steamer actually did graze each rock and scraped the bottom. The passengers were none too easy, as they paced the floor "looking as they were about to be hung." Swiftly, however, they found their way to peaceful waters and to less agitated thoughts.

And so they came to Cairo, after a week on the Ohio, which poured its stream of mud far down into the Father of Waters. Everywhere at villages boys came down to the wharves to watch them go by, or looked down from their aeries on the bluffs. Flowing south for a thousand miles, the great Mississippi, taking tribute from half a dozen states, seemed to Whitman the very heart of the democratic empire of his dreams. Its physical appearance, like the life on board ship and at the stopping places, was now familiar to him, and his notebook jottings ceased. But the inner eye had its work to do, and for this there was no time like the night. Whitman would sit on deck long after all unimaginative souls had retired to their state-rooms, and gaze at the shadowy shore-line, at the stars and murky clouds overhead. He wrote a poem, the last he should compose for some time, for now he was entering a life which, more congenial to art and enjoyment than Brooklyn had been, would satisfy body and soul with its luxurious lassitude.

> How solemn! sweeping this dense black tide!
>   No friendly lights i' the heavens o'er us;
> A murky darkness on either side,
>   And kindred darkness all before us!
>
> Now, drawn nearer the shelving rim,
>   Weird-like shadows suddenly rise;
> Shapes of mist and phantoms dim
>   Baffle the gazer's straining eyes.
>
> River fiends, with malignant faces!
>   Wild and wide their arms are thrown,
> As if to clutch in fatal embraces
>   Him who sails their realms upon.-
>
> Then, by the trick of our own swift motion,
>   Straight, tall giants, an army vast,
> Rank by rank, like the waves of ocean
>   On the shore march stilly past.
>
> How solemn! the river a trailing pall,
>   Which takes, but never again gives back;
> And moonless and starless the heavens' arched wall,
>   Responding an equal black!
>
> Oh, tireless waters! Like Life's quick dream,
>   Onward and onward ever hurrying—
> Like death in this midnight hour you seem,
>   Life in your chill drops speedily burying!

In the stanzas just quoted from the manuscript as Whitman wrote it on board the *St. Cloud,* the symbolism of nature is hackneyed and indefinite; it expresses a vague feeling vaguely. But long after, when the experiences of that year were little more than memories, the poet revised the poem for publication among his juvenilia, dropping one rime in each quatrain and adding several suggestive stanzas. These are the lines added:

> Tide of youth, thus thickly planted,
>   While in the eddies onward you swim,
> Thus on the shore stands a phantom army,
>   Lining forever the channel's rim.
>
> Steady, helmsman! you guide the immortal;
>   Many a wreck is beneath you piled,
> Many a brave yet unwary sailor
>   Over these waters has been beguiled.
>
> Nor is it the storm of the scowling midnight,
>   Cold, or sickness, or fire's dismay—
> Nor is it the reef, or treacherous quicksand,
>   Will peril you most on your twisted way.
>
> But when there comes a voluptuous languor,
>   Soft the sunshine, silent the air,
> Bewitching your craft with safety and sweetness,
>   Then, young pilot of life, beware.

As he approached New Orleans Whitman scarcely realized the strength of certain forces that were warring for the mastery within him. Even his patriotism, though it had been put to more than one test, had sometimes betrayed him, as in the case of the Mexican War, to strenuous advocacy of a cause unworthy of the country he loved. This was because he had allowed his desire to love and defend something outside himself to take counsel of conventional ideas on which he had been brought up rather than of independent convictions. He was not critical of congenial ideas, preferring to spend his energy in expressing them as individually as he might. But it does not occur to a man, particularly a young man, to stress a cause whose rightness he takes for granted. He is most militant when he fights a hidden foe, an inarticulate protest within his own nature. Every poet must make terms with sex, since so much poetry is an expression, crude or sublimated, of the sex instinct. But what did this young poet know of sex? When, at twenty-one he had first made up his mind some day to do a significant book on human nature and government, that which seemed to him most important was the tyranny of material things, the American mania for acquiring money. Such an ambition allowed too little time for loafing and enjoying one's soul. But of women he had declared that he would say nothing, for the very sufficient reason that neither by experience nor observation had he learned anything about them. As he sailed down the Mississippi he was, it would seem, as innocent of sex as he was naïve in thought. Not that he was indifferent to woman. Writing his editorials in the *Eagle* office, he had often paused to admire the Brooklyn belles on their way to the ferry.

"They have those lithe graceful shapes such as the American women only have—the delicately cut features, and the intellectual cast of head. Ah, woman! the very sight of you is a mute prayer of peace. Without your refining presence the late sulky weather 'wouldn't be a beginning' to the darkness that would spread over the earth."

But what if he should meet the rich womanhood of warmer climes with features sensuous rather than delicate, emotional rather than intellectual? Would he then be able to keep his distance and the integrity of his complacent puritan soul? The editor of the *Eagle* had advised all young men to marry, but it was "to do the state some service," not to appease a hunger which he himself understood. But in New Orleans, as truly as in Paris, the fact of sex was taken as a matter of course, and provided for. And New Orleans would be his teacher.

Swinging around the big bend in the river on the northern bank of which the old, historical, and respectable sections of the city lie, the *St. Cloud,* brilliantly lighted, found her way among a multitude of similar steamers to a mooring at the cobblestone

WHITMAN AT THIRTY

wharf. It was ten o'clock, on Friday, and the Whitmans had opportunity only to find a bed for the night. The next morning Walt set out in the rain to make arrangements for board. A room was found at Poydras and St. Charles streets, but it proved to be so unclean that they had to seek more comfortable quarters. These they found at the Fremont, next door to the St. Charles Theater and just across the street from the St. Charles Hotel, both, in their day, rated by travelers among the best in the world. Walt was to know both of them intimately. The former presented on its boards the favorites he had applauded at the Park and the Bowery—Macready, Booth, and Edwin Forrest, the last just now retiring from the stage. There was also Dr. Collyer's "Model Artists," a review of whose tableau performances led Whitman into his first defense of the nude in art. In the hotel Whitman had perhaps his best opportunity to see a cross-section of the population of all but the *vieux carré,* or old French and Spanish Creole city; for the St. Charles was in the municipality where American enterprise had taken the lead in commerce, politics and civic improvement. He loved to loiter there, especially on those hot days when, as he phrased it, one could "get the full good of sherry cobblers, umbrellas, shady sides of the street, and equanimity of temper." He long remembered the handsome bar, its "cobblers" topped with strawberries and snow, its mild French brandy and exquisite wines, which the author of "Franklin Evans" did not scruple to enjoy. He was most interested in observing the strange mixture of men in this cosmopolitan city. The Trist treaty with Mexico had just been signed but had not yet been ratified, and the city was still full of uniforms. To its customary brilliancy, gayety and freedom were added the abnormal excitement and irresponsibility of war time. The American armies had debarked from New Orleans, and were now returning thither. General Taylor himself was in town, and General Pillow. Whitman talked with both and later saw them at a theater where they were given an ovation. But there were many types drinking their countless toddies and mint juleps at the St. Charles who had been attracted to the Queen City of the South for other than patriotic reasons: adventurers, gamblers from Saratoga, dandies, fugitives from justice in the States or in South America, planters, steamboat captains, *bon vivants*.

The life of the workers was no less strange and picturesque, as he observed on his early morning or noonday strolls about the town and the levee.

"Got up early," he records, "from my bed in my little room near Lafayette. The sun had scarcely risen and every object seemed lazy and idle. On some German ship moored to the levee I saw about a dozen stalwart sailors with bare legs, scouring the decks. They seemed to be as happy as lords, although their wages are sometimes not more than six dollars a month. . . . Saw a negro throw a large stone at the head of his mule, because it would not pull an empty dray—wished I owned the negro—wouldn't treat him as he treated the mule, but make him a present of a cow-skin, and make him whip himself. . . . Saw a poor longshoreman lying down on a bench; had on a red shirt and blue cottonade pantaloons; coarse brogans, but no stockings. He had spent all his money in a tippler's shop the night previous for grog, and when his last picayune was discovered to be gone, he was kicked out of the house. Thought that there were some landlords who deserved to be bastinadoed. . . . Saw a shipping master riding at full speed upon a small pony. He would have been willing to have freighted every ship in port, if he could have been 'elected.' Saw him go on board a vessel, and come off again, with, in all probability, a flea in his ear. He kicked the pony in his sides, and after dismounting went into the nearest grog-shop. How he kept 'his spirits *up* by pouring spirits *down*.' He didn't get the freight of that ship. . . . The sun has just showed his golden face above the gray clouds of the horizon, and bathes with lustre the distant scenery. Now come the bustle and business of the day. Shop-keepers are opening their stores; stevedores are hurrying aboard their respective ships. Those stevedores! they are for the most part honest men, and, physically speaking, work much harder than any other class of the community. Many of them have little tin kettles on their arms which contain their simple dinner repast. When their work is over they get their 'bones,' and then separate for their different homes to woo 'tired nature's sweet restorer'—sleep; or mayhap to spend their day's earnings in a grog-shop. . . . There's a big, red-faced man walking hastily up the levee. He's a Customhouse officer, and is hurrying on board his vessel for fear that if not there by sunrise the Captain may report him to the Collector. . . . Went into St. Mary's Market, saw a man, a good old man in a blue jacket and cottonade pantaloons, with a long stick of sugar cane in his hand. Wondered who he was, and much surprised to find out that he was a lawyer of some repute. At the lower end of the market there was a woman with a basket of live crabs at her feet. Although she loved money, she had no particular affection for a press from the claws of the ungainly creatures that she handled with a pair of iron tongs. Saw the 'cat fish' man, who declared that his fish were just caught, and were as tender as a piece of lamb. Went up the Market and saw rounds of beef, haunches of venison and legs of mutton, that would make a disciple of Graham forswear his hermit-like appetite. . . . Came down town—shops all open —and heard the news boys calling out the names of the different papers that they had for sale. These boys are 'cute' as foxes and as industrious as ants. Some of them who now cry out 'ere's yer—, here's the—, here's the—,' may in time be sent to Congress. . . . Went down town further—all was business and activity—the clerks placing boxes upon the pavements— the persons employed in fancy stores were bedecking their windows with their gaudiest goods, and the savory smell of fried ham, broiled beef-steaks, with onions, etc., stole forth from the half unshut doors of every restaurant. . . . Passed down Conti street and looked at the steamboat wharf. It was almost lined with steamboats; some were puffing off steam and throwing up to the sky huge columns of blackened smoke—some were lying idle, and others discharging sugar, molasses, cotton, and every-

thing else that is produced in the great Valley of the Mississippi.
Came to the conclusion that New Orleans was a great place
and *no* mistake. . . . Went still further down—visited the
Markets and saw that every luxury given to sinful man by sea
and land, from a shrimp to a small potato, were there to be
purchased. Came home again and took breakfast—tea, a
radish, piece of dry toast, and an egg—read one of the morning
papers, and then went about my business."

But he did not always dine so frugally. Until he learned
that overeating interfered with his work, he was fond of fre-
quenting the justly famous oyster houses of the city as a change
from the less appetizing fare of the Fremont. Such was the
city, doubtless the most romantic, the most European, the most
picturesquely quaint in the United States, one whose social
order, though not her business life, was the product of Latin
traditions. The city was, politically, three cities, or "municipalities"; but though the American section was in many ways in the
lead, even the Americans had lost some of their stiffness, their
avarice, their cautious reserve, and their pioneering earnestness,
in a desire to imitate those graces of life which grow only in a
civilization rooted in the past. On a Sunday morning Whitman
must have heard the soft music of the guitar played in the street
and reflected that this would have landed a man in jail in New
York or Boston—but why should it? What a man, or a city,
does in his leisure hours is often more indicative of his true
character than his efforts to make a livelihood. And New
Orleans did everything. To quote a writer in the *Crescent,*
probably Whitman himself: "If there be any individual in the
community who has Santa Anna's favorite passion on the apex
of his heart—which remark meaneth a furious desire to be
present when the Gallic emblem of nationality spurs himself for
the fight—he can at all times be accommodated in the lower
municipalities. In certain locations he will be permitted to cry
—'Crow, Chapman—Chapman, crow!' to the fullest extent of
his lungs. Does the gentleman desire to see the Attakapas bull
(just imported from Havana) speared by an *artiste* of celebrity?

If so, his wish can be fulfilled by visiting Algiers [the most law-less section of the city, on the southern bank of the river] and the Third Municipality, in the pleasant season of our Southern summer. As for masquerade Balls, we can only be beaten by gay, gallant, chivalrous Paris: and in the way of operas we can't be beaten at all. There's the French opera at the Orleans Theater; and occasionally we have those addicted to music from the 'Father-land,' who sing to our uneducated ears strains of the most mysterious sweetness.—Again, once or twice in the course of the theatrical season, we have gems of genius from the 'sunny skies of fair, classic Italy,' who sing as if their very blood had been intermixed with the red currents that flow from the hearts of nightingales. Therefore, as Bombastes says—

'Since music is the food of love,
Play Michael Wiggins once again!'

"If a person wishes to perforate his intimate friend or in-solent enemy, he has only to go to some one of the numerous shooting-galleries in New Orleans, and by the joint aid of a few dimes and three days' practice, he can be taught to split a bullet against the edge of a pen-knife, at the distance of ten paces. Those, too, who are fond of playing with edged tools, will, by applying to some of our fencing-masters, be taught how to 'pink' a gentleman in a manner that Chevalier Bayard would have wept at. More than this could not be desired.

"Now, as far as our National Drama, we have all the materials necessary. Stars from Europe, from Britain, and, aye, sometimes from our own wild Western states, appear week after week at the different Theaters—which 'temples of the drama' are, we suppose, better patronized than any others in 'the land of the free and the home of the brave.' Those who come to visit us, albeit for a season, must never think that the Queen City of the South is deficient in amusements—for they can enjoy themselves at anything in the way of drinking, from a glass of the waters of the muddy Mississippi, up to a golden goblet filled with Roman punch;—in the way of eating, from a moldy sea biscuit with a slice of rusty bacon, up to a broiled pompano with terrapin eggs and asparagus; and in the way of music, from the tooting of a penny whistle, up to a soul-entrancing strain of a silver bugle, in the still, solemn hours of night.

"The fact is, that in this goodly city, we can go through the whole alphabet of enjoyment, and, as they say in the West, 'not miss a letter from A to Izzard.'"

And enjoy it Whitman did. Physically, he had never felt better. And if there had ever been any social timidity, born of his own humble origin, to keep him from the parlors of the élite in Brooklyn and New York (though he had sometimes attended functions as a reporter), his appearance in a hospitable, easy-going city where he was quite unknown would do much to give him courage, if not discretion. One evening in May he accompanied some friends to a ball in the suburb known as Lafayette. He wore unaccustomed, and uncomfortable, evening clothes, perhaps for the first time in his life; and as he drew the white kid gloves on his large hands, he burst them, so that they looked, as he said, like "cracked dumplings." "But," he added with characteristic nonchalance, "I didn't care; so I put my hands behind my back and made my first debut amidst the chivalry, beauty, loveliness, and exquisite grace congregated in that social hall." Had Whitman gone merely as a reporter, he need not care greatly whether he were noticed or not; but already he had been in the social capital of the South long enough to begin to think of his personal relation to it. He had seen the Creole beauties, and all those varying shades of feminine loveliness which made the city famous, on the streets, in the parks, and at the theater. At the opera he had doubtless noted the elegance of the San Domingan beauties, "free women of color" whose tincture of a more passionate race could hardly be detected under the gas light which fell upon their jewels as they sat in the second tier reserved for them. And seeing so many lovely women, intelligent but certainly not with "the intellectual cast of head" he had admired in Brooklyn, the poet in him responded, before he knew it. So, on this night, he was wondering if he might not at the ball find the woman Nature intended for his mate.

"The room was overflowing with the beauty of Lafayette, with a sprinkling from New Orleans and Carrolton. A promenade was in order when I entered and I watched each graceful form and lovely face as they approached like sylphs of some fairy tale, in plain, fancy and mask dresses. Each one, methought, was more lovely than the other; but no, the object of my heart,—she who has caused me so many sleepless nights and restless days,—she whom I have seen so often in my dreams and imaginings, was not among the unmasked. I rose from my seat with a heavy heart, walked into the [bar] and took a drink of lemonade *without* any brandy in it. I looked upon it with stoic indifference—*she* was not there, and not being there, the place or persons had no charms for me.

"While musing to myself that I would emigrate to Europe or China—get wrecked, perhaps—find her on some barren isle, etc. —I caught a glimpse of what I conceived the very pink of perfection, in form, grace and movement, in fancy dress. Doctor Collyer would give the world for such a figure. My eyes were riveted to the spot. My head began to swim. I saw none but her. A mist surrounded all the others, while she moved about in bold relief. She turned. I saw her face, radiant with smiles, ecstacy, delight. ' 'Tis she!' I ejaculated, as if tossed by a pitchfork, and caught the arm of a manager, to introduce me. He didn't know her. It was her first appearance in the ballroom. I imagined it was an auspicious coincidence. It was also my first appearance. Seeing a gentleman conversing with her, I watched my opportunity, and seeing him alone, I requested him to introduce me. Never saw him before in my life; but what cared I—my case was getting desperate. He willingly consented; and off we started toward her. To describe my feelings while approaching her, is impossible. I was blind to all but her.

"The agony was over; she spoke; and the deed was done. I found that she was everything that I imagined—accomplished, pleasing in her manners, agreeable in conversation, well versed in the authors, from Dryden down to James—including all the intermediate *landings*—passionately fond of music, she said; and by her musical voice I *knew* she could sing. I was happy in every sense of the word—delighted beyond measure. She kindly consented to promenade—would carry me through a cotillion if I'd go—but, knowing nothing about the poetry of motion, I had to decline; and she,—noble, generous creature as she was!—preferred rather to talk and walk than dance. I admired her, nay, I will confess, for the first time in my life, I felt the 'tender passion' creeping all over me. *I was in love!* I could not restrain myself. Candor compelled me to speak openly—I told her I had been looking for *her* since I was 18 years of age. 'Looking for me!' she exclaimed with astonishment. 'If not you,' I answered, 'some one very much like you.' She guessed my object, saw and understood all, and invited me to call and see her.

"I was, in my own opinion, as good as a married man—at length my toils and troubles were to cease—I was about to be repaid for my constancy, by having the one for my wife that nature intended. Just at this moment where, in any other place, I would have been on my knees, the gentleman who had introduced me, came up and said—'Wife, ain't it time to go home?' 'Yes, my dear,' she responded. So taking his arm, casting a peculiar kind of look at me, and bidding me good night, they left me like a motionless statue on the floor."

And there we will leave the youth, sadder and wiser, to laugh at his rashness as best he can. Who was she? She may have been any fashionable woman who, bored with a husband, thought to amuse herself with the novelty of coquetting with the foreign young man from New York. Or she may have been one of those beautiful and accomplished vampires which infested the New Orleans of that day, who, finding that her intended victim was financially unpromising, gave the wink to her wedded accomplice, and so shook him without more ado. He would get over it in a week, though his writings for the *Crescent* the next day bore traces of a sentimentally distraught mind. Yet the Whitman who awoke knew more about himself and his needs. There were other women in New Orleans, and this dazzling experience impressed him with the fact that he was a man.

Know I am a man, attracting, at any time, her I but look upon, or touch
    with the tips of my fingers,
Or that touches my face, or leans against me.

So Stevenson was to boast of his power over the correlative sex. Whitman's friends doubtless took him also to the quadroon balls, the amusement *par excellence* to be shown to all visiting gentlemen. But with Jeff, or alone, he found his way to the many other points of interest the city afforded. There were the Sabbath throngs who carried flowers to the strange "ovens" in the cemeteries, the dueling oaks, the Metairie race course, the Spanish Fort, the Cabildo, the primitive negro dances in Congo Square, the old St. Louis Hotel with its slave block in the basement, the battlefield at Chalmette. Like the battle-field of Brooklyn, this last stirred his imagination. He had once, as a boy of fourteen, seen Andrew Jackson when, as President, the gray-haired "hero and sage" had been welcomed in Brooklyn. Whitman wandered also in the *Place d'Armes* and thought of its eventful history. Doubtless he had pointed out to him the blacksmith shop of Jean Lafitte, pirate and patriot. Quaker though he was, he was fond of the old cathe-dral, where religion was beautiful without falling into the ostentation he had deplored in the rich and gaudy churches of New York. His brother Jeff was less impressed by such Old World beauty. "On Sunday morning," he wrote home, "we took a walk down to the old French church and an old looking thing it is too. Every one would go up and dip their fingers in the holy water and then go home and *whip* their *slaves*. One old black took a bottle full home to wash the sins out of the family." But Walt was more catholic, more comprehending.

"The tall, gray Cathedral reared its ancient spire to Heaven: but the towers wherein were the bells that have tolled the death knell, and rung the merry marriage music of thousands, were silent. It was a day dedicated to the 'King of Kings'—it was the Holy Thursday of Passion Week. It commemorated the occasion of the 'Last Supper' of our Saviour, who, when surrounded by his disciples, gave them his last earthly blessings. There were over two thousand communicants kneeling at the altars, at various periods of the day, and all seemed fully sensible of the solemnity of the occasion. Grand Mass was celebrated—after which many persons came in to adore or communicate in spirit with the 'Son of Man.' . . . Our dark-eyed Creole beauties, with their gilt-edged prayer books in their hands, would walk with an air that seemed to say that beauty was a part of religion. Dipping their taper fingers into the holy water and crossing their foreheads, they would then walk up the aisle and kneel down to prayer. We saw many women there whose garments betokened that some dear friend had not long been laid in the grave. They knelt before the picture of Christ carrying his cross, and prayed, no doubt, that they might have strength to carry theirs. Persons of all classes went down before the shrine of Religion. There was the broken-hearted man of the world—the gray-haired man, whose feet were on the brink of the grave—the blooming girl whose charms were budding into womanhood—and the wrinkled, care-worn widow, to whom love was but a memory. Then again, were the servants of ancient families; and then ragged, pale-faced creatures, who looked as though they did not dare to approach too near the altar. The whole scene was beautiful and solemn, and calculated to impress the heart with the purity of virtue, and endow the soul with full reliance in the power of Him who rules above."

A religion which could, even for the moment, bring all classes of a city to think so humbly of God that they were equal in their penitence and their adoration, and do this with perfect naturalness and peace, could not fail to impress a democratic Quaker

poet to whom religion was always much less a creed intellectually
apprehended, a code sustained by the self-sacrificing will, than
it was a mode of living, a spirit of brotherhood toward men and
filial piety toward the Creator.

Such a romantic city should be blessed of Nature. As a matter of fact, it was flat, and so poorly drained that epidemics of
cholera and yellow fever were almost annual scourges. Whitman missed the hills of his native North. But Nature lavished
her grace on tree and shrub.

I see where the live-oak is growing, I see the yellow-pine, the scented bay-
  tree, the lemon and orange, the cypress, the graceful palmetto . . .
The cactus guarded with thorns, the laurel-tree with large white flowers,
The range afar, the richness and barrenness, the old woods charged with
  mistletoe and trailing moss,
The piney odor and the gloom, the awful natural stillness,
  (here in these dense swamps the freebooter carries his gun, and the
  fugitive has his conceal'd hut;)
O the strange fascination of these half-known half-impassible swamps,
  infested with reptiles, resounding with the bellow of the alligator, the
  sad noises of the night-owl and the wild-cat, and the whirr of the
  rattlesnake,
The mocking-bird, the American mimic, singing all the forenoon, singing through the moon-lit night.

And as in Paris, flowers everywhere gladdened the drab of city
street-corners, sold by bewitching young grisettes. One of these
Whitman selected to stand for the type, studying her as she
stood nightly under his window, and perhaps making her
acquaintance in her home, or in the French market where he
loved to take the morning cup of black coffee which, in New
Orleans, is considered almost an obligation.

"Miss Dusky Grisette is the young 'lady' who takes her stand
of evenings upon the pavement opposite the St. Charles Hotel,
for the praiseworthy purpose of selling a few flowers by retail,
showing off her own charms meanwhile, in a wholesale manner.
She drives a thriving trade when the evenings are pleasant.
Her neat basket of choice bouquets sits by her side, and she has

a smile and a wink for every one of the passers-by who have a smile and a wink for her.

"Mademoiselle Grisette was 'raised' in the city, and is pretty well known as a very pretty *marchande des fleurs*. She can recommend a tasteful bunch of posies with all the grace in the world, and her 'buy a broom' style of addressing her acquaintance has, certainly, something very taking about it. She possesses pretty eyes, a pretty chin, and a mouth that many an heiress, grown oldish and faded, would give thousands for. The *em bon point* of her form is full of attraction, and she dresses with simple neatness and taste. She keeps her eyes open and her mouth shut, except it be to show her beautiful teeth—ah, hers are teeth that are teeth. She has sense enough to keep her tongue quiet, and discourses more by 'silence that speaks and eloquence of eyes' than any other method—herein she is prudent.

"Grisette is not 'a blue' by any means, rather a *brune,* or, more prettily, a brunette—'but that's not much,' the vermillion of her cheeks shows through the veil, and her long glossy hair is *nearly straight*. There are many who affect the *brune* rather than the *blonde,* at least when they wish to purchase a bouquet —and as

'Night
shows stars and women in a better light,'

they have a pleasant smile and a bewitching glance thrown into the bargain whilst purchasing a bunch of posies.

"What becomes of the flower-girl in the day time would be hard to tell: perhaps it would be in bad taste to attempt to find out. She is only interesting in character and association. Standing at, or reclining against, the door-cheeks of a store, with the brilliancy of the gas light falling favorably, and perhaps deceptively, upon her features and upon her person, with her basket of tasteful bouquets at her feet, and some of the choicest buds setting off her own head-dress. As such she looks

in character as a *jolie grisette,* as she is, and will excite the
notice of those who, beneath the light of the sun, and in the
noontide gaze of men, would spurn and loathe such familiar-
ities."

The little witch was evidently a member of that class whose
existence gave New Orleans a social code that would be
strange, if not immoral, in any other American city—the octoroon woman, beautiful and passionate victim of racial amalgama-
tion.   All testimony agrees that she was a marvel of physical
charm.   Sometimes her complexion was clear and her hair
flaxen, without a single condemning wave; sometimes her hair
and eyes were dark, her skin shot through with only an Italian
hint of a duskier hue, her voluptuous lips alone betraying her
standing in a society that had made her what she was.   So
lovely was she, and often so rich and cultivated, that she was
allowed to wear her mask at the "quadroon balls," to which
none but gallants of the superior race might come, and to which
they often did come, leaving their own ladies to "make
tapestry" at more exclusive soirées.   But she could escape
neither her origin nor her destiny, both of which had reference
to the lust of man.   Nor was she altogether to be blamed if
she sought to mate above rather than beneath her, even though
the law forbade a regular marriage.   Thus only might her children climb another step toward social recognition and culture,
until ultimately should be erased all traces of the shadows on
her past.   Whitman never forgot these women, and in old age
feelingly described them to a young friend to whom he tried to
tell the greatest personal secret of his life.

"I have been in New Orleans—known, seen, all its peculiar
phases of life.   Of course my report would be forty years old
or so.   The octoroon was not a whore, a prostitute, as we call
a certain class of women here—and yet she was too; a hard class
to comprehend; women with splendid bodies—no bustles, no
corsets, no enormities of any sort: large luminous bright eyes:
face a rich olive: habits indolent, yet not lazy as we define lazi-

ness North: fascinating, magnetic, sexual, ignorant, illiterate: always more than pretty—'pretty' is too weak a word to apply to them."

A picture which strikingly fits this description was found pasted in one of Whitman's personal notebooks.

Whitman's situation in the *Crescent* office, for a time, was congenial and promising. Mr. Hayes and Mr. McClure, the proprietors of this enterprising and independent newspaper, were both kind to him, and paid him well. He saved his money; and when he had been away from Brooklyn a month, in his homesickness at hearing that his mother, who had not written him, was ill, he even contemplated going back. But he wanted first save a thousand dollars, now that he had the chance, so that they could buy a quiet little farm of their own and live together in family affection. Jeff also worked on the paper, giving the five dollars he received each week to Walt to save, and adding to it the proceeds from the exchange papers his brother gave him to sell. One of Walt's duties on the *Crescent* was to read the exchanges, excerpting articles of interest and writing editorials about them, though most of the leaders were written by a Mr. Larue, while a Mr. Reeder was city editor and a certain DaPute translated the Mexican items. These exchanges were interesting to Whitman. They told of the enthusiasm in New York over the establishment of France's Second Republic, and of Greeley and Bryant and others of his friends drawing up resolutions of salutation to the new democracy. Even in the *Place d'Armes* he could hear a hundred guns saluting the freedom of a land which was more truly a mother to the city than any other could ever be. He knew, too, that the Free-soilers were busy and that, though he had been defeated in his fight with the *Eagle,* the fight was being carried on by others.

Aside from writing some whimsical, post-Addisonian sketches of the motley New Orleans life as it appeared to a pair of strange but observant eyes, Whitman showed little qualification for covering the news of the city in any broad way. But he was sent almost daily to the recorders' courts to get the stories of those who fell under the displeasure of the law. This sort of reporting was largely new to him, and opened his eyes to yet another stratum of humanity which needed to be taken into account by one who would celebrate the average life of America. Promptly at ten o'clock each morning, when the local Rhadamanthus, Recorder Baldwin or Ramos, sat down on the bench beneath its dingy canopy, the court would awake to life and a semblance of order. Before him swarmed the second-rate lawyers who thrive on humanity's more inglorious woes, and beyond them the tiers of greasy benches occupied by witnesses and visitors. From behind the bars to the left peered out the anxious or sullen faces of men, women, and even children who had spent a night in the calaboose. Opposite these culprits sat those unofficial judges, the reporters, who would publish abroad with ridicule or sympathy the stories of the night before. When the Recorder came in, the reporters would take out their pencils and make ready to write, their chairs tipped against the greasy wall.

One common class of culprits was the negro slaves. Sometimes they had run away to the swamps and had been caught. Sometimes they had found a grog-shop that would break the law by selling liquor to them, and had created a disturbance. Often they were up for thieving. But often, too, they were present to complain of cruelties suffered at the hands of the ruling race. Whitman hated slavery, but he knew that slaves also could do wrong, and he tried to be just to accused and accuser alike. His nature revolted at the sight of women in the chain gang, yet he was able to see also the other side of slavery. One day the *Crescent* printed the story of a slave woman who, running away from her master's plantation near the city, had voluntarily returned from Ohio, preferring slavery to such liberty as she had known in her two years in the North. No, Whitman would never write an "Uncle Tom's Cabin" out of one-sided sympathy for the slave, however he might deplore the evils of the system; for he knew, like Emerson, that there

are, and will always be, slaves wherever man has not attained
the mastery over himself.

Those who were cruel to animals, as most of the negro teamsters were, he excoriated, as he did the drivers of omnibuses
who·endangered the lives of pedestrians. Drunkards, for the
most part, he laughed at.

The various grades of prostitution to be found in New
Orleans were not then segregated or regulated as they are to-
day. But the more notorious types were somewhat localized in
the region of Magazine, Perdido and Philippa streets. The
section was of course often represented in the police court.
Once Whitman limited his article to this type of vice and mis-
fortune.

"Isle of Cyprus.—Recorder Baldwin's dock was yesterday
metamorphosed into the Isle of Cyprus upon a very small scale.
The police were unusually active on Wednesday night last, and
by way of experiment arrested no less than twenty-three of the
frail Cyprians who reside in Magazine, Perdido and Philippa
streets. Let's sketch the picture. In one side of the dock sits
a woman with a brazen face and a don't-care-a-pennyish air.
She has on a splendid black silk dress, and wears a large gold
chain about her neck. Her fine muslin collar is fastened by an
enormous brooch, and her fingers glitter with jewels made of
glass, colored to suit her fancy. She evidently belongs to the
'upper ten thousand' of those of her *caste,* and purses up her
mouth at her humbler companions. By the side of this Cleo-
patra of Perdido street, is a woman with red hair, no shoes, a
pug nose, and a very dirty calico gown. All the time she pats
her foot upon the floor, and when 'sent down' ogles the police
as she goes out. Then again, seated in one corner is a creature
who owes much of the beauty of her form to one of the staples
of the South—cotton. She has on the smallest bonnet that possibly could be obtained, and a green veil long enough for the
drop-curtain of a small theater shades her features. Ever and
anon she makes mathematical problems with the end of her
parasol on the floor and seems to be in a great anxiety 'to leave.'

Her companion in the red muslin dress seems utterly a stranger to shame, and with her white bare arms crossed over her breast, patiently awaits her fate. She tasted vice's poisoned chalice early. See! there is a woman rocking herself to and fro, apparently unconscious of what is going on. When called on by the Recorder, she starts to her feet and looks vacantly around. She is laboring under the influence of *mania-a-potu,* and her bed will soon be her grave!

"How unlike her frail sister who sits beside her! She has ruddy cheeks, sparkling eyes, coral lips, and a bust like that of Venus. Little cares she whether the Recorder sends her down or not. She has plenty of friends to help her out of the scrape. Ever and anon she takes out her gold watch, not exactly to see what time it is, but merely to let the police know that a female who has a gold watch could not possibly belong to the society which she was in. When the Recorder tells her that she must find a voucher, she perks up her nasal organ and sails out of the dock with the air of a queen. Poor old Jane! that friendless creature who sits in one corner with her hands clasped over her eyes. She is bare-footed, and, like Lazarus of old, is 'clothed in rags.' Yet that wretched Magdalene was once innocent, and perhaps the pride of doting parents. Now she is a drunken dotard, and would not 'turn upon her heel to save her life.' Close by her side there is a masculine-looking woman, who is all the while giggling and smiling at every one who looks at her. When asked what her occupation is, she states in a tragic voice, 'I'm a actress.' The Recorder orders her to make an exit to the workhouse. In yonder group are those who have passed through almost every stage of vice and misery—to whom life is but a curse, and death a blessing. Shunned by their own sex, they seek companions among the lowest of the low, and day by day like loathsome worms creep and crawl nearer and nearer to their graves. Well might we exclaim with the poet,

'There is no sight on earth so piteous
As woman lost to honor and to shame!'

"The poor wretches, for the most part, were sent to the workhouse, upon the ground that they followed no honest occupation."

On another day the reporter's sympathy was evoked by another girl who, though a member of the *demi monde,* was not lost to shame.

"In another corner there was a pale, thin-visaged woman, who sat shivering, as it were, and hiding her head from the audience by covering it with her apron. Her face bore the impress of beauty; and her soft, white, taper fingers told that once she had been a lady—and better than that, a woman! How changed the scene! This creature, once, perhaps, the idol of a lordly household, had become dishonored—dismayed and lonely. Even as one step is above or below another, so we sink down or rise in the estimation of the public. Life has its steps—its days are but the rounds upon the ladder, like that seen by Jacob —which must carry the true and just to happiness and heaven." And again, "There was the woman who, in her dishevelled hair and hectic cheek, cursed in her inmost heart the wretch who destroyed her. And then again, one who had just fallen from the brink of ruin, with the last tinge of the spring bloom of life upon her care-worn cheeks. The scene was a sermon to the preacher and a lesson of the changes of life to all. Each of these poor Magdalenes might have known a mother's love, but never had they knelt at a Saviour's feet.—Even by a humble police report, the noblest precepts may be inculcated, and virtue made to wave her scepter over the dark abode of vice." For once the preacher in him asserts itself—against what? His tendency, so apparent in some of his police reporting, to describe misfortunes cynically, even jestingly? How different that from the Whitman of the *Eagle* editorials. But the sympathy he felt for women whose misfortunes had debarred them from motherhood, his ideal for all good women, that was sincere.

When Whitman had been writing these easy-going, whimsical, sometimes puerile sketches for the *Crescent* for three months, his connection with the paper came to a sudden end. He probably was unable to see himself just how it happened; and certainly he was not prepared for it. One day he sent down to the counting room a request for a small sum of money. To his chagrin Mr. McClure sent back a statement of what money he had drawn and declined to make any further "advances." It is true that a certain coldness had been observed in both Mr. Hayes and Mr. McClure for some time past. They had ceased to consult Whitman about the policies of the paper. This had provoked in him an equal reserve. And now, his pride being touched, he returned a memorandum showing that he was not their debtor and suggested that the connection be dissolved. This was agreed to, and in two days the Whitmans began their return journey.

What had caused the coldness of his proprietors? Possibly they had seen that his slovenly writing, often below the tone of that he had done for the *Eagle,* would add distinction to no paper. Perhaps he was as hard to get along with in New Orleans as newspaper proprietors in New York and Brooklyn had found him to be. Or perhaps the owners of the *Crescent* had heard the gossip going around among the newspaper men that Whitman had taken up with a woman, one of the class at once most fascinating and most accessible, an octoroon. This in itself would probably not be sufficient to declass a man, especially a journalist, in a city like the New Orleans of 1848. But if it affected his work, or the regularity of his hours, as it would be certain to do, then that was another matter. He had been reading Byron and was fond of quoting the line,

"A change came over the young man's dream."

And it is clear that a change did come over Whitman's dream of life about this time. That Whitman was no stranger to woman is evident to any reader of his verse. That he was never married he himself has declared. All the evidence points to New Orleans as the place where he learned what can be taught by romantic passion. Though we perhaps shall never know a great deal concerning the circumstances attending the progress of his entanglement, it is essential to the story of Walt Whitman to fit that episode into his history as truthfully as we can. The portrait which Eakins painted of him he thought the best, though, as he said, it included "too much of Rabelais instead of just enough"; that touch was more essential than the curls in the "parlor portrait" by Gilchrist. The plan of our story does not permit us here to sift all the evidence concerning Whitman's *affaire de cœur;* but though in the nature of the case, Whitman himself having been very reticent about it, dates and names cannot be supplied, I am convinced by many years of study and investigation that the gossip which linked the young journalist with the peculiar *demi monde* of New Orleans was substantially true.

A dozen years later, in preparing an edition of his poems, he wrote,

Once I passed through a populous city, imprinting my brain, for future use, with its shows, architecture, customs, traditions,
Yet now, of all that city, I remember only a woman I casually met there, who detain'd me for love of me,
Day by day and night by night we were together,—All else has long been forgotten by me,
I remember I say only that woman who passionately clung to me,
Again we wander—we love—we separate again,
Again she holds me by the hand—I must not go!
I see her close beside me, with silent lips, sad and tremulous.

But he was careful to hide the key to this poem, though publishing it elsewhere at the same time; and after a few years he threw it away altogether. It was this:

Singing what, to the Soul, entirely redeemed her, the faithful one, the prostitute, who detained me when I went to the city;
Singing the song of prostitutes.

But we must hasten to make a distinction, even as Whitman did in describing the octoroon. Though a "prostitute," she is not necessarily to be associated with the class on whom Whitman had bestowed his pity and his scorn as a police reporter. Even were there no direct evidence, it is more probable, as it is more charitable to suppose, that she was a Creole octoroon. In that case she may have been respectable in everything except her opportunity to marry into the ruling race, and she may have been too self-respecting to marry elsewhere. But apparently Whitman's justification for her lay in the fact that she was faithful in her love for him, even as Anne of Oxford Street was faithful to DeQuincey and Claire to Stevenson. A self-reliant young man without experience with women would have been strong to have hesitated, in that exotic atmosphere, to return a love so offered to him, if only out of pity for the woman. Had not Melville yielded to the charms of his Fayaway? Whitman knew enough about literary biography to understand that boldness in sex matters had been the rule rather than the exception with great poets; and for once, with a beautiful woman to love him in his large manliness, he could be bold. It is true that he was something of a sluggish Dutchman, but in this woman with the warmth of summer in her veins, he found what could stir him. And once stirred, his imagination quickly released her from her past and made her a woman redeemed by her love—as Hester Prynne thought herself pure because her love, being single, had a consecration in itself.

Biography cannot, should not, be too minute in recording the details of a poet's first love. That belongs forever to him. But the impress it left upon him, and through his mind upon his verse, is a part of his legacy to his kind. When we turn to that verse we see records of other loves, no less unhappy perhaps but less unconventional; but this first love wrote itself into lines of such abandon that the poet himself later wished them unwritten. Perhaps they were an easing of the secret, a kind of self-torture, whereby the Puritan in him, on his return to a more typical American environment, sought to expose the "caresser of life" in the market-place of public print, as Hester Prynne was exposed in Salem village. Even when, his lesson learned,

he began to pass for a saint among the pure, he sometimes could
with difficulty endure their praises:

Oh admirers, praise not me—compliment not me—you make me wince,
I see what you do not—I know what you do not.

The dogmatic prude was gone forever. / Whitman had found
himself akin, through the flesh, with all mankind.   In two
spheres men meet and really 'comprehend each other—in their
loftiest ideals and in their most animal desires.   Whitman seeks
the ideal community, being a poet and an idealist. / But such
communion is possible only among the few who have imagination; so Whitman also emphasizes the common origin in us of
the many passions wherewith we individualize our lives.   But
at first Whitman was engrossed with the fact, so recent and
so powerful with him, that man was an animal.   Like Rousseau,
he chafed under the limitations of society.

O the puzzle, the thrice-tied knot, the deep and dark pool, all untied and
    illumin'd!
O to speed where there is space enough and air enough at last!
To be absolv'd from previous follies and degradations, I from mine and
    you from yours!
To find a new unthought-of nonchalance with the best of Nature!
To have the gag remov'd from one's mouth!
To have the feeling to-day or any day that I am sufficient as I am.

O something unprov'd! something in a trance!
To escape utterly from others' anchors and holds!
To drive free! to love free! to dash reckless and dangerous!
To court destruction with taunts, with invitations!
To ascend, to leap to the heavens of the love indicated to me!
To rise thither with my inebriate soul!
To be lost if it must be so!
To feed the remainder of life with one hour of fulness and freedom!
With one brief hour of madness and joy!

The floodgates of a highly sexed nature, the "pent-up rivers" of himself, gave way, and Whitman returned to nature. For the time he lost his sense of proportion, his reverence for the wisdom of the race. Sensation opened to him the gates of novel joys, and, that conscience might be kept at bay, he quickly found in the purity of his passion reasons why his love was pure. He took out his notebook, when the passion had a little spent itself but was still vivid in his memory, and wrote down, in lines as free of poetic convention as his life has been free from social convention, the story of the tyranny of passion, the revelation of sex.

One touch of a tug of me has unhaltered all my senses but feeling
That pleases the rest so, they have given themselves up in submission
They are all emulous to swap themselves off for what it can do to them.
Everyone must be a touch
Or else she will abdicate and nibble only at the edges of feeling.

They move caressingly up and down my body
They leave themselves and come with bribes to whatever part of me
    touches,—
To my lips, to the palms of my hands, and whatever my hands hold.
Each brings the best she has,
For each is in love with touch.
I do not wonder that one feeling now does so much for me,
He is free of all the rest,—and swiftly begets offspring of them, better
    than the dams.
A touch now reads me a library of knowledge in an instant.
It smells for me the fragrance of wine and lemon-blows.
It tastes for me ripe strawberries and melons,—
It talks for me with a tongue of its own,
It finds an ear wherever it rests or taps.
It brings the rest around it, and they all stand on a headland and mock
    me
They have left me to touch, and taken their place on a headland.
The sentries have deserted every part of me
They have left me helpless to the torrent of touch
They have all come to the headland to witness and assist against me.—
I roam about drunk and stagger

I am given up by traitors,
I talk wildly I am surely out of my head,
I am myself the greatest traitor.
I went myself first to the headland. . . .

Pass as you will; take drops of my life, if that is what you are after
Only pass to someone else, for I can contain you no longer
I held more than I thought
I did not think I was big enough for so much ecstasy
Or that a touch could take it all out of me.

The descent to nature is simple and swift. The atavism of sex in itself relieves the tension of civilized man's ill-fitting inhibitions, meanwhile stimulating through physical beauty that imagination which is able to create beauty of more enduring form. But man cannot become an animal by simply disregarding "others' anchors and holds." He cannot divest himself of his past nor of his dreams for his future. For that reason cultivated men who, wearied with the limitations of society, have sought to become "children of Adam" in some far South Sea isle or other, have generally returned to seek the freedom which is under law —the law of regarding others as well as themselves. The author of "Compensation" might have taught Whitman that one cannot have his cake and eat it—that when one seems to be doing so it is time to examine the quality of the cake. This the sensitive young Whitman was quick to do. He realized what he was losing. But he also was conscious of the new powers liberated in him—powers of sympathy as well as a new confidence in his own personal identity. He had broken the law, perhaps, but he was not yet damned. Indeed, the fruit of the tree of knowledge had made him wiser as well as sadder. His struggle with a weakness within would last many years, but his very first reaction taught him the indestructibility of his soul— he knew he was made neither selfish nor callous by his experience, but rather had learned to feel that all men are more strangely akin than he had thought.

Ah poverties, wincings, and sulky retreats,
Ah you foes that in conflict have overcome me,
(For what is my life or any man's life but a conflict with foes, the old
  incessant war?)
You degradations, you tussle with passions and appetites,
You smarts from dissatisfied friendships, (ah, wounds the sharpest of all!)
You toil of painful and choked articulations, you meannesses,
You shallow tongue-talks at tables, (my tongue the shallowest of any;)
You broken resolutions, you racking angers, you smother'd ennuis!
Ah think not you finally triumph, my real self has yet to come forth,
It shall yet march forth o'ermastering till all lies beneath me,
It shall yet stand up the soldier of ultimate victory.

If Whitman soon found in such an entanglement that which
threatened his independence and his future career, so that on
losing his position on the *Crescent* he was willing at once to depart from the South and the woman who loved him, he at least
never forgot her. She is the dark lady of his sonnets. Of
all the unfortunates for whom our civilization is responsible, he
singles out the class which she represented for special compassion in his verse. Poems of abandon he might set down in order
to record his own emotional experiences with her; but other
whole poems were written, and still others planned, to express
his tenderness for such outcasts—poems which he would not
leave out though the very life of his book was at stake.

BOOK III

THE SPIRIT SPEAKS

AKING two days to pack his few belongings and to make his adieus, Whitman, with Jeff, went aboard the *Pride of the West* at dusk on May 26. The steamer was a fast one, and put them in St. Louis almost as quickly as the *St. Cloud* had borne them downstream. Yet the passage was monotonous, especially to one who had recently made it; and Whitman, stimulated by no new excitement, had time to reflect on the experiences of the past three months. They had been very different from anything he could have expected of himself. They had released the bohemian in him, had taught him how sensitive he was to beauty and to sex, and had made it clear that henceforth romance was to be a part of his life. Perhaps he was glad to be leaving behind him a city wherein was no great opportunity for his ambition and where a yielding to the senses might even prove his undoing. In any case, his strong puritan training, having now an opportunity to reassert itself, doubtless threw into uncomfortable relief his recent "caressing of life." His sense of family responsibility made him realize, too, that Jeff's lot in New Orleans had been far from ideal. He had had to work harder than Walt thought he should, the water did not agree with him, and he was terribly homesick. There would be relief and safety in getting back to the accustomed standards and influences of Brooklyn.

Landing in St. Louis the following Saturday, Whitman reserved passage on an Illinois River steamer for La Salle, and while waiting for it to start, rambled over most of the town. The night trip up the Illinois was unpleasant. The steamer was overloaded with freight, and the passenger list was so large that Whitman had to sleep on the floor. To add to his discomforts, a storm blew up, making it necessary to tie the vessel to the shore. The next day Whitman inspected Peoria, as he did other cities on the route, inquiring the price of land and the demand for labor. Wonderful farm land, he found, could be had for four or five dollars an acre. From La Salle the brothers made their slow way to Chicago in a canal boat. The next morning, on board the *Griffith,* they started up Lake Michigan, the young poet admiring its "bright, lively color, so beautiful and rare."

He inspected the Wisconsin towns with interest, remembering that this state had the most advanced constitution in the Union, a constitution which safeguarded the rights of women as well as those of men. "It seems to me," he wrote in his diary, "that if we should ever remove from Long Island, Wisconsin would be the proper place to come to."

Crossing Lake Huron was uneventful.—On Lake Erie they passed over the scene of Perry's battle a generation before. On the evening of June 11 they arrived at the attractive little town of Cleveland, about which the Whitmans rambled in the dark. Erie was rough, and Whitman was all but seasick, but he cheered himself with anticipation of the stop at Buffalo and a visit to the show place of the New World, Niagara Falls. But when he saw the giant cataract he was unprepared for its grandeur. "Great God! What a sight!" was all he could exclaim.

A day and a night of further travel brought them to Albany. There a Democratic convention was in session; but finding it to be one of Hunkers, Whitman passed it by. With the old party that had committed itself not only to slavery as a temporary and a local institution in the South but to the morally unjustifiable extension of the virus into the free soil of the Union, Whitman would have no more to do. His residence in the South having taught him that slavery was not an unmixed evil for the negro at his present state of development, his attitude was not one of mere sentimental humanitarianism, like that of the Abolitionists; but he knew that slavery was inimicable to the development of the West by self-reliant, free pioneers, and for their opportunity he meant to fight. After all, he was a fighter, and felt that personal enjoyment could never satisfy him as an end in itself. The life that he knew, the power that he felt, the dreams that he enjoyed, must somehow be made available for his fellowmen. For this he was willing, for the time, to work through politics as the most available method of reform.

But he was never a reformer engrossed in one idea. When he saw anything to enjoy, he enjoyed it without asking why. Such a sight was the varied and imposing scenery of his own "lordly" Hudson River, down which he sailed in the *Alida*. He was immensely relieved to find that his mother, from whom he had heard but infrequently, was well, as were the other members of the family.

At the time when Whitman broke with the *Eagle* in January, the liberals in the party, as we have seen, finding their communications excluded from the only Democratic paper in the city, talked of starting a journal of their own, with Whitman as editor. Both Bryant and Greeley heard the rumors and encouraged them in their own papers. But for some reason, perhaps because financial backing could not at the time be had, the matter was dropped, at least so far as Whitman was concerned. But the ending of the war during his absence in the South gave new urgency to the problem of excluding slavery from the immense domains acquired by conquest. Whitman had not been back in Brooklyn more than a week when Henry Lees, English editor of the *Advertizer*, announced the return of "Mr. Barnburner Whitman." Lees had been the *Eagle's* chief political foe, and there had been many sharp passages of editorial arms between them, not always avoiding vulgar personalities. But Whitman as an ally in fighting the locally successful bosses of the *Eagle* was a different person entirely. The Freesoilers might not ultimately be absorbed by the Whigs, but on the dominant issue before the country they were fighting side by side. After recounting the history of Whitman's break with the *Eagle*, Lees says:

"But lo! whom should we meet, on the sidewalk in Fulton street yesterday afternoon, with his brown face smiling like a wicker vessel filled with wooden particles cleft from timber, but our Barnburner friend himself? 'Rienzi hath returned.' Dame Rumor tells some tales of a forthcoming gazette, in which old Hunkerism is to be handled without gloves.—Put that and that together and see what it works out. As for us, we 'say nothing to nobody,' in the way of positive information; but we like, at least by hints, to keep our readers well informed of what is going on in this blessed city of churches, and (if we may speak of them in the same sentence) *such* 'democrats' as have hitherto pulled the wires of their party.

"One thing we will predict, as a dead certainty: if our Barn-burning friend does put forth a daily here in Brooklyn, there'll be fun. No bull dog ever clutched determinedly on cattle's nasal membrane (that tender spot)—no Grimalkin ever worried horror-stricken mice—more than our amiable locofoco friend, the ex-editor of the *Eagle,* will be likely to clutch and worry Old Hunkerism in Kings County."

And the prediction was more than a guess. Judge Samuel E. Johnson, an ardent Free-soiler—"Nigger-catcher" he was called by his enemies, so zealous was he in underground-railroad-ing—put up the money and early in September Whitman brought out the first number of a weekly campaign sheet, the *Freeman.* The intention was to change it into a daily, should the results of the election insure its wider support. Whitman was the nominal proprietor and threw himself heart and soul into this his last political reform, as an outlet for the new sense of power he had found through his recent emotional awakening. He took part in local politics, and went to Buffalo as delegate to the Free-soil Convention, of which Judge Johnson was vice-president. This convention nominated Van Buren for the Presidency on a platform which affirmed the power and duty of Congress to exclude slavery from the territories. The Brooklyn mass meeting which ratified this platform elected Whitman one of its vice-presidents, his old friend Alden Spooner being one of the secretaries.

Lucky as he was in always finding some new and congenial

task of journalism, he sometimes drew a bad hand. The *Freeman* had modestly established itself in a basement at 110 Orange street (in the same building with the *Star*), just off Fulton. On Saturday morning, September 9, the first number had come from his press, to be complimented on its appearance by most of the newspapers of Brooklyn and New York. But that night a fire broke out in an upholstery establishment at 122 Fulton street and spread with such rapidity that the volunteer firemen, operating hand-pumps, could not gain control of it till many blocks in the heart of Brooklyn had been destroyed, including the *Freeman* plant in Orange street. Nor was there any insurance. Whitman's strongest characteristic, however, was dogged perseverance, a characteristic shared with the other enemies of slavery, so that in two months the *Freeman*, now published at 96 Myrtle Avenue, again jumped into the pre-election fight. "This time," declared the energetic young editor, "we are determined to go ahead. Smiles or frowns, thick or thin, we shall establish a Radical Newspaper in Kings County. Will it remain to be said that the friends of Liberal Principles here give it a meager and lukewarm aid?"

The *Freeman* has apparently been quite lost to history, but it was supported for a time so well that Whitman was hopeful of getting the city advertising. Indeed, he soon boasted that he sold two and three times more papers than the *Eagle* or the *Star*. He employed a number of the lively newsboys just coming into use, and the price of the paper was only a penny. Of course the election went against him, not only because that is the all too common fate of third-party protests, but because both the old and well organized parties had side-stepped the issue of free-soil. Long before Kansas should again make acute the issue, or even before the Fugitive Slave Law should arouse the free spirit of the North, Whitman would again have lost his job. The *Freeman* went so well, indeed, that, notwithstanding the defeat of the party, it was possible to make of it a daily paper, similar to what the *Eagle* had been under Whitman's management. This was in the spring of 1849. It looked as if Whitman, the wanderer, was going to settle down. He built a two-story house on the corner of Myrtle and Bridge, using the ground floor for a printing office and bookstore and the upper rooms for the family residence. But there were forces working against him, perhaps behind his back. The *Eagle* had cause to wish to draw the teeth of the *Freeman,* and this it seems to have done. In any case, this would be a natural result of the action taken by the Free-soil convention at Utica in September, consolidating its ticket with that of the regular wing of the party and led in doing so by Van Buren himself. At any rate, just a year after its first unlucky issue the editor of the *Freeman* found himself stranded again. His successor pretended to be equally independent until just before the fall election, when he endorsed the same ticket that the *Eagle* was supporting. But Whitman went out with colors flying—as the new editor said, in accounting for the change of policy, "He took his flag with him." And he did it with a cry of defiance and scorn, intended perhaps not only for his immediate enemies but for the whole tribe of petty politicians to whom personal interest was more than the interests of the people they pretended to serve. On September 11 he announced:

"After the present date, I withdraw entirely from the *Brooklyn Daily Freeman.* To those who have been my friends, I take occasion to proffer the warmest thanks of a grateful heart. My enemies—and old Hunkers generally—I disdain and defy the same as ever.—Walter Whitman."

He was through. In time he would join the Republican party and support Fremont and Lincoln, and he would edit one more Brooklyn newspaper; but henceforth, if he could not hitch his wagon to a star, he would not hitch it to a snail. At least he would have such a wagon as he could hitch to himself. He might do odd jobs in newspaper offices, as a means of making enough to supply his simple needs, but his life ambition would be connected with something which he could control, even as it controlled him. What was wrong with the country was simply the people in it, especially the people who had not his courage to vote and speak as conscience might direct. Now he would attempt to "disseminate culture among the masses," as Emerson had long counseled the young reformers to do.

But what was he to do? A year and a half before, when he was in a similar position, he was glad enough to get away from the scene of his defeat and to indulge the romance in his nature by a visit to the country of his dreams. He had now more than the *Wanderlust,* the need of change, to impell him to the open road again; he had memories of the woman of his dreams. As a man of affairs, he belonged in the North, where his work lay; but as a lover, his heart was in the South. Would not that woman who had so loved him now understand, if not his problems, yet his moods, his hunger for appreciation, as even his own adored mother could never do? Surely then, if ever, he felt the "longings for home"—longings which he would later write poetry about, disguising it with general terms.

O magnet—South! O glistening perfumed South! my South!
O quick metal, rich blood, impulse and love! good and evil! O all dear
    to me! . . .
O longings irrepressible! O I will go back to old
    Tennessee and never wander more.

Certainly he went back at some time, and what time more likely than this? If out of his love a child had been born (and he confided to a friend late in life that such was the case) it would now be six months old. Perhaps, when it grew old enough to understand or to remember, it would have to be kept away from him in the interest of its own social standing and peace of mind. Perhaps it would have to be given to the Church to raise, as love-children of the *demi monde* in New Orleans are to this day. But Whitman, the lover of children, the prophet of a grand paternity, would have to see it once. Of this or any later trip to the South he left but little record, but it would seem clear that he loitered on the way. At the Mammoth Cave, in Virginia, he stopped to gratify his curiosity, exploring its mysterious depths and talking with Proctor, his host at the Cave Hotel. At Blennerhassett Island, in the Ohio, he was entertained by a farmer named Johnson. Brooding on the scene of natural loveliness, and perhaps finding in it, as he found in all nature, now that he was becoming more and more subjective in his writing, a symbol of his own experiences, he wrote a poem and gave it to his appreciative but uncomprehending host. It had little inspiration, emotional freedom or *élan*, but it was far different from the verse he had written on the Mississippi the preceding year. He now discards rime and regular meter, relies more on the bold suggestiveness of his imagery, more on the poetic value of the object described, than on conventional tricks of expression. He grows surer of himself, and more daring.

> Bride of the swart Ohio,
> Nude, yet fair to look upon,
> Clothed only with the leaf,
> As was innocent Eve of Eden,
> The son of grim old Alleghany,
> And white-breasted Monongahela
> Is wedded to thee, and it is well.
> His tawny thighs cover thee
> In the vernal time of spring,
> And lo! in the autumn is the fruitage.
> Virgin of Nature, the holy spirit of the waters enshrouds thee
> And thou art pregnant with the fruits
> Of the field and the vine.
> But like the Sabine maid of old,
> The lust of man hath ravished thee
> And compelled thee to pay tribute to the
> Carnal wants of earth.
> Truth and romance make up thy
> Strange, eventful history,
> From the cycle of the red man,
> Who bowed at thy shrine and worshiped thee,
> To the dark days of that traitor
> Who linked thy innocent name to infamy.
> Farewell, Queen of the waters,

I have slept upon thy breast in the innocence of a babe,
But now I leave thee
To the embraces of thine acknowledged lord.

Perhaps on this journey to the South Whitman visited the "other states than Louisiana" in which he declared himself to have traveled, either to satisfy his boundless curiosity concerning America or possibly to follow dim traces of a happiness, which, untreasured at the time, had already slipped from his view. Whether he found her we do not know, but in any case he was to discover that only by opening vistas to more and more spiritual loveliness can the beauty of the senses make terms with its own mortality. At any rate, by 1850 he was a different man. His hair was now well streaked with gray, and his manner of life was altered so strangely that the older picture of the conventionally, even daintily, dressed young editor has been blotted from the memory of those who knew him.

But Whitman had other mistresses. One of them was his country, and no one ever loved her more devotedly. In the spring of 1850 she seemed, to his partial eyes, in sore distress. The plague spot of slavery appeared sure to spread to the West, for even the most temperate men in the nation, Webster and Clay, were counseling compromise. To Whitman this was, on Webster's part, not the moderation of a broad-minded statesman, but betrayal by a coward or a mercenary. And not only Webster, but all the Whig and Free-soil Democrats of the North, were unworthy of his ideal for "Libertad." He would scourge the time-serving misrepresenters of the people from the temple of Democracy. The South had her extenuations if not her excuses, but he could see no excuse in the North for compromise on a moral question. He cried out, as an orator cries, in lines of lyric passion, scorning the conventional tricks of poetic rhetoric:

Virginia, Mother of greatness,
Blush not for being the mother of slaves.
You might have borne deeper slaves—

Doughfaces, Crawlers, Lice of Humanity—
Terrific screamers of Freedom,
Who roar and bawl, and get hot i' the face,
But, were they not incapable of august crime,
Would quelch the hopes of ages for a drink—
Muck-worms, creeping flat to the ground,
A dollar dearer to them than Christ's blessing;
All loves, all hopes, less than the thought of gain,
In life walking in that as in a shroud:
Men whom the throes of heroes,
Great deeds at which the gods might stand appalled,
The shriek of a drowned world, the appeal of women,
The exulting laugh of untied empires,
Would touch them never in the heart,
But only in the pocket.

But the hope of the future lies in its youth, and to them the poetic cavalier sounds his battle cry.

Arise, young North!
Our elder blood flows in the veins of cowards—
The gray-haired sneak, the blanched poltroon,
The feigned or real shiverer at tongues
That nursing babes need hardly cry the less for—
Are they to be our tokens always?

And when Webster advocated that legalistic abomination of abominations in the North, the Fugitive Slave Law, Whitman went to Greeley with a poem, "Blood-Money," charging that statesman with being "guilty of the body and the blood of Christ." It was not very good poetry. Sudden outbursts of scorn seldom are, even Whittier's "Ichabod" written on the same occasion. But it was better than a newspaper editorial. And it suggested to Whitman a new way to address the conscience of the nation. Yet Whitman could not have loved his country so much, loved he not liberty more. When, by the summer of this year, it became apparent that the revolutions in Europe had, for the most part, failed in establishing the rights of the average man, or even the independence of little nations, his spirit, though saddened, lost none of its intrepidity. It was something at least for them to have asserted their manhood.

> God! 'twas delicious!
> That brief, tight, glorious grip
> Upon the throats of kings.

The failure of the revolutions abroad and the apparent failure of the spirit of freedom at home, resulting in the compromises of 1850 and the extinction of the Free-soil party, robbed Whitman, for the time, of a cause and gave him leave to meditate how he might work in more enduring materials than the surface movements of massed mankind. Having made his peace with Lees, he wrote a little for the *Advertizer*—anonymously, out of pride and political sagacity. He corresponded a little for Bryant's *Evening Post*. But he was practically footloose. He still had his printing shop, and did what printing he could, sometimes for the Kings County Board of Supervisors. Later he helped his father in housebuilding. But all these occupations were flexible ones, and he enjoyed having, at the same time, a sense of enlarged personal power and more leisure to cultivate it. He became a bohemian, not to affect a fad, but because it was congenial to his spirit and habits. He did not mind if people noticed a certain eccentricity in him—they would then leave him the more alone with his inner communings. Moreover, he was cultivating the society of artists.

One day in 1851 he went to the exhibition of paintings given by the young artists of the Brooklyn Art Union. He was struck both by the artists and the work they were doing. He was pleased to see that others were working for the expression of native themes, as he had urged singers and dramatists to do, and novelists and painters. Instead of making portraits of the nobility, or the landscapes of palace grounds, William Mount and Walter Libby were picturing simple country boys, black or white. "The stamp of class is, in this way, upon all the fine scenes of the European painters, where the subjects are of a proper kind; while in this boy of Libbey's, there is nothing to prevent his becoming a President, or," he added with a sarcastic smile at the current incumbent of that office, "even an editor of a leading newspaper."

The artists, the young bohemians, should be encouraged, he told the readers of the *Evening Post*.

"There are at the present moment ten thousand so-called artists, young and old, in this country, many of whom are working in the dark, as it were, and without aim. They want a strong hand over them. Here is a case for the imperial scepter, even in America. . . . What a glorious result it would give, to form of these thousands a close phalanx, ardent, radical and progressive. Now they are like the bundle of sticks in the fable, and, as one by one, they have no strength. Then, would not the advancing years foster the growth of a grand and true art here, fresh and youthful, worthy this republic, and this greatest of the ages?" The children in the schools, he now sees, should not be taught merely the arithmetic of the counting house, but something of the quest for beauty. "Nearly all intelligent boys and girls have much of the artist in them, and it were beautiful to give them an opportunity of developing it in one of the fine arts."

But first of all comes the Artist. He may be bohemian, but he is the finest specimen of the race for all that. "With warm, impulsive souls, instinctively generous and genial, but mean and sneaking never—such are these rapidly increasing ones. Unlike the orthodox sons and daughters of the world in many things, yet it is a picturesque unlikeness. For it need not argue an absolute miracle, if a man differ from the present dead uniformity of 'society' in appearance and opinion, and still retain his grace and morals. A sunny blessing, then, say I, on the young artist race! for the thrift and shrewdness that make dollars, are not everything that we should bow to, or yearn for, or put before our children as the be all and the end all of all human ambition."

California was still luring thousands away with its elusive

gold; and Mammon in less romantic but more respectable dis-
guise was trying to tempt our young artist at home. Brooklyn
was on a building boom, wages were high, sales were ready.
For want of an easier way to make what money he needed,
Whitman for a time turned to his father's trade, for the old
man was nearing his grave and his hand was losing its cunning.
Jeff was working on the city waterworks and advancing rapidly
in his profession as a surveyor. George and the other able sons
were at work with Mr. Whitman. So Walt took up the tools
of a carpenter, building house after house. The Whitmans
would build a residence, live in it from one "moving day" to
the next, and then sell it as population in the rapidly growing
city increased the demand and the price. Thus they shifted
from Myrtle avenue to Cumberland, from Cumberland to Skill-
man, and then to Ryerson and Classon. The expansion halting,
they came back nearer the center of town to live in 1859, and
there they remained till the war scattered their family forever.
But no pressure from the family could induce Whitman to put
his carpentering above the things that concerned his inner growth
and his country's future. "His big opportunity missed!" they
sighed, little understanding the nature of the stake that he was
playing for. Had he amassed a competence at this time in the
manner approved by the average American, his life would no
doubt have been far easier in many ways. Even his philosophy
of life might have incorporated some of the shrewd worldly
wisdom of Franklin, who respected riches as a safeguard of virtue. He might have been less inclined to make a virtue of
poverty. But, on the other hand, only by convincing himself
that he was better off without the respectable responsibilities of
wealth could he devote all his energies to that which would lift
him, by sheer excellence, above the plebeian class in which he
was born. For in spirit he was a noble Greek, associating with
the masters as with friends and equals.

Whenever possible he went to lectures on Greek and Roman
civilization. The classical tradition was at this time more congenial to him than the English, because it was more distinct.

Though not dead to him, it was something to be joyfully apprehended in all its clarity rather than to be absorbed through a multitude of emotional contacts, as was the life about him. And this was the more delightful as a precipitant of his own inner purposes, since a change was coming over him which, above his mere will, was to remove him in a sense from the *milieu* about him—remove him into the future rather than into the past. His family noticed it, but were powerless to affect it or even to get his ear for their criticism of his increasing strangeness. He would pick up his big soft hat just as a meal was being laid on the table by his mother and sisters and go off on some impulse of his own, without explanation or apology, returning, if need be, to eat in solitude. Night after night he was out, at the opera or the theater, atop the stage coaches, or studying the life of the city in less conspicuous retreats. But the young artists understood him, or at least they comprehended that he understood them, which was sufficient. So they invited him to deliver an address on a March evening in 1851. He prepared himself carefully, rounding out his periods till they were almost poetic, playing on just the right emotions to sway the young radical—the scorn of conformity and style, the reverence for the truly heroic, the sublimity of enduring beauty in a life or in a picture of life. Now that he had a select and appreciative audience, he could afford to drop the platitudes of the stump speech and the condescending colloquialism whereby he had sought to widen the circle of his newspaper readers.

"Among such a people as the Americans," he began, "viewing most things with an eye to pecuniary profit—more for acquiring than for enjoying or well developing what they acquire—ambitious of the physical rather than the intellectual; a race to whom matter of fact is everything, and the ideal nothing—a nation of whom the steam engine is no bad symbol—he does a good work, who, pausing in the way, calls to the feverish crowd that in the life we live upon this beautiful earth, there may, after all, be something vaster and better than dress and the table, and business and politics."

That would be his function henceforth, to pause in the way and to point as persuasively as he could, as defiantly as he must, to the beauty of that truth which the Orientals had for centuries made the end of their existence. Having himself tasted of power and of love, and found them both more easy to lose than to gain, he was making no great sacrifice, if, with "Asiatic complacency" and artistic subjectiveness, he should render himself immune to the cruder slings of outrageous fortune.

But music was more closely related to his own artistic needs than was drama or painting. There was one tenor singing in New York at this period whom Whitman adored as much as he did the contralto Alboni. This was Bettini, whose singing of *La Favorita* he remembered, with gratitude, to his dying day. The time was mid-summer, a hot evening in August. Finishing an early supper, Whitman struck off on foot for the ferry, passing the aristocratic Heights section on his way. There the breeze from the bay met him on the hill; so, baring his head and crushing his great soft hat behind him, he watched the gorgeous sunset behind the New Jersey marshes. He might be late, but his eye was as hungry as his ear, and here a divine musician was playing a nocturne on the color-organ of the heavens.

"Sails of sloops bellied gracefully upon the river, with mellower light and deepened shadows. And the dark and glistening water formed an undertone to the play of vehement color above.

"Rapidly, an insatiable greediness grew within me for brighter and stronger hues; oh, brighter and stronger still. It seemed as if all that the eye could bear were unequal to the fierce voracity of my soul for intense, glowing color.

"And yet there were the most choice and fervid fires of the sunset, in their brilliancy and richness almost terrible.

"Have you not too, at such a time, known the thirst of the eye? Have you not, in like manner, while listening to the well-played music of some band like Maretzek's, felt an overwhelming desire for measureless sound—a sublime orchestra of myriad orchestras—a colossal volume of harmony, in which the thunder might roll in its proper place; and above it, the vast, pure Tenor—identity of the Creative Power itself—rising through the universe, until the boundless and unspeakable capacities of that mystery, the human soul, should be filled to the uttermost, and the problem of human cravingness be satisfied and destroyed?"

A romantic nature is this, and conscious, now, of its romantic needs! But music could solace him, the music of Donizetti, and the music that would soon be his own. This very hunger for the sweet, august voice of Creation would in time be somewhat appeased by a poem he was to compose, partly in memory of this evening, one of the grandest nature poems to flow through the soul of man—"Proud Music of the Storm."

Now the great organ sounds,
Tremulous, while underneath, (as the hid footholds of the earth,
On which arising rest, and leaping forth depend,
All shapes of beauty, grace and strength, all hues we know,
Green blades of grass and warbling birds, children that gambol and play,
    the clouds of heaven above,)
The strong base stands, and its pulsations intermit not,
Bathing, supporting, merging all the rest, maternity of all the rest,
And with it every instrument in multitudes,
The players playing, all the world's musicians,
The solemn hymns and masses rousing adoration,
All passionate heart-chants, sorrowful appeals,
The measureless sweet vocalists of ages,
And for their solvent setting earth's own diapason,
Of winds and woods and mighty ocean waves,
A new composite orchestra, binder of years and climes, ten-fold renewer,
As of the far-back days the poets tell, the Paradiso,
The straying thence, the separation long, but now the wandering done,
And man and art with Nature fused again.

The sun sank, the colors faded, and Whitman, coming back to reality, reminded himself that the opera was yet before him. Walt ascended to the balcony. In such a setting he was to write many a poem, to the inspiration, if not to the tune, of the opera, just as he was to compose many another at home while Jeff played his violin in an adjoining room. Below him chattered the society of the metropolis, but he was not conscious of any envy of that society. To his reader he said:

"Come, I will not talk to you as one of the superficial who saunter here because it is the fashion, who take opera glasses with them and make you sick with shallow words upon the sublimest and most spiritual of the arts. I will trust you with confidence; I will divulge secrets.

"The delicious music of 'the Favorite' is upon us. Gradually we see not this huge amphitheater, nor the cropped heads and shaven faces of the men, nor coal-scuttle bonnets, nor hear the rattle of fans nor even the ill-bred chatter. We see the groves of a Spanish convent and the procession of monks; we hear the chant, now dim and faint, then swelling loudly, and then again dying away among the trees. The aged Superior and the young Fernando we see. In answer to the old man's rebukes and questions we hear the story of love."

Then Whitman recounted the old familiar story of the young Fernando, a novice whose heart was given to the things of the spirit but whose young body colored his visions with dreams of woman's delicious loveliness. He went out into a strange world to seek her. He found her at the court, and she loved him in return. Serving well the state in war, he claimed her hand in marriage as a guerdon from his sovereign. Too late he discovered that she was the favorite mistress of that sovereign, deposed only by a recent order from the Pope. Brokenhearted and disillusioned, he returned to his mission. When his love finds him and explains that she had told all in a letter he had never received, he forgives her and she dies.

"Now we approach the close of the legend. We see again the dark groves of the convent. Up through the venerable trees peal the strains of the chanting voices. Oh, sweet music of Donizetti, how can men hesitate what rank to give you! "With his pale face at the foot of the cross kneels the returned novice, his breast filled with devouring anguish, his eyes

showing the death that had fallen upon his soul. The strains of
death, too, come plaintively from his lips. Never before did you
hear such gushing sorrow, poured forth like the ebbing flood,
from a murdered heart. Is it for peace he prays with that appealing passion? Is it the story of his own sad wreck he ut-
ters?

"Listen. Pure and vast that voice now rises, as on clouds,
to the heaven where it claims audience. Now, firm and unbroken, it spreads like an ocean around us. Ah! welcome that
I know not the mere language of the mere words in which the
melody is embodied; as all words are mean before the language
of true music."

The artist in the poet answered the artist on the Castle Garden stage, and knew himself to belong to the same race, "as
souls only understand souls."

> Composers! mighty maestros!
> And you, sweet singers of old lands, soprani, tenori, bassi!
> To you a new bard caroling in the West,
> Obeisant sends his love,

he sang a score of years later; but through the *Post* he sent his
appreciation at the time:

"Thanks, great artist! For one, at least, it is no extravagance to say you have justified his ideal of the loftiest of the
arts. Thanks, limner of the spirit of life, and hope and peace;
of the red fire of passion, the cavernous vacancy of despair and
the black pall of the grave.

"I write as I feel; and I feel that there are not a few who
will pronounce a 'yes' to my own confession."

Never had Whitman written so enthusiastically of the drama
or of any other music. Was it indeed the power of Bettini?
Even so, how could the young music critic judge of that performance unless he had passed through the storms of passion
and the fires of painful loss himself? Had he already lost, by
death or eternal separation, his own "favorite," and now first

comprehended how much solace there might be for him, if, like Heine, he might make a song out of his great pain?

The stranger casually meeting the large rough figure of Whitman, dressed in workman's clothes, the neck of his red flannel shirt wide open, his pace slow rather than elastic, would not have suspected that his body was probably the most sensitive organism in the city, his sense of hearing and smell exceptionally acute, and his touch so highly developed that personal force went out of him at each contact of the hand with properly sensitive hands.

> Mine is no callous shell,
> I have instant conductors all over me whether I pass or stop,
> They seize every object and lead it harmlessly through me.

The observer would still less have imagined what a delicate mental and emotional organism was within, responsive to suggestions of childhood's "trailing clouds of glory," as likely as Jeanne d'Arc to commune with spirits and to believe them. And into this organism, emerging from the protracted discord of adolescence so common in men of genius, there was soon to come a harmony, which, if it did not eliminate the fundamental paradoxes which composed his temperament, would reduce them to a state of balanced peace. But this could never have happened without a certain enervation, a certain resultant weakness or failure elsewhere, had there not been a compensating objectivity, an animal delight in sense experiences, a child's unreflecting wonder at outward shows. Before telling the story of that inner change, we must take a glimpse of Whitman in the presence of his fellow man and of nature.

Whitman had a peculiar genius for friendship, which grew in proportion as he abandoned the ordinary strife for the ordinary prizes. It was akin to the friendship man has for nature, impartial, receptive, kindly uncritical. Like Byrant, he loved to watch humanity pass by on its petty personal missions, himself remaining inert the while. It was not Diogenes in his tub, seeking to reduce experience to the formulæ of philosophy, but rather the open-eyed child who has forgotten to grow up. He was never tired by repetition of the same sight, provided it were natural or human. And nowhere could a man of this type find sights more to his taste than on Broadway. The grand processions of presidents and generals, distinguished foreign visitors, ambassadors and artists, all passed there. Yet common humanity was sufficient on any fine day to warrant a two-hour ride on an omnibus. Before the day of horse-cars, these omnibuses were, relatively, as numerous as taxicabs are to-day. It would almost have been possible to walk on their tops from the Astor house to Wall Street. And handsome stages they were too, drawn by two or four horses and ornamented by the brushes of the best decorators. Passengers entered by a side door or a door at the rear, passing their fare up to the driver through a hole in the roof. And those drivers were a race of originals, "strange, natural, quick-eyed and wondrous race," a study and a delight for Rabelais, Cervantes, Shakespeare—or Whitman. "Powerful, uneducated persons" they were, eating, drinking, loving women, telling vivid stories with the mimicry of born raconteurs, quick to know a man from a nincompoop. Their stage lines, like their own nicknames, were individual and picturesque as no mode of transportation will ever be again—the Yellow Birds, the Red Birds, the Knickerbocker, not to mention the lines named for Broadway, Fifth Avenue, Fourth Avenue and so forth. One day Whitman, who knew them all, set down in his notebook the names of as many drivers as he could recall: Shortly—Deadbodie—Letloose—Graball—Christmas Johnnie—Doughnuts—Poggy—Codmouth—Black Jack—Broadway Jack—Dressmaker—Harlem Charley—Pochuck—Dry Dock John—Raggedy—Jack Smith's Monkey—Emigrant—Buffalo—Wild Man of Borneo—Elephant—Baltimore Charley—Blind Sam—Santa Anna—Long Boston—Pretty Ike—Mountaineer—Rosy. What a great, overgrown boys' world it was! At first, they were a little suspicious of Whitman, he knew so much about books. But when, one winter, a driver lay ill and Whitman quietly took his place on that

driver's box to support his family, they knew he was of the
right breed. Then the whole race of drivers, with the clan-
nishness of boys, admitted him to their fellowship. He would
stand at the curb and a driver would draw up, casting at him a
friendly and inquiring glance of invitation. Without a word,
if he were so minded at the moment, Whitman would seize the
handle and swing up with a springing and elastic motion to
light on the off side of the box, as quietly, he put it, "as a hawk
swoops to its nest."   No wheel on Broadway was rubber-tired,
and the street was paved with cobblestones; so that the din was
a continuous rumble, over which no voice could carry far.
Sometimes, feeling exuberant, he would shout passages from
"Richard II" or Homer over the heads of the pedestrians.   Or
he would listen to the stories or the life history of his host.   At
other times, he would brood upon the panorama, his dull eyes
fixed in a kind of half-dream, interrupted only by the frequent
salutes he must give, boy-like, with raised arm and upright hand,
to four out of every five of the drivers who passed him.   It was
an ideal vantage point for a poet who wished not only to observe, but, without breaking his solitude, to be personally in
contact with the living stream his soul was fishing in.   In return for their uniform courtesy, there was little Whitman could
give these drivers, save his friendship, for they could receive
little.   But when one of them died, he could at least write a
fitting requiem and place it in his portfolio, doubtless the only
poem ever written on the theme.

A reminiscence of the vulgar fate,
A frequent sample of the life and death of workmen,
Each after his kind.

Cold dash of waves at the ferry-wharf, posh and ice in the river, half-
     frozen mud in the streets,
A gray discouraged sky overhead, the short last daylight of December,
A hearse and stages, the funeral of an old Broadway stage-driver, the
     cortege mostly drivers,
Steady the trot to the cemetery, duly rattles the death-bell,

The gate is pass'd, the new-dug grave is halted at, the living alight, the
hearse uncloses,
The coffin is passed out, lower'd, and settled, the whip is laid on the
coffin, the earth is swiftly shoveled in,
The mound above is flatted with the spades—silence,
A minute—no one moves or speaks—it is done,
He is decently put away—is there anything more?

He was a good fellow, free-mouth'd, quick-temper'd, not bad-looking,
Ready with life or death for a friend, fond of women, gambled, ate
hearty, drank hearty,
Had known what it was to be flush, grew low-spirited toward the last,
sicken'd, was helped by a contribution,
Died, aged forty-one years—and that was his funeral.

Thumb extended, finger uplifted, apron, cape, gloves, strap, wet-weather
clothes, whip carefully chosen,
Boss, spotter, starter, hostler, somebody loafing on you, you loafing on
somebody, headway, man before and man behind,
Good day's work, bad day's work, pet stock, mean stock, first out, last
out, turning-in at night,
To think that these are so much and so nigh to other drivers, and he
there takes no interest in them.

And still, as always, Walt frequented the ferry-boats, the
stages of the river. He wanted to know everything about the
boat; there was no plan, no conscious selection in his acquisition
of information. And there would be as little rejection when he
sat down to write. "Tell me all about it, boys," he would say,
"for these are the real things I cannot get out of books." And
when they told him he remembered, never missing the technical
phrases of the many occupations he studied. Tiring of long
reading in the libraries or of composition at home, he would
seek his ferry friends and tell them stories, repeat what he had
read, or make sharp criticisms of the events of the day. When
there were few passengers, sometimes he would sing snatches
from the operas, or recite from Shakespeare in his best manner. When he had awakened an interest in some writer, Homer

or Shakespeare or Epictetus, he would say to his young friend and willing pupil, "My boy, you must read more of this for yourself," cramming his own volume into the pocket of the sailor's monkey-jacket.

Whitman was always fascinated by expositions. Indeed, the plan of his first book was to make an exhibition, not only of an individual as such, but as a repository of all the hetereogenous displays his age and land had afforded him. When, on July 14, 1853, the Crystal Palace fair was opened in New York, Whitman began his visits, which were to be kept up through a whole year. So curious and persistent was he in his study of whatever specially interested him that he excited the attention of the police, who exercised particular surveillance over him. It was beyond the intelligence of a simple policeman to comprehend how a roughly dressed visitor could stand for hours before Thorwaldsen's marbles unless he were premeditating a theft. When, sometime later, Walt made the acquaintance of these same policemen, they confided to him, to his amusement, their former fears and precautions.

But Whitman did not belong altogether in the city. His birthplace was in the country, and there he spent a part of almost every summer. If he were editing a newspaper, he would, like Bryant, leave it to shift without him, sending back correspondence while he was away. This getting back to nature was quite as important, as an element in keeping him sane and wholesome, as was his getting close to the humanity he was now living to serve and enjoy.

It is one o'clock on a fine day in the summer or early fall. Leisurely pushing his way into the throng gathered about the platforms at the foot of Atlantic Avenue at the hour for the Long Island railroad train to start on its slow daily trip to Greenport, Whitman, carpet-bag in hand, makes his way into one of the primitive, high-wheeled coaches. Raucous newsboys, friends shouting farewells as if for a hazardous journey or an indefinite separation, Irish women vending peaches and oranges, the crude locomotive filling the air with smoke and giving forth ominous rattles—a symbol of America indeed. The bell rings, the train starts, and ambitious youngsters, seeking final sales, run along to poke their wares through the windows. But soon the scene is lost as the train plunges into the darkness of a tunnel, cold and damp. Fifth Avenue is passed, the hills of Greenwood Cemetery and the sight of Gowanus are left behind, the residential section of Bedford, with its ample shade trees is passed, and the train pulls into East New York. It is, or was, a boom town, battening its hopes on the speculations bred of the United States Bank, to which Jackson's veto put such a summary end. Whitman was himself asked, years before, to go there and start a village newspaper; but he seems to have had an instinct for the future. The next stop is Jamaica. Whitman can remember when it was nothing but a long street, lined with stores and taverns, a stopping place for the market wagons making their way from the island to the metropolis. At twenty he lived there himself, teaching school a few miles down the road and helping James Brenton, familiarly called "Dr. Franklin," get out the *Long Island Democrat.* He lived with the Brentons, but his fondness for loafing on his back under the apple trees, looking up at the sun, was to be longer remembered in the household than anything he ever wrote for the paper. Yet he contributed a good deal—puerile, melancholy rimes on death and human vanity or ambitious philosophizing about the nature of man and the duty of brotherly love. He was already given to moods not unlike a trance, and he cultivated the mystical outlook on life. Yet at Jamaica he was ready on occasion to cast all care aside and make one of a party to go sailing or clamming on the Great South Bay, or, in winter, spearing eels through holes in the ice. Those were happy care-free days, filled with healthful body-building exercise, far from the city with its woes and responsibilities.

At Mineola the train stops and detaches a car to be drawn by horses two miles south to Hempstead. There too Whitman once taught school for a few months and wrote for the local pa-

per. Sweeping southeast the turnpike threads the south-side
towns he knew and loved so well in his youth—Babylon, Pat-
chogue, and the Hamptons. There at the Hamptons, when a
boy, he all but saw a steamer wrecked. Its terror so horrified
his impressionable soul that he ran away for miles. Directly to
the north lies the village of Jericho, birthplace of Elias Hicks, a
Quaker community, and near by is Cold Spring, the homestead
of his Dutch ancestry, the Van Velsors. In that neighborhood
was another of his many schools. The farm which was once
his father's lies a little farther to the east, near the high
ground at West Hills, a stronghold of democracy and a fertile
and well wooded region. East of Jamaica, along the railroad
which runs through the center of the island, extends a great
plain, sterile, covered with kill-calf and huckleberry bushes, and
pasturing hundreds of milch cows. As the train puffs along in
the late evening Whitman can make out the clanking of copper
cowbells, as the kine file slowly homeward. Land monopoly
keeps it from cultivation, whereas, with the fish fertilizer being
used by the farmers along the South shore, it might otherwise
give homesteads to thousands. As a democrat, Whitman
naturally protests against such a parceling out of the gifts of
nature. The farther east he rides, the worse the country looks,
the more deserted. Scrub oak and pine everywhere, and now
and then, as darkness comes on, he can make out the fires of the
charcoal burners. But the stations are merely a few ragged
houses, often unoccupied, a few lazily tended gardens, a few
nondescript, barefooted children. Now and then he catches
sight of roads which lead to places he knows, roads he has
traversed as a lad, hunting adventure in a wilderness all his own.
Some of these roads lead to the schools he has taught, and remind him of youthful friends and of evenings in the homes of
sturdy, self-reliant farmer folk. Up there at Huntington he
started his first newspaper, and delivered its weekly issues
through the whole region on Saturdays, riding his own pony.
The scrub-oak wilderness is devoid of interest, however, save
that supplied by memories of his youth, and now he has an ex-

cellent opportunity to take stock of his life. He is in his early thirties, full of ambition, full of the love of life; and yet is he not a failure? He has had many opportunities, but where are they now? He has fought in many causes, but which of them has he won? Was he not in fact merely fighting some contrary tendency in himself in each case? Has he won the fight for self-mastery? He does not, cannot know, but he is sure of one thing: by so much as he has been growing through all these experiences, he is the more indifferent to the outward fates of his life. Moreover, he is becoming conscious that he is different from other men, in his ambitions, his affections, his powers. He cannot tell what he will do, but in one way or another it shall be to learn the art of living more largely than the rest, more largely because he will live less for himself.

These simple folk with their unconstrained mentality give him courage. They represent the things which endure—simple personal qualities. And like them are the hardy fishermen with whom he will consort when he reaches the terminus of the road at Greenport. Having come to the country to escape the city, he is displeased to find the boarding houses there trying to make city tourists feel at home, with pianos, mahogany chairs, fashionable carpets and flummery in general. What he desires is simplicity, cleanliness, and plenty of wholesome country fare. Nor can he understand the value of coming to the country, as most of his fellow New Yorkers do, to keep out of the sun and air. "They evidently preserve all the ceremoniousness of the city —dress regularly for dinner, fear to brown their faces with the sun, or wet their shoes with the dew, or let the wind derange the sleeked precision of their hair." Such people, unable to stand up with dignity or ease when stripped of the corseting of convention, interest Whitman before a background of wild nature even less than when they appeared, in evening costume, at Castle Garden. He determines to go out among real persons, however humble, seeking what they may teach him about the mystery, the fascinating heterogeneity, of life.

It was the farmer folk, like the mechanics and stage drivers

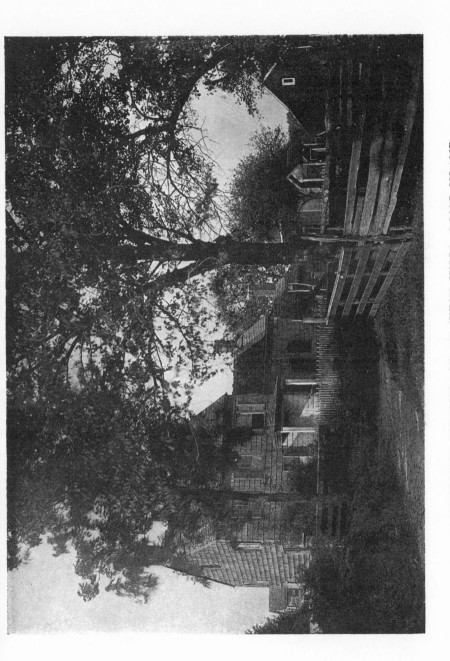

WHITMAN'S BIRTHPLACE AT WEST HILLS, LONG ISLAND

of New York, with independence enough to make their lives fit
their personalities, that Whitman counted on as the bulwark of
the republic. He had had enough experience in politics to
cause him to doubt that the voice of the people, taken numeri-
cally, is the voice of God; but he believed that the people,
properly addressed, would recognize that voice. With the com-
munistic experiments of Fourier, of Brook Farm, of Fruitlands,
he would have nothing to do; for he knew that he could not endure to live in any standardized society, or even to work in a
factory or with an organization wherein division of labor and
responsibility would ultimately divide the man as well. He
dreamed of the industrial exploitation of the country, but in
those dreams was no room for the factory system wherein the
rapidly increasing use of steam was already creating a new set
of problems for government, a new barrier between the North
and the South.

Though there were few books in the Whitman home and
though he was not now receiving review copies as a newspaper
editor, we are not to suppose that he was reading no more. He
was especially fond of magazines, English or American, caring
little if they were second-hand and a bit old. What he wanted
was information about the parts of the world his eye had never
explored, knowledge of how the rest of mankind lived, or had
lived long ago—what religions, what art and architecture, what
ideas of immortality they had. He was interested, too, in those
newer subjects just beginning to be taught in the schools,
chemistry, astronomy, physiology. He would tear out the
magazine article, stuff it into his big pocket, and take it with
him to the seashore or to the shade of some hillside, to ponder
over and annotate it at his leisure, always feeling free to gloss
what he read with comments of his own. He frequented old
bookstores, too, for there he could always find cheap copies of
the classics, his masters. The *Enchiridion* of Epictetus filled
him with a sense of personal sufficiency, thrilled him with the
conception of a sage giving moral lessons to his fellows in words

fitly chosen. Homer, Sophocles, Shakespeare, the Bible, and a little later, Dante—all kept him company on the deserted but far from lonely shores of Coney Island, or in some sequestered wood. Thither he would go alone for the week-end, taking with him a book to read and paper on which to jot down such inspirations as came to him. For by this time he knew certainly that he was himself about to bring forth a book of some sort. Even when carpentering he would slip into his lunch basket a book to read at the noon hour. One fortunate day the book selected was the "Essays" of Emerson. It proved to be the needed precipitant, as it has been to many a young man and woman since.

The mind and soul of Whitman, the American, lay fallow, and ready for the seed sown by the germinative mind of Emerson. For the latter was no dry, pedantic formulator of a philosophic system; he was a concrete American interpretation of the abstractions of German transcendentalists and Eastern mystics. He "sold" the idea of the inner life of man to certain classes of the American people. But this he did more by poetizing it than by rationalizing it. From such persuasiveness one may turn away, but against it argument is futile. Emerson spoke of things that he knew, and there is no way to deny his testimony as such. On testimony, by word or life, every religious or spiritual movement advances or recedes; creeds and institutions but mark its progress and consolidate its gains. Now, when a man has observed the world attentively a long while, if he be not a mere child lost in unreflective wonder, its diversity and apparent contradiction, transferred to his inner consciousness, begin to embarrass him. Low souls select some simple, material end in life, such as amassing a fortune, or adding pleasure to pleasure, seeking thus a simple solution of their existence by denying all else. But more heroic minds crave a unity which will reconcile this diversity, making a beautiful cosmos of what, to the senses, is but chaos. If the intellect predominate over the imagination, the man becomes a philosopher, achieving peace of mind in proportion to the universality of his analysis

of the world he has known.   He discards what cannot, by his
scientific method, be reduced to a semblance of form.   But if
he be a man of imagination, sensitive to much that can never
pass through the conscious mind to be dissected by the blunt
scalpels of the reason, he becomes a poet.   Then he seeks
in some form of mysticism a "solvent and a setting for it
all."   And this is what Emerson, and all the Transcendentalists,
were doing, and had been doing for twenty years.   Nor were
they pioneers in this attitude toward life, even in America,
though they were the first to unite the artist with the priest,
the lover of beauty with the lover of a beautiful life.   Mysticism has always flourished as a protest when formalism, legal-
ism, unimaginative creed-worship have too long repressed the
aspiring, loving soul of man.   And when, in the eighteenth century, the Great Awakening came, producing Methodism, the religion of personal experience, to be preached eloquently and
with popular success in England by the Wesleys and in America
by Whitefield, Jonathan Edwards and the circuit riders of
the frontier, it had a very definite doctrine of mystical union with
God.   The phrase by which it was known to-day seems as obso-
lete as the doctrine itself; it was suggestively called by John
Wesley the "witness of the Spirit."   Religious experience was
considered not fully consummated until the believer knew for
himself that he had been transfigured by a glimpse of the Unseen Spirit of Life.   But in Methodism, unlike the nihilism of
Gautama or the feudalism of Brahma, and unlike some of the
daintier forms of Transcendentalism, this inner ecstasy was not
to be enjoyed in monastic asceticism, but was definitely related
to a life of humanitarian service.   In this respect, it had much
in common with the practice of the Quakers.   It is not difficult
to understand, then, how well prepared was Whitman, in his
early thirties, for such an experience.   He had been brought up
to believe in the "inner light."   He had that repose, that re-
ceptivity, that sluggishness of the motor and muscular organism
that is conducive to "quietism" and to visions.   It was as if our
world were throbbing with radio waves bearing hints of another

and diviner world, capable of being caught only by the most sensitive receiving set. And Whitman, the silent man, was alway listening for signals from this far country. When a friend of his, unable to comprehend the mystery of mysticism, finally experienced a sort of illumination during a period of convalescence, his spirit filtered by the sickness of his body and for the time ceasing to struggle with life, he remarked the fact to Walt, who replied, "I suppose a poet is always convalescent." He, too, had ceased to "sweat through fog with linguists and contenders." Moreover, he had known love, which, when pure, more perfectly than any other human experience symbolizes the transports of the *exalté*. For as in love man achieves at least a momentary release from the prison of the body through the meeting and merging of two souls, so with the mystic the individual soul seems to itself to be swallowed up in the absolute Soul of the universe.

Our story of Walt Whitman could not go on without such a digression as this, for the reader would otherwise be sure, at this point, to lose his man in a cloud and ever after doubt that Whitman was a normal person. Unlike such mystics as Swedenborg, St. Francis and St. Paul, however, Whitman was unwilling to surrender his grasp on reality entirely to the control of these experiences. He thought that a mysticism which cannot transfigure man's human lot is, if not fanatical, at least useless and cowardly. But it should not be difficult to believe that mysticism itself is under law, as truly as is poetic inspiration or musical genius.

Let us now go away from familiar sights and sounds, with only the constant symbolism of nature about us, and look over the young poet's shoulder as he turns the pages of his Emerson. He had already known Emerson's writings; he perhaps had heard him lecture in Brooklyn in 1850 and read his "Representative Men" in that year. But there is a time to read Emerson, and Whitman's time came in 1853 or 1854. It was then that Emerson "brought the simmering pot to a boil."

"The superiority of Emerson's writings," he said, "is in their character—they mean something. He may be obscure, but he is certain. Any other of the best American writers has in general a clearer style, has more of the received grace and ease, is less questioned and forbidden than he, makes a handsomer appearance in the society of the books, sells better, passes his time more apparently in the popular understanding; yet there is something in the solitary specimen of New England that outvies them all. He has what none else has; he does what none else does. He pierces the crusts that envelop the secrets of life. He joins on equal terms the few great sages and original seers. He represents the freeman, America, the individual. He represents the gentleman. No teacher or poet of old times or modern times has made a better report of manly and womanly qualities, heroism, chastity, temperance. His words shed light to the best souls; they do not admit of argument. As a sprig from the pine tree or a glimpse anywhere into the daylight belittles all artificial flowerwork and all the painted scenery of theaters, so are live words in a book compared to cunningly composed words. A few among men (soon perhaps to become many) will enter easily into Emerson's meanings; by those he will be well-beloved. The flippant writer, the orthodox critic, the numbers of good or indifferent imitators, will not comprehend him; to them he will indeed be a transcendentalist, a writer of sunbeams and moonbeams, a strange and unapproachable person."

What were the written words that could affect the well-read Whitman like that? As he lounges on the grass, turning the pages, slowly pondering the passages here and there and compounding them with his own experience, we note a few—enough to suggest the tenor of them all:

"Man is a stream whose source is hidden."

"We live in succession, in division, in parts, in particles. Meantime within man is the soul of the whole; the wise silence; the universal beauty, of which every part and particle is equally related, the eternal One."

"The soul in man is not an organ, but animates and exercises all the organs; it is not a function, like the power of memory, of calculation, of comparison, but uses them as hands and feet; it is not a faculty, but a light; it is not the intellect or the will, but the master of the intellect and the will; it is the background of our being, in which they live—an immensity not possessed and that cannot be possessed. . . . When it breathes through his intellect, it is genius; when it breathes through his will, it is virtue; when it flows through his affection, it is love."

"The soul circumscribes all things. As I have said, it contradicts all experience. In like manner it abolishes time and space."

"The soul looked steadily forwards, creating a world before her, leaving worlds behind her. . . . The soul knows only the soul, the web of events is the flowing robe in which she is clothed."

"In youth we are mad for persons. Childhood and youth see all the world in them. But the larger experiences of man discovers the identical nature appearing in them all. . . . There is a certain wisdom in humanity which is common to the greatest men with the lowest, and which our ordinary education often labors to silence and obstruct."

"We are wiser than we know. If we will not interfere with our thought, but will act entirely, or see how the thing stands in God, we know the particular thing, and every thing, and every man."

"A certain tendency to insanity has always attended the opening of the religious sense in men, as if they had been 'blasted with excess of light.' "

"Much of the wisdom of the world is not wisdom, and the most illuminated class of men are no doubt superior to literary fame, and are not writers. Among the multitude of scholars and authors we feel no hallowing presence; we are sensible of a knack and skill rather than of inspiration; they have a light, and know not whence it comes, and call it their own; their talent is some exaggerated faculty, some overgrown member, so that their strength is a disease. . . . But genius is religious. It is a larger imbibing of the common heart. . . . The great poet makes us feel our own wealth, and then we think less of his compositions."

"This energy does not descend into individual life on any other condition than entire possession. It comes to the lowly and simple; it comes to whomsoever will put off what is foreign and proud; it comes as insight; it comes as serenity and grandeur."

Those words were written as with authority, and not as mere scribes might mumble a tradition. Whitman could not doubt them when their proof lay in the strange sense of peace and power which flowed over him. He had been thinking along this line for many years, but now it was the hour for thinking, properly speaking, to cease. Something ineffable happened to him. Description here is of necessity but suggestion, since the language in which he must speak to other men was not fashioned for such uses. But he recalled it thus:

I believe in you my soul, the other I am must not abase itself to you,
And you must not be abased to the other.

Loafe with me on the grass, loose the stop from your throat,
Nor words, not music or rhyme I want, not custom or lecture, not even the best,
Only the lull I like, the hum of your valvèd voice.

I mind how once we lay such a transparent summer morning,
How you settled you head athwart my hips and gently turn'd over upon me,
And parted the shirt from my bosom-bone, and plunged your tongue to my bare-stript heart,
And reached till you felt my beard, and reached till you held my feet.

Swiftly arose and spread around me the peace and knowledge that pass all the argument of the earth,
And I know that the hand of God is the promise of my own,
And I know that the spirit of God is the brother of my own,
And that all the men ever born are also my brothers, and the women my sisters and lovers,

And that a kelson of the creation is love,
And limitless are leaves stiff or drooping in the fields,
And brown ants in the little wells beneath them,
And mossy scabs of the worm fence, heap'd stones, elder, mullein and
poke-weed.

The sexual imagery in this description, a form of symbolism
very common in religious writings, reminds us that the mystic is
in love—in love with the universe—and that without the insincerity we associate with the charlatan. In love with an illusion,
if one will. Yet illusions are the creators of reality. In the
cooler light of reason it may come to no more than this: the
mystic's god is a sudden crystallization of his hitherto nebulous
subconscious mind; he sees everything transfigured because he is
not really looking at the so-called outer universe at all but at
its reflections, or refractions, in his own glorified soul. Yet,
since all religious mystics see the same order in the world, an
order in which love is law, for all men thus to hypnotize themselves would make far simpler the outward adjustment of their
ideas and interests by supplying each with a motive for adjustment in the interest of all.

But could a man, particularly a man with no more ascetic
nature than Whitman had inherited, live half a lifetime in that
key? No man can make tents in which to dwell for long on the
mounts of his own rare transfiguration; few have such disci-
plined wills as long to hold even a living memory of life's highest moments. But at least it is something to have definitely appeared, to have made terms with one's deeper self. With Whitman the trance was to return more than once, but perhaps
never would he again see it in this first glory of mid-manhood.
But one glimpse of heaven is, after all, as good as eternity;
and increasing art, in the remembered light of that high noon,
might gradually perfect the expression of what he had seen.
Twenty years later, through the lips of Columbus, whose faith
also had been rewarded by the discovery of a new world, the
poet offers a prayer to his Muse, his God.

I am too full of woe!
Haply I may not live another day;
I cannot rest O God, I cannot eat or drink or sleep,
Till I put forth myself, my prayer, once more to Thee,
Breathe, bathe myself once more in Thee, commune with Thee,
Report myself once more to Thee.

Thou knowest my years entire, my life,
My long and crowded life of active work, not adoration merely;
Thou knowest the prayers and vigils of my youth,
Thou knowest my manhood's solemn and visionary meditations,
Thou knowest how before I commenced I devoted all to come to Thee,
Thou knowest I have in age ratified all those vows and strictly kept them,
Thou knowest I have not once lost nor faith nor ecstasy in Thee,
In shackles, prison'd, in disgrace, repining not,
Accepting all from thee, as duly come from Thee.

O I am sure they really came from Thee,
The urge, the ardor, the unconquerable will,
The potent, felt, interior command, stronger than words,
A message from the Heavens whispering to me even in sleep,
These sped me on.

When Isaiah, the son of Amos, greatest of Hebrew mystics before Jesus, had a similar overpowering vision of the pure God he
worshiped, in which "the whole earth was full of his glory",
his reaction was one of personal unworthiness. "Woe is me,"
he cried, "for I am undone; because I am a man of unclean lips,
and I dwell in the midst of a people of unclean lips: for mine
eyes have seen the King, the Lord of hosts." But when his
lips had been purged and made eloquent by a live coal from off
the mystical altar, he was ready for the commission implicit in
every such vision. "Also I heard the voice of the Lord, saying,
Whom shall I send, and who will go for us? Then said I,
Here am I; send me."

Whitman had been reading Isaiah on the barren shores of
Coney Island, and his Quaker education created in his mind no
prejudice against the doctrine of continued revelation. He
doubtless now saw, perhaps in bewilderment, that he too was

among the prophets. But might he not argue that he lacked
Isaiah's commanding style?

> Speech is the twin of my vision, it is unequal to measure itself,
> It provokes me forever, it says sarcastically,
> *Walt, you contain enough, why don't you let it out then?*

If he should caution himself that the irregularities of his personal life unfitted him to bear such a message, yet there stood
St. Augustine, and St. Paul, and many another saint to answer him. Moreover, it was not a mere repetition of older
prophecies that he thought to be the need of his day and land.
The Modern Man was to be neither a monk nor a sentimental
philanthropist. He would live his message rather than preach
it; and to live it he must be complete, as God made him.
Were such a germinant vision as this that came to Whitman
planted in the arid soil of a pious asceticism, as so often it had
been, only impotent and visionary results could grow from it;
but, if sown in a well developed intellectual and emotional nature, while it might put forth some ugly weeds unfamiliar
to Transcendental herbariums, it would certainly in time make
glad the soil with leaves of wholesome, democratic grass. That
were better than growing lilies in a hothouse. Whitman's own
experience had taught him that evil is only the shadow of good,
the coarse soil from which good may spring. But if, as we shall
see, he was a "caresser of life wherever flowing," and no ascetic,
he nevertheless addressed himself to his task in heroic manner.
What he says to the young poet aspiring to sing worthily of
America, he had done, or was to do, himself: "Love the earth
and sun and the animals, despise riches, give alms to every one
that asks, stand up for the stupid and crazy, devote your income and labor to others, hate tyrants, argue not concerning
God, have patience and indulgence toward people, take off your
hat to nothing known or unknown or to any man or number of
men, go freely with powerful uneducated persons and with the
young men and with the mothers of families, read these leaves
in the open air every season of the year of your life, reëxamine

all you have been told at school or church or in any book, dismiss whatever insults your own soul, and your very flesh shall
be a great poem and have the richest fluency not only in its
words but in the silent lines of its lips and face and between the
lashes of your eyes and in every motion and joint of your body."

But is the illumination of genius a cause, a new creation, or an
effect of hidden causes, just now rising, like a volcanic mountain,
above the level of the conscious sea? There can be no doubt
that the genius himself, particularly if his imagination be great
and his caution small, at first looks upon it as a personal incar-
nation of something supernatural. His first impulse is to fall
down and worship this great I AM. But if so, we are dealing
with religion, with facts above scientific scrutiny, with an example not to be emulated. We are dealing with mythology, and
are in need of a priest, not a biographer. As for Whitman, for
all his faith in the spirit world, he did not believe any less in the
dominance of law even there.

Every one has sought rest in slumber after a day of earnest
but fruitless mental struggle, only to waken in the morning with
the clarifying point of view uppermost in his mind. Some fairy
has been laboring for him while he slept. But though we do
not know the method of that magic, we now know that the fairy
burrows in the subconscious brain, waiting only for the aban-
donment of vain surface tension in order to put forth in his
service his own larger powers of perception and memory. But
the poet, less distrustful of his intuitions than others, is served
by them even when he is awake. And what he speaks he speaks
with conviction, because the whole man communicates with the
reader. It may even be to the surprise of that fragment of his
own mind which is under conscious control. This is what Emerson meant when, calling for a new race of American thinkers
("scholars"), to transfigure her life and to objectify her deeper
self, he declared that such a leader must be not a thinking man,
merely, but Man thinking. It is doubtful if the Muse, in her
visitations, ever adds anything in the way of language, or special knowledge, or artistic talent. "Kubla Khan" might indeed

be composed, word by word, in an opium dream; but it is significant that nothing like it ever was composed by a man who had not cultivated a sense of verbal harmony and who had not been reading books of oriental mystery and charm. Emerson was right in declaring that the soul is not a faculty, but a light to reveal our faculties. The divine fire may indicate the pleasure of Heaven in consuming the goods upon the altar, but it is the man's task, not the god's, to heap the sacrifice there. And it would indeed make the life of genius immoral to expect any great world-lighting fire upon an altar that could boast but a few soggy and malodorous sticks upon it. In this respect, as Whitman says, "All that a person does or thinks is of consequence." To comprehend the literary offspring of Whitman's rare experience, then, we must go back a little, in order to examine, not only the efforts he had been making to produce the book which, from the age of twenty, had been the secret dream of his life, but to discover also, if we can, the half-conscious motives which supplied the energy behind his work.

Aside from his normal human ambition for literary, political and personal honors—the adolescent manifestations of a great ambition—Whitman had developed two cardinal desires. One was for himself, one for his country. They were so fundamentally interrelated that they must be satisfied together or not at all. Had he been a sensualist, he might, with his rare capacity for sense enjoyment, have withdrawn into the arcanum of some private lust, or, taking Nature for his mistress, might have learned to dwell as a hermit in some simple Walden, untouched by the fate of his book or the fortunes of his country. But the price he had to pay for drawing so heavily as he did upon the life of his age for his personal growth and joy, as well as for the epic significance of his poetry, was that he should be tied to that larger life by the umbilical cord of his genius, never to be severed. In a sense this meant that, whatever he might learn or learn to think in the ordinary method of self-taught men, he must always remain, as he said, "a child, very old."

The dominant note in his personal ambition, once he had passed the fluctuating, melancholy moods of a prolonged adolescence, was to be himself, "a simple, separate person," developing his emotions, his tastes, his sense of expression, his unbounded curiosity, his hunger for love and friendship, to the utmost, whatever this might cost in worldly success, in time, or in the comfort which attends conformity. For his country, as we have seen in his editorials, he craved the same experience. She must be independent, not merely politically and materially, but in her spirit, her drama, her music, her literature, her genius;, and with all her diversity, she must, at whatever hazard, be a Union, capable of preserving the opportunity of each section and individual, and ultimately passing these blessings to the less favored nations of the earth. He would be at peace with himself only when these two ambitions should coalesce into one and a way be opened for their accomplishment through some task suited to his powers. Undeterred by the failure, or apparent failure, of the particular reforms he had fought for and advised, he attacked the problem at its root; he quietly set about "a modern image-making creation" which, like a pillar of fire in the wilderness, would give purpose and direction to the aimless, blinded, wasting spiritual efforts of his people. When this could have its perfect work through a new race of writers, "plowing up in earnest the interminable average fallows of humanity—not 'good government' merely, in the common sense," then at last the state would be the people, democracy would be a spiritual reality as well as a political dream, and by controlling the "ballads" of the nation, the men of vision might easily control its laws. The conception of such a life-work was worthy of a genius, the motive behind it worthy of a saint. Looking back after thirty years of effort in this direction, he calmly described it as "a feeling or ambition to articulate and faithfully express in literary or poetic form, and uncompromisingly, my own physical, emotional, moral, intellectual, and æsthetic Personality, in the midst of, and tallying, the momentous spirit and facts of its immediate days, and of current America—and to exploit that personality, identified with place and date, in a far more candid and comprehensive sense than in any hitherto poem or book." But a man must be possessed by a spirit which raises him above timidity and personal pride to dare a thing like that. And here lies the significance of Whitman's mystical experience, fusing his deep desires—perhaps likewise the unrealized desires of the race of which he was a part—in a subconscious manner which relieved him of the doubts that properly attach to the results of our fallible, conscious cerebration. "I fulfilled in that an imperious conviction," he declared, "and the commands of my nature as total and irresistible as those which make the sea flow, or the globe revolve." No wonder that he should take Nature as the standard and the judge of his message and his art, and seek to catch in his dithyrambs the rhythmic surge of the sea.

At about the age of thirty Whitman had begun to jot down in little notebooks, some of which have been preserved, incoherent ideas, figures of speech that had struck his fancy, descriptions of his ideal man, his ideal country. As yet he had no plan, no special inspiration, though with an instinct common to all artists he felt that something would come of these experiments. His first rule for composition was: "Be simple and clear.—Be not occult." His language was always to be more or less racy and concrete; but he was to find that he had things to report which could only be suggested. So that when the work was finally done he could declare, "I have not been afraid of the charge of obscurity . . . —because human thought, poetry or melody, must leave dim escapes and outlets—must posses a certain fluid, aërial character, akin to space itself, obscure to those of little or no imagination, but indispensable to the highest purposes. Poetic style, when addressed to the soul, is less definite form, outline, sculpture, and becomes vista, music, half-tints, and even less than half-tints." So far had he gone beyond his patronizing review of Carlyle.

Describing the superiority of the "true, noble expanded American Character" over the gentlemanly products of European and Oriental feudalism, he obviously was looking in a mirror as he wrote: "It is to be illimitably proud, independent, self-possessed, generous and gentle. It is to accept nothing except what is equally free and eligible to anybody else. It is to be poor, rather than rich—but to prefer death sooner than any mean dependence." He took very literally the Jeffersonian doctrine that in a democracy the individual citizen is the ultimate governor, should "carry himself with the finished and haughty bearing of the greatest ruler and proprietor," adding, "I never yet knew how it felt to think I stood in the presence of my superior." So the Quaker was trained to compensate himself for his humility before God by standing "hatted and high-headed before kings," unaware, it may be, that such an affectation only confessed an inferiority complex. His long brooding on the surface phantasmagoria of life and nature had taught him the secret of the sympathetic imagination, that "a man is only interested in anything when he identifies himself with it," and that by such identification "the universal and fluid soul impounds within itself not only all good characters and heroes, but the distorted characters, murderers, thieves," and even the inanimate creation. This Oriental straying out of himself to dwell comprehendingly in the lives of others caused him to be "always conscious of myself as two—my soul and I." And thus a glorious sense of wealth came over him, known only to imaginative lovers, for "the wisest soul knows that no object can really be owned by one man or woman any more than another." It was something worth teaching, something he had for many years wished to teach. But how? Such perception cannot be communicated by teaching. "I will not be a great philosopher, and found any school, and build it with iron pillars, and gather the young men around me, and make them my disciples," as his Greek masters had done, "that new superior churches and politics shall come.—But I will take each man and woman of you to the window and open the shutters and the sash, and my left arm shall hook you around the waist, and my right shall point you to the endless and beginningless road along whose sides are crowded the rich cities of all living philosophy, and oval gates that pass you in to fields of clover and landscapes clumped with sassafras, and orchards of good apples, and every breath through your mouth shall be of a new perfumed and elastic air, which is love. Not I—not God—can travel this road for you."

There was doubtless much self-will and stubbornness in Whitman in all he did, but there was at this period little conscious selfishness. He looked longingly for a messiah, whose coming into the world of democracy might be comparable to the advent of the religious teachers of antiquity; but he was not conscious of seeking such a rôle as a means of personal aggrandisement. Yet the moment he could clearly envisage the rôle, he began to feel, like Ernest in the legend of the "Great Stone Face," that he must himself be the deliverer. "Why," he cried, "can we not see beings who by the manliness and transparence of their natures, disarm the entire world and bring one and all to his side [their side] as friends and believers!—Can no father beget, or mother conceive, a man child so entire and elastic that whatever action he do or whatever syllable he speak, it shall be melodious to all creatures, and none shall be an exception to the universal and affectionate Yes of the earth?" He waited for some modern Orpheus, whose lyre, taught of nature, might make even the trees to dance when he played. Then, in the notebook comes his first strumming of the instrument so mysteriously slipped into his own hands:

> I am the poet of slaves, and of the masters of slaves,
> I am the poet of the body
> And I am the poet of the soul,
> I go with the slaves of the earth equally with the masters
> And I will stand between the masters and the slaves,
> Entering into both, so that both shall understand me alike.

This is the rare democratic man, averaging high and low by reducing all to the level of their common spiritual heritage. Pride and sympathy, equally necessary in a democracy, so unite in the genuine poet that he may celebrate his own experiences

And here are my slave-gangs, South,
at work upon the roads, the women
indifferently with the men — see you,
how clumsy, hideous, black, pouting,
grinning, sly, besotted, sensual,
shameless;
And this of a scene afar in the
North, the arctic — those are the corpses
of lost explorers, (no chaplets
of roses will ever cap those icy
graves — but I put you a
chaplet here, you, English heros;)
But here now, copious — see you, here,
the Wonders of eld, the famed Seven,
The Olympian statue this, and this
the Artemesian tomb,
Pyramid this, Pharos this, and this
the shrine of Diana,
These Babylon's gardens, and this Rhodes'
high-lifted marvel,

PAGE FROM MANUSCRIPT POEM "PICTURES," circa 1853

Courtesy of Mr. Henry Goldsmith

and those of others together, as though there were actually a community of life in the world. In the subconscious of the religious artist all life blends in God. Well, it was begun. He had set his hand to the plow, and was not made of the stuff that turns back. He might never write another line, might never even perfect what he had written, but in his heart he had established contact with the Muse—he was a poet in his own right. Lowell, himself more a critic than a poet, had put it well:

> In creating, the only hard thing's to begin;
> A grass-blade's no easier to make than an oak,
> If you've once found the way, you've achieved the grand stroke.

For about two years after his chief illumination Whitman labored on the book. Believing that in any art or craft "he is greatest forever and forever who contributes the greatest original practical example," Whitman wrote a motto in his bold uncompromising script and placed it above his desk:
"*Make the Works.*—Do not go into criticisms or arguments at all. Make full-blooded, rich, flush, natural *works*. Insert natural things, indestructibles, idioms, characteristics, rivers, states, persons, etc. Be full of *strong sensual germs.*"

His task completed, Whitman published his book in July, 1855, at the age of thirty-six. He had no publisher, nor did he now have a printing office of his own. But he had friends who liked him and believed in him. Tom and James Rome had a little shop at the corner of Fulton and Cranberry, and there he set up "Leaves of Grass," as the thin large-page volume was to be christened. Everywhere within it were evidences of the personal touch and taste, even the idiosyncrasy, of the author. The very lettering on the back was symbolical, little roots in gold foil reaching down from the words in the title. There was no author's name, only his photograph as signature. But for all that it was a pleasing book to read, a fascinating book to look at. Almost no copies were sold, but returns were had from some of the review copies. A few of these found their way to England and in time brought forth a crop of defenders

in the author's hour of distress. One historic copy sent to
Emerson elicited a letter of thanks which made up for all unsold
copies; not only because it meant the "well done" of his master,
but because the book was a call for friends and it made Emerson
his lifelong friend. One can imagine the look of exaltation, perhaps the joyful years of success, that transformed Whitman's
face as, breaking the seal of this letter, he read its unqualified
sentences. For no first author is ever quite at his ease till the
critic he most admires and fears has spoken, much less the author of a book the like of which had never before appeared in
America. "When Emerson's letter came he was set up," says
brother George, in his uncomprehending way; "I took no account of it." Very well, Walt's family of friends would grow
as his book slowly made its way, till a little neglect on the part
of the unprepared, even in his own household, could not matter
much. But let us see Emerson's opinion of the pot that had
now come to a boil.

"Concord, Mass., July 21st, 1855.
"Dear Sir,—I am not blind to the worth of the wonderful gift
of 'Leaves of Grass.' I find it the most extraordinary piece of
wit and wisdom that America has yet contributed. I am very
happy in reading it, as great power makes us happy. It meets
the demand I am always making of what seems the sterile and
stingy Nature, as if too much handiwork or too much lymph in
the temperament were making our Western wits fat and mean.
I give you joy of your free and brave thought. I have great
joy in it. I find incomparable things, said incomparably well,
as they must be. I find the courage of treatment which so delights us, and which large perception only can inspire.

"I greet you at the beginning of a great career, which yet
must have had a long foreground somewhere, for such a start.
I rubbed my eyes a little to see if this sunbeam were no illusion;
but the solid sense of the book is a sober certainty. It has the
best merits, namely, of fortifying and encouraging.

"I did not know, until I last night saw the book advertised in a newspaper, that I could trust the name as real and available for a post-office.

"I wish to see my benefactor, and have felt much like striking my tasks, and visiting New York to pay you my respects.

"R. W. Emerson."

The letter was obviously written somewhat on the impulse, and the pride it expressed was, with equal obviousness, a little the pride of paternity. Yet no ordinary book had ever stirred that impulse in Emerson, and he never wrote a second letter like this. It was not given as a matured judgment, it is true, but it was as simple, as manly and sincere as the book which called it forth. Whatever Emerson might later do about it, he could never retract the feeling of that moment, and Whitman was overjoyed at the testimony it gave to his personal and literary power.

But, however authentic and compelling the command to create, Whitman soon found that it was almost like ordering him to make bricks without straw. The dream might be clear, but the artist must have a medium—parian marble, fit models, a language that would convey his meaning. Lacking this, he would have to coin it out of himself and wait for his recognition until readers should have learned the idiom in which he spoke. That is what Whitman had to do; and it is significant that readers who like him at all enjoy him more as they grow familiar with his language and form. How he envied Shakespeare! To an interviewer he once said:

"Shakespeare had his boundless, rich material, all his characters waiting to be woven in. The feudal world had been, had grown, had richly flourished for centuries—gave him the perfect king, the lord, the finished gentleman, all that is heroic and gallant, and graceful and proud, and beautiful and refined—gave him the exquisite and seductive transfiguration of caste—sifted and selected out of the huge masses, as if for him, choice specimens of noble gentlemen, and gave them to him—gave him all the varied and romantic incidents of the military, civil, political, and ecclesiastical history of a thousand years. All stood up, ready, as it were, to fall into the ranks for him. Then the time comes for the sunset of feudalism. A new power has appeared; and the flush, the pomp, the accumulated materials of those ages, have all the gorgeousness of sunset. At this time Shakespeare appears. By amazing opportuneness, his faculty, his power, his personal circumstances come—and he is their poet.

"But I, for *my* poems—what have I? I have all to *make*. The feudal poet, as I say, was the finder and user of materials, characters, all ready for him—but I have really to make all, except my own inspiration and intentions—have to map out, fashion, form and knit and sing the ideal American. Shakespeare, and all, sang the past. I project the future—depend on the future for my audience."

But writing, as he did in his first volume, largely out of his subconscious inspiration, much of this planning was done for him. The ideal man he sang was—had to be—himself. He accepted this necessity, though he seems never to have fully realized its limitations. "I know perfectly well my road is different. Most of the great poets are impersonal; I am personal. They portray characters, events, passions, but never mention themselves. In my poems, all revolves round, concentrates in, radiates from myself. I have but one central figure, the general human personality typified in myself. But my book compels, absolutely necessitates, every reader to transpose himself or herself into the central position, and become the living fountain, actor, experiencer himself or herself, of every page, every aspiration, every line."

Thus one novel thing about this book, in its general conception, was that while it had an epic purpose it used the lyric point of view, yet without becoming dramatic in form. This was due in part to the technical limitations of the author who confessed himself deficient in dramatic ability and pictorial talent; but it was more profoundly due to the requirements of that twin ambition which was to celebrate himself while celebrating his country.

The Hartford Wits—Dwight, Barlow and Trumbell—filled
with a shallower patriotism, had sought to put the new country
on the literary map by composing Columbiads and such epics,
but they failed through imitation, blind to the fact that no man
can rise to the proportions of an epic hero in this country except
he be the reflection of the spirit of the average masses of his
day. This Whitman truly felt and accepted.

A fifth of the book was a prose preface stating, in terms of
youthful conviction, what the author was about. This pronun-
ciamento, despite a certain oracular incoherence shared with
Emerson and other mystics, was full of beautiful suggestiveness,
many a well-turned phrase betraying the fact that the author had
polished it with care. Moreover it, like the book, emanated
"buoyancy and gladness," the jocund spirit of the morning.
The preface announces as a personal fact what, in the "American
Scholar" address, Emerson had twenty years before voiced as
an aspiration—that America should realize herself through her
writers, no longer betraying her provincial inferiority either by
rejecting or by imitating the past. The author then describes
the sort of character which has resulted from the conditions of
our colonization, our pioneering, and our crude experiments in
democracy, and finds in it a poetry that awaits "the gigantic and
generous treatment worthy of it." This leads him to describe
the poet who is to do justice to such a subject. He is to be no
mere mellifluous historian; "here the theme is creative and has
vista." Of all this life he is not only the observer but himself
a *magna pars*. "In war he is the most deadly force of the war
—he can make every word he speaks draw blood. The time
straying toward infidelity and confections and persiflage he
withholds with his steady faith. He sees eternity less like a
play with a prologue and dénouement . . . he sees eternity in
men and women. He is a seer . . . he is individual . . . he is
complete in himself." His function is to "indicate the path between reality and their souls." The soul is beautiful in itself,
and to convey that beauty an art suggestive of even the sublimest of man's creations becomes "an obscuring curtain," a "per-

fume" less wholesome than the sun-shot air. Looking as he does toward the future, such a poet naturally makes friends with the scientific spirit, which works by slower, if not surer, methods to the same end. And, like the scientist, he is the champion of liberty, without which there cannot long be life. Having made his peace with the Universe, he is conscious of the encompassing laws of life, justly compensating for all effort that is worthy, punishing, without the aid of man, the knave and the fool. The poet thus becomes the priest of mankind, a priest who does not mediate but only inspires. Whitman concludes with a high tribute to the English language as a vehicle for such an epic, a language which, living after the institutions of feudalism were dead, still breathed the spirit which was dominant in America, "the powerful language of resistance . . . the dialect of common sense . . . the speech of the proud and melancholy races and of all who aspire." Whether the nation follows the path of greatness indicated by the poetic prophet or not, he has saved his own soul: "An individual is as superb as a nation when he has the qualities which make a superb nation." In this assurance, he is willing to wait for appreciation at the hands of his people, when "his country absorbs him as affectionately as he has absorbed it."

I exist as I am—that is enough;
If no other in the world be aware, I sit content;
And if each and all be aware, I sit content.
One world is aware, and by far the largest to me, and that is myself;
And whether I come to my own to-day, or in ten thousand or ten million
    years,
I can cheerfully take it now, or with equal cheerfulness I can wait.
My foothold is tenon'd and mortis'd in granite;
I laugh at what you call dissolution;
And I know the amplitude of time.

This was his program; the performance in the first experimental edition was not always up to it. One poem, written in 1854, when Boston was, he thought, disgraced by her failure to resist the operation of the Fugitive Slave Law, was included, though strangely out of keeping with the others. It was a satirical poem, called "A Boston Ballad"; but it was no ballad, in theme, narrative manner, point of view or verse form. It appeared to attempt satire by means of ridicule; but this was the very error which he had warned himself against. Indeed, humor seems always to be an incumbrance to a prophet. Why this is true will appear when we look at another of the poems. I do not refer to the first, the principal poem—one often approaches Whitman most successfully by some of his own indirection—but to a poem called, originally, "Sleep Chasings." The superficial critic finds in this poem only an attempt to describe realistically the phantasmagorical effect of actual dream activity—the strange but never incongruous succession of images in the mind of the sleeper. But it does more; it gives us a clue to the whole poetic mentality of Whitman. Indeed, had he known as much about psychology as we do to-day, he might not have had the temerity to publish such a book. And yet, until some other writer has emptied the contents from all the pockets of his mind, even more completely than Sherwood Anderson or Theodore Dreiser has done, and a balance has been struck between what is noble and what mean, it is too soon to declare that, while Whitman's method may have been good, he was not the man to make such public use of it. Besides, there is in dreaming a moratorium on morality. Not only does the dreamer realize the ideal state in which, as Madame de Staël phrased it, "to know all is to forgive all," but his critical faculty, always more or less under the control of the moral will, is on vacation. Hence the universal absence of humor in a dream.

The material out of which dream images are fashioned is, of course, all supplied by experience, personal or imaginative. In his poem, Whitman refers to the events of his dream as "past-readings," or records of what he had seen, "whether in the body or out of the body." Some passages we can recognize as his actual experience, such for instance as the terror inspired by a shipwreck, and some were doubtless consciously fashioned rather than remembered from sleep. But the significant point is that the psychology is accurate; everything might have happened in an actively dreaming mind. And it would stream along in just that formless, ever-changing way. Such a method was typical of all his early poems, without beginning or end. I do not mean there was no architectonic; that he had a plan is apparent enough. But the art is an attempt to catch the flux of nature, just as it appears in sleep. Later, when the novelty of such inspiration began to wear off, and when, with increasing study of poetic art, Whitman began to "finish specimens," there is form aplenty, even metrical form; but now he has merely made rhythmical the incoherent ejaculations and gnomic sayings of mystical inspiration. Another fact of importance to us, if not of revelation to him, is that in these images, aspirations, experiences, desires, tossed up into consciousness by the fatal waves of sleep, there is a certain law, the personal equation. Science has discovered that in day-dreaming eighty per cent of the experiences are ego-centric, a protective mechanism against the assaults of the active world in which one has proved himself less heroic than he could wish. By necessity all the images in a dream of the night are ego-centric; so that we have in his method of composition the explanation of Whitman's apparent egotism. Awake, he recognizes a certain element of brag in his verses which does less than justice to his moral nature, his cultivated generosity and fairness; so he sings for the other man as well as for himself, even though he knows, or should know, that in the mind of the average man no such songs are being smothered.

> I know perfectly well my own egotism,
> Know my omnivorous lines and must not write any less,
> And would fetch you whoever you are flush with myself.

Much less can he speak for those strata of American life which he not only did not know, but which he deeply envied—the aristocracy of the Brahmin, the culture of the Cavalier, the learning of the schools. He protested rather too much that they were un-American, unfitted for the future. For he was, by his own very program, seeking to create a race of great individuals. When through literary success, through the purifying of his personal motive in war-time service, he had conquered the sense of inadequacy which prompted his declaration that he had no superior, he would write poems truly democratic; he would rely less upon his uncensored dreams. For these early "radical utterances out of the abysms of the Soul . . . following only its own impulses" were already beginning to reveal the strange fact that a man may be religious, in the mystical sense, and yet not be moral according to the code of his day. The inner light exposes what is there, and in the "Sleepers" the predominance of sexual images, the imaginary promiscuity, the hints of childish exhibitionism and even of a more savage past, all betray the fact that our poetic medium is no St. Theresa, and that if he is to be the prophet of a new religion it will, perforce, be one in which evil is included as well as good, thus projectng into philosophy and theology his own anthropomorphic limitations, as now he was doing in his conception of the average man of the future. In "Chanting the Square Deific" this final sublimation of the paradox of evil later actually took place.

That this is the true interpretation of this poem, and a key to the First Edition, appears from its close, a parable in which the night represents his mind when engaged in mystic dreaming, the day standing for the mind of normal, common sense.

I too pass from the night,
I stay a while away O night, but I return to you again and love you.

Why should I be afraid to trust myself to you?
I am not afraid, I have been well brought forward by you,
I love the rich running day, but I do not desert her in whom I lay so long,
I know not how I came out of you and I know not where I go with you,
  but I know I came well and shall go well.

I shall stop only a time with the night, and rise betimes,
I will duly pass the day O my mother, and duly return to you.

That the subconscious mind forgets nothing may well be believed when one turns the pages of this book, with its interminable lists of things thrown up under rhapsodical inspiration in this passive, mystical state, or fished up by memory-hooks to complete the author's rough plan. The little poem "There Was a Child Went Forth" explains how the poet became what he was by the impress of innumerable experiences.

And the first object he looked upon, that object he became.

The early lilacs, the democratic, symbolical grass, the sights of the farm, the fish in the sea, the people he met on the street or in the country road,

His own parents,
He that had father'd him, and she that had conceiv'd him in her womb, and birth'd him,
They gave this child more of themselves than that.
They gave him afterward every day—they became part of him.
The mother at home, quietly placing the dishes on the supper-table;
The mother with mild words—clean her cap and gown, a wholesome odor falling off her person and clothes as she walks by;

The father, strong, self-sufficient, manly, mean, anger'd, unjust;
The blow, the quick loud word, the tight bargain, the crafty lure,
The family usages, the language, the company, the furniture—the yearning and swelling heart,
Affection that will not be gainsay'd—the sense of what is real—the thought if, after all, it prove unreal,
The doubts of day-time and the doubts of night-time—the curious whether and how,
Whether that which appears so is so, or is it all flashes and specks?

The first poem, longer than all the others together, only carries this catalogue further, with the author's interpolated comments. Of course such a method involved contradictions, not only in matter but in mood. Life is paradoxical, nowhere more so than in the United States, and no poet who does not in his nature and training embrace more than a single tradition, a single racial strain, can hope to speak for the country at large. A national poetry could come out of New England no more than out of Scotland. Even Whitman needed the experiences of the Civil War, fusing North and South, East and West, in a common ideal, before he could really be an epic as well as a lyric poet. However, his mixed ancestry of English, Dutch and Welsh stock, his residence in a cosmopolitan city, his travels and his journalistic experiences were all preparing him to embrace and in a measure resolve the paradox which was America.

> Do I contradict myself?
> Very well, then, I contradict myself;
> (I am large—I contain multitudes.)

The same diversity is embraced in the consciousness of every man, though not always with the same childlike complacency. Only in our outward lives, regulated by conscious, prudent selection of word and impulse, is there consistency. Yet for Whitman it was enough to know that there was something, he called it "Identity," beneath all these experiences and persisting through them. Apparently it did not occur to him to ask why the "identity" of one person responded to one set of stimuli, of interests, of ambitions, while another identity no less vital, responded only to a different set. The answer to that question might have forced him to select more carefully from among his companions, his sense satisfactions. He preferred to loaf and invite his soul, passively "observing a spear of summer grass" or humanity "magnificently moving in vast masses."

Whitman's point of view sometimes limits itself to pictures of a single kind, as when he takes an imaginary promenade up the street and paints in words the various faces he meets, seeing in every countenance the man's own faithful epitaph. Or he lets his mind roam over all the occupations he knows, celebrating not so much the feelings that actual workingmen experience as the poet's youthful joy in watching the world at work. So too in the poem "Great are the Myths," a series of oracular approvals, endorsing the concepts whereby man has

released his growing energies. Similarly the poet elsewhere
makes a blanket confession of all the faiths that man has ever
known, feeling, like the Darwinians soon to be reading the
"Origin of Species," that he was "an acme of things accomplished, encloser of things to be." But in some respects the
most harmonious poem in the book is the one which most closely
follows the prose of the preface, "Now List to My Morning's
Romanza," a description of the great poet, who makes answer
to the riddle of the Sphinx. At any rate, in the story of Walt
Whitman we are more interested in it.

Him all wait for—him all yield up to—his word is decisive and final,
Him they accept, in him lave, in him perceive themselves, as amid light,
Him they immerse, and he immerses them.

. . . .

He puts things in their attitudes;
He puts to-day out of himself, with plasticity and love;
He places his own city, times, reminiscences, parents, brothers and sisters,
  associations, employment, politics, so that the rest never shame them
  afterward, nor assume to command them.

. . . .

A man is a summons and challenge,
(It is vain to skulk—do you hear that mocking and laughter? do you
  hear the ironical echoes?)

. . . .

Books, friendships, philosophers, priests, action, pleasure, pride, beat up
  and down seeking to give satisfaction,
He indicates the satisfaction, and indicates them that beat up and down
  also.

. . . .

Whichever the sex, whatever the season or place, he may go freshly and
  gently and safely by day or by night,
He has the pass-key of hearts, to him the response of the prying of hands
  on the knobs.
His welcome is universal, the flow of beauty is not more welcome or
  universal than he is.

. . . .

WHITMAN AT THIRTY-FIVE

Every existence has its idiom, every thing has an idiom and tongue,
He resolves all tongues into his own and bestows it upon men, and my
man translates, and any man translates himself also,
One part does not contradict another part, he is the joiner, he sees how
they join.

He says indifferently and alike *How are you friend?* to the President at
his levee,
And he says *Good-day my brother,* to Cudge that hoes in the sugar-field,
And both understand him and know that his speech is right.

He walks with perfect ease in the Capitol,
He walks among the Congress, and one Representative says to another,
Here is our equal appearing and new.

Then the mechanics take him for a mechanic,
And the soldiers suppose him to be a soldier, and the sailors that he has
followed the sea,
The authors take him for an author, and the artists for an artist,
And the laborers perceive that he could labor with them and love them;
No matter what the work is, that he is the one to follow it, or has fol-
lowed it,
No matter what the nation, that he might find his brothers and sisters
there.

. . . .

The gentleman of perfect blood acknowledges his perfect blood;
The insulter, the prostitute, the angry person, the beggar see themselves
in the ways of him—he strangely transmutes them,
They are not vile any more—they hardly know themselves, they are so
grown.

As we have seen, and shall see, this is autobiographical in
the fullest sense. The author himself was the original poem,
of which the book was but a transcript; and in his person as in
his poems there was an effect of physical health and overflowing spirits. He had a right, if any one did, to be a poet of the
body as well as a poet of the soul. And in his first edition he
included a single poem of a sort later to be given more prominence, celebrating man the animal as a suitable pedestal for man

the dreamer. Or it was as if one might see man as he is in himself, stripped of the clothes which hide both his body and his mind. "Sartor Resartus" had done this for satirical purposes. In Whitman's view, nothing in the creation was impure save when the impure mind of man had made it so. He longed for a return to the graceful athleticism of the Greeks, their flowing garments placing a premium on bodily health and poise. Such "exquisite realization of health" gave him joy, not only as an artist but also as one who thought much about the generations of Americans to follow his own. In "man or woman, a clean, strong, firm-fibred body is beautiful as the most beautiful face." How necessary such a preachment was in 1855 may be seen by examining the styles of dress then worn, or by noting how modern form-revealing clothes and athletic exercises have improved the pride of men and women in their bodies. In New Orleans Whitman had seen slaves auctioned in the basement of the old St. Louis Hotel, a custom graphically described by Fredericka Bremer; and though he knew how bestial and savage the slave sometimes was, he could not bear to see a human body sold as merchandise. Even a slave's body had a relation to the soul. Trace it back far enough, he said, and every life will be found to emerge from some form of slavery. The slave of to-day must therefore be looked upon as

 not only herself—she is the teeming mother of mothers;
She is the bearer of them that shall grow and be mates to the mothers.

BOOK IV

ON THE OPEN ROAD

UBLISHING "Leaves of Grass" was not unlike addressing an open letter to the country, intended for personal and private reading. And such a letter has accomplished its purpose only when proper replies are evoked. So, after fondling his first-born book, doubtless with more affection than most authors feel, in proportion as his personality was more identified with it, Whitman began to be anxious as to whether he had hit the mark. Emerson's prompt letter was reassuring, and yet the book had not been addressed to the Emersons. They were of the household and their approval was not unmixed with loyalty. He had sent a copy to Whittier also. That poet, because of his own pioneering "Songs of Labor" and his interest in abolition, might have found in the new bard a brother but for the fact that Whitman substituted for the orthodox Quaker humility a certain arrogant pride of man in himself and especially because he was too frankly masculine for the chaste and sentimental bachelor accustomed to sing in borrowed tunes. So this other poet of the people, adopting the attitude of the people themselves, threw the book into the fire. The public bought hardly a copy. But Whitman had sent review copies to the press, and the press was heard from. The *Eagle,* now that Whitman was no longer a potential political foe, was willing to notice his book at length. Admitting that the extraordinary deliverance staggers him with the strangest "compound of transcendentalism, bombast, philosophy, wit and dullness which it ever entered into the heart of man to conceive," the reviewer is yet open-minded enough to realize that it defies criticism, and so refrains from pronouncing judgment upon it. "It is a work that will satisfy few upon a first perusal; it must be read again and again, and then it will be to many unaccountable. All who read it will agree that it is an extraordinary book, full of beau-

ties and blemishes, such as nature is to those who have only a half-formed acquaintance with her." The reviewer had himself been puzzling with the book before attempting to give it a stamp, for his review did not appear for two months after he had received the book. The London *Leader* was likewise cautiously complimentary to this "rough, devil-may-care Yankee who riots with a kind of Bacchanal fury in the force and fervor of his own sensations." It pointed out that "much remains of which we confess we can make nothing; much that seems to us purely fantastical and preposterous; much that appears to our muddy vision gratuitously prosaic, needlessly plain-speaking, disgusting without purpose, and singular without result." But he adds that "there are so many evidences of a noble soul in Whitman's pages that we regret these aberrations, which only have the effect of discrediting what is genuine by the show of something false; and especially do we deplore the unnecessary openness with which Walt reveals to us matters which ought rather to remain in sacred silence. It is good not to be ashamed of Nature; it is good to have all-inclusive charity; but it is also good, sometimes, to leave the veil across the temple." Similarly the London *Critic* was willing to "grant freely enough that he has a strong relish for Nature and freedom, just as an animal has; nay, further, that his crude mind is capable of appreciating some of Nature's beauties; but it by no means follows that, because Nature is excellent, therefore art is contemptible. Walt Whitman is as unacquainted with art as a hog is with mathematics." He who said "all things can be forgiven him who has perfect candor" ought not to have found fault with this criticism for its plain-speaking; rather he might well have pondered its attack on his fundamental conception of art. Except to make his verse free, it is doubtful if Whitman had as yet given a great deal of attention to art in writing. With a certain tendency to make a virtue of whatever was congenial to his disposition, he was, after all, in this first book, presenting not the mountain and the sea so much as rough blocks of experience, chiseled a bit here and there perhaps, but not yet arranged with painstaking art. But when neglect and attack alike made him alive to the fact that it is of no use to sing unless one has the art of catching the ear of a listener, he eventually learned to carve his stone till it could speak for itself. Many of the reviews were wholly unfavorable; but in fairness to the reviewers we must remember that artistically Whitman's first book was his worst, though the freshness of its mystical inspiration and the vigor of his robust optimism might compensate for this in the minds of those who were not balked by a form at that time novel in America. These critics did not have the benefit of the later work or the poet or the judgment of history to assist them; and yet sometimes they found vulnerable points in Whitman's armor. The pity is that he was temperamentally incapable of profiting by their advice without being crushed by their scorn. This was in part due to his o'erleaping ambition, not only to create a new literature in America, but to do it by a sudden explosion. Had he included a single poem in conventional form, appropriate to some of his own conventional sentiments, but in original and picturesque language—as with pains he was quite capable of doing—it would have disarmed his critics at the start, and forced them to estimate the thing he was trying to do on its own merits. He was condemned to suffer from the defects of his qualities. For instance, the New York *Crayon* struck home when it said: "To Walt Whitman, all things are good—nothing is better than another, and hence there is no ideal, no aspiration, no progress to things better." For precisely that reason the Socialist of a more recent day found that Whitman, rightly understood, was too complacent to be the poet of reform. Whitman's rejoinder would have been, of course, that he made everything ideal. But the result on the evolutionary urge in man is the same. The *Crayon* goes on to say, "With a wonderful vigor of thought and intensity of perception, a power, indeed, not often found, 'Leaves of Grass' has no ideality, no concentration, no purpose—it is barbarous, undisciplined, like the poetry of a half-civilized people and, as a whole, useless save to those miners of thought who prefer the metal in its unworked state." This, of course, is hardly accurate; and yet in that first volume, so wholly spun out of the author's personal life of aimless observation, so undisciplined, subsisting so little on the language of form, there were autobiographical revelations which the author naturally did not too carefully examine. "Putnam's Monthly" called the book a "compound of New England Transcendentalism and New York rowdy." Not that the rowdy had absorbed the transcendental teachings and now gave forth a version in the vulgate, for in that case he would have ceased to be a rowdy and would have felt the need of language more delicately suggestive; but it was as though the searchlight wherewith Concord had been accustomed to scan the heavens for some new planet of an idea had by Whitman been turned upon the streets of New York, in the hope that divinity might be found in human clay. Of course, the public did not know of Emerson's endorsement, but Emerson himself had difficulty in getting others to see what he had found in the book. This made him hesitate to send it to that acrid satirist of democracy, his friend Carlyle, though the latter as well as himself might have recognized something of his "Sartor Resartus" in more than the style of the book. At last he did send it, timidly. "The book," he wrote Carlyle, "throve so badly with the few to whom I showed it and wanted good morals so much, that I never did [send it]. . . . After you have looked into it, if you think, as you may, that it is only an auctioneer's inventory of a warehouse, you can light your pipe with it." Had Emerson then seen the second installment of the "Leaves," to appear the next year, he would have suggested that it looked like the inventory of the earth, the sea, and all that in them is. There can be no doubt that the tendency to catalogue damned the book with critics almost as much as did its occasional conflict with the customary prudish reticence. As I have said, Whitman himself came to see this, and to realize that "size," even in a poem, "is only development," that a truly reverent faith "leaves the best untold." For a poet consciously appealing to the future, even in a rough and youthful country, it was fortunate that he abandoned a childish formlessness; for his nation, following an immutable law, was to become more complex rather than more simple, and form is the language of the complex races. However, there was a form, as Rodin has shown, and as Whitman was to guess, which might at once have unity and suggest the larger, cruder creation of which it was a part.

In his letter to Whitman Emerson had expressed an impulse to visit the Brooklyn bard. Before he did this, however, he recommended Moncure Conway to do so. "Americans abroad may now come home," he said with pride in his discovery; "for unto us a man is born." The eager-minded and talented young Virginian needed no second hint from such an oracle. On the boat trip to New York he read "Leaves of Grass" and was struck by its points of similarity to the oriental books he had been perusing in Emerson's library. His visit fell on one of the hottest days of September, a Sunday, when the mercury was climbing toward the century mark. Any one who has been in Brooklyn when that happens can realize that young Conway's enthusiasm was not easily deterred. For on the last "moving day," four months before, the Whitmans had gone to the very edge of town, on Ryerson Street. There, just before his book came off the press, Whitman had seen his father end the struggle and pain which were his life. The preceding year his parent had felt the end coming, and at his request, Walt had conducted him out to the Island to say farewell with his eyes to the old home-place.

Conway did not find Whitman at home; that is, not at home in the house. He was equally at his ease, however, where the young visitor did find him. This was not until his caller had searched carefully the sunburnt grass of a treeless meadow near the house, to which he had been directed by the poet's mother. It really looked like a case of protective coloration. If Whitman's workingman's costume of gray, his blue-gray shirt, iron-gray hair, and his sunburnt face and open neck, as he moved into a room or down Broadway with an elephantine roll, threw him into picturesque relief against the more conventional people of his day, they only served to blend him in with the landscape here, a modern Antæus, not only touching foot to his mother earth, but lying at full length upon her breast, and gazing like an eagle out of his pale blue eyes at the midday sun. That was how he composed much of his poetry, and it is no wonder that his poems should have lacked the perspective the *Crayon* reviewer had found wanting.

"Don't you find this sun rather hot, Mr. Whitman?" asked Conway, by way of opening conversation.

"Not at all too hot," said the child of nature. For all that, he had a sunstroke about this time and was sensitive to the heat for twenty years. But, courteously remembering that in any event his visitor was uncomfortable in the heat, he led the way back to his room. Its appointments were marked with simplicity, if not poverty. There was no bed, but only a small cot, no bureau, but a little wash-stand over which a small mirror was hung against the wall. A pine table, with pen, ink and paper handy, completed the furniture. On the wall hung an old line drawing of Silenus and another of Bacchus, which were to hang in Whitman's room to the end. The original god Bacchus; not a frenzied bacchante, but the proud and perfectly formed caresser of life. There was but a single window, and it gave upon nothing but the barren plain. The average laborer could boast as much.

It was hardly the place to cultivate the acquaintance of this young gentleman. So they packed themselves off to Staten Island where they might have plenty of shade, miles of secluded beach, in which to open their souls to each other. When they undressed and took sun baths and sea baths, it appeared to the younger man that Whitman himself might in another age have given rise to the myth of Bacchus, so perfectly formed was his body, so graceful his slow movements, so fervent his embrace of the sea. It was the gesture of a child, animated by the full-blown passions of a man. But as they talked, fervor of a more inward sort gave a subtler, finer impression. The poet's gentle clear voice was slow, his eyelids drooped, and his words, his look, communicated kindness and sincerity.

They liked each other so well that they agreed to meet again a few days later for a stroll through New York, Whitman's other world. A strange magnetism had attracted Conway when he left Whitman and, though no fool, he felt a tendency to leave all and follow this happy, powerful, natural individual, even imitating his unconventional attire. A strange magnetism, but strange perhaps only because most of us are so perfectly insulated by custom and reserve as to neutralize it, for what can be the proof of man's worth to man if he have no power of personally attracting his kind?

The place of appointment was a printing office, doubtless that in which Whitman had set up the "Leaves." Already Whitman was thinking of a second edition, in which he meant to include a sheaf of reviews of his first, both favorable and unfavorable. Indeed, in some copies of the first edition, bound late, he had included a number of these criticisms. On this morning he was at the case setting up in type for this purpose an article from the "Democratic Review." Probably Conway did not linger to read the copy, for had he done so he would have been troubled by a vague suspicion.

"An American bard at last!" it began. "One of the roughs, large, proud, affectionate, eating, drinking, and breeding, his costume manly and free, his face sunburnt and bearded, his posture strong and erect, his voice bringing hope and prophecy to the generous races of young and old. We shall cease shamming and be what we really are. We shall start an athletic and defiant literature. . . .

"For all our intellectual people, followed by their books, poems, novels, essays, editorials, lectures, tuitions and criticisms, dress by London and Paris models, receive what is received there, obey the authorities, settle disputes by the old tests, keep out of rain and the sun, retreat to the shelter of houses and schools, trim their hair, shave, touch not the earth barefoot, and enter not the sea except in a complete bathing dress. Where are the gristle and beards, and broad breasts, and space, and ruggedness, and nonchalance, that the souls of the people love? . . ."

At this, remembering the style of the book he had read, and the manner of man he had seen, Conway would have turned to find a familiar signature—which was not there.

"Self-restraint, with haughty eyes, assuming to himself all the attributes of his country, steps Walt Whitman into literature, talking like a man unaware that there was ever hitherto such a production as a book, or such a being as a writer. . . . He must recreate poetry with the elements always at hand. He must imbue it with himself as he is, disorderly, fleshy, and sensual, a lover of things, yet a lover of men and women above the whole of the other objects of the universe. His work is to be achieved by unusual methods. Neither classic nor romantic is he, nor a materialist any more than a spiritualist. . . . Undecked also is this poet with sentimentalism, or jingle, or nice conceits, or flowery similes. . . . Here comes one among the well-beloved stone-cutters, and announces himself, and plans with decision and science, and sees the solid and beautiful forms of the future where there are now no solid forms. . . . His rhythm and uniformity he will conceal in the roots of his verses, not to be seen of themselves, but to break forth loosely as lilacs on a bush, or take shapes compact, as the shapes of melons, or chestnuts, or pears.

". . . He drops disguises and ceremony, and walks forth with the confidence and gayety of a child. . . . The first glance out of his eyes electrifies him with love and delight. He will have the earth receive and return his affection; he will stay with it as the bridegroom stays with the bride. The cool-breath'd ground, the slumbering and liquid trees, the just-gone sunset, the vitreous pour of the full moon, the tender and growing night, he salutes and touches, and they touch him. The sea supports him, and hurries him off with its powerful and crooked fingers. Dash me with amorous wet! then, he says; I can repay you.

". . . Nature he proclaims inherently clean. Sex will not be put aside; it is a great ordination of the universe. He works the muscle of the male and the teeming fiber of the female throughout his writings, as wholesome realities, impure only by deliberate intention and effort.

"Especially in the 'Leaves of Grass' are the facts of eternity and immortality largely treated. Happiness is no dream, and perfection is no dream. Amelioration is my lesson, he says with calm voice, and progress is my lesson and the lesson of all things. . . .

"If health were not his distinguishing attribute, this poet would be the very harlot of persons. Right and left he flings his arms, drawing men and women with undeniable love to his close embrace, loving the clasp of their hands, the touch of their necks and breasts, and the sound of their voices. All else seems to burn up under his fierce affection for persons."

A cooler and a more impartial observer might have questioned whether such overweening affection, however ideal, were the token of absolute health. Possibly the big body and the smooth functioning which kept the doctor forever away misled him as to the normality of the large soul within. Possibly too he was, unknown to himself, striving to sublimate in an unnatural way what could not be wholly satisfied in a natural way. As to his poetic mission, did he really have perfect faith, cheerfully waiting for his recognition, instead of writing an anonymous review to counteract what he considered the misapprehension of other reviewers? "To be great," Emerson had said, "is to be misunderstood"; but he did not add that great art needs to explain itself. The deception implicit in anonymous self-puffing had aroused Walt's ire as an editor; but now his own ox was gored, an ox that was too valuable to die. His nervousness about the success of his ambitious undertaking betrayed itself also in other reviews of the sort, and in ways which shall be recounted presently. But doubtless all this was lost on his young visitor eager to inspect New York with Whitman as cicerone. So many workmen greeted Walt with a warm hand-clasp that Conway, with the instinct of a reporter, interviewed them to see how the democratic poet really impressed the *demos*.

"What sort of man is he?" he put to one.

"A fust-rate man is Walt. Nobody knows Walt but likes him; nearly everybody knows him, and—and *loves* him."

But they knew nothing of his writing. What power he showed there was but the overflow of his personal contacts. Some biographers are inclined to tell the story of Walt Whitman as though the book he wrote were essentially greater than the man, thereby betraying their lack of comprehension of either. How could it be?

In a visit Conway and Whitman paid to the Tombs it became evident that the latter had been there before. The inmates crowded around him, as to a father confessor, unburdening their various complaints. One man, held on some petty charge, had been confined in a foul and unhealthy cell. Whitman went to the warden and stated the complaint, forgetting to explain who he was—or perhaps preferring to speak without introduction, on his personal authority. He ended his complaint with quiet emphasis: "In my opinion it is a damned shame." Unaccustomed to such a command from any one so coarsely clad, the warden hesitated, as if considering whether his interlocutor should not himself be in jail; but the serene look of offended justice in Whitman's eyes, marked by no trace of fear, caused him rather to order a subordinate to make the transfer requested.

A few days later Whitman returned Conway's visit, calling on him and his sister at the Metropolitan Hotel. He wore a baize coat and an inexpensive checked shirt; but it was immaculate, and the Southerners found his manner pleasing.

With a curious mixture of pride and dependence in these days when the prophet felt himself to be without adequate honor in his own country, he carried about with him the precious letter from Emerson. He showed it to his friend, Richard Henry Dana, Jr., managing editor of Greeley's *Tribune*. But when

Dana, who was likewise a friend of Emerson, asked permission to publish the letter, as an offset to so much hostile and uncomprehending talk in the press, Whitman hesitated on the score of propriety. He was himself writing reviews to which he considered it impolitic to attach his own name, but he paid Emerson the compliment of supposing that the latter never wrote anything he was unwilling to see over his name in print, particularly when it was so well written and when, as Whitman was all too willing to believe in those days of confused emotion, what Emerson said was profoundly true. Indeed, with some effort, he convinced himself that Emerson must have meant it for use. So when Dana persisted, Whitman gave in, and the letter came out in the *Tribune*. Emerson did not see it there, but if Whitman could have seen him when he heard of it from Bellews he would have been sorry he had published it.

"I wrote at once," said Emerson to Bellews, "a letter to the author, congratulating him."

"Yes," I replied, "I read it."

"How? When? Have you been to New York?"

"No; I read it in the New York *Tribune*."

"In the New York *Tribune?* No, no! impossible! he cannot have published it!" he exclaimed with much surprise. Being assured that such, nevertheless, was the case, he muttered:

"Dear, dear! that was very wrong, very wrong indeed. That was merely a private letter of congratulation. Had I intended it for publication I should have enlarged the but very much— enlarged the but," biting the word off with his lips and looking thoughtfully out the window, as he meditated upon the lack of taste in the people's poet whom he had taken for protegé.

But Emerson's thought of the book was not conditioned by his opinion of the man, and though he was annoyed by the position in which the publication of the letter placed him as the unqualified sponsor of the book, he did not retract what he had written. And when he came to see the author he realized that the error was more of the judgment than of the heart, and he forgave him it, as one would a child. But, as we shall see, Whitman, having once conquered his scruple, went still farther in his questionable exploitation of Emerson's friendship. Once he had committed himself to a course of action, he was likely to persist in it, even if he knew he was wrong.

It was clear by this time that to complete his plan of the "Leaves" by publishing additional sections along the lines he had sketched in the first edition Whitman would undertake a thankless job. Was it worth while? Had a man, even a man of genius, the right to trust himself so completely, disregarding what revelation of truth might have been committed to other men? The transcendentalists had dodged this problem by frankly disclaiming the right of the reason to demand a philosophy of life and, with characteristic self-sufficiency, drank only that water which was drawn from their private wells. Was not all water alike if pure? For his part, Whitman needed time to think it over. For he was still conscious of his limitations, and his whole training taught him to be wary of those who were committed to a single point of view. So he struck out for the region about Peconic Bay, and spent the fall there. Away from men, far from the city with its suggestions of selfish and temporary ambitions, he made the great decision of his life: he would go on with his plan and do the best he could with it, for after all he was not pretending to be perfect but only to put a genuine man for once into a book. If the book revealed the imperfections of the man, it might at least provoke a better man to do a better book; but in any case he would have made the most of his talent. And he would frankly admit the evil in himself as well as the good—indeed, he would almost brag of it, if only to insist that an emasculated literature can never be a virile force in life.

I have called this a decision; that is perhaps not quite the word. As he once said to his reverent biographer, Dr. Bucke, "I have hardly done anything in my life of set purpose." He wrote the book because he wanted to, because it gave him a certain pleasure to assert himself through such an experiment in making the world better and happier. It was religious to him in the sense that it satisfied an imperative demand of his subconscious affection; but it was also pleasing to him personally inasmuch as it gave him a picturesque rôle such as he could never hope to attain by competing with poets, orators, statesmen on their own ground. If thus his twin ambition had in it a little pose, it had also, as history has now shown, the significance of a national service.

The new volume was ready the following July. It was printed by Fowler and Wells, a prosperous firm which had made much of the fad for phrenology. But it did not bear their imprint; like other publishers they feared the terrible power of Puritanism in the United States and this volume was sure to provoke more caustic comment than the first. It dropped the prose preface of the earlier edition but, without greatly altering the lines, incorporated much of it in various new poems. Both poems and preface being essentially declamatory, this was not difficult to do. The new poems, though more numerous than those in the first edition, added only as many more pages.

A man who has published a book out of his soul is never quite so subjective afterwards, for part of him is now on the outside of his consciousness, a picture for himself as well as for others to look at and criticize. Perhaps this was less true in Whitman's case than in most, inasmuch as he had strangely caught in his book not only his ideas and feelings, but deeper meanings which he could not understand and hence could not criticize. Nevertheless, his next book showed clear evidences that he was beginning to think more of the laws which govern the artistic impression of others as well as of the spontaneous expression of himself.

Although the first, dazzling effect of his interior illumination was now beginning to take its place in Whitman's mind as a dominant phase of his thought, it was not the only phase. He had been led to it in part, as we have seen, but the rapidity whereby his dreams for an ideal civilization had outrun the power of the reformer to make over a nation in the likeness of those youthful dreams. He had never celebrated the past, or even the present; concerning them he, being a journalist, had few illusions. And when the light of his mystical vision revealed things in the future, he could but contrast them with the actuality about him, the actuality which would put him down, not only as a dreamer, but a dreamer with a nightmare. Such a situation is the test of the idealist. He may react in one of two ways: if his patience, his ability and his faith be limited, he will turn satirist, seeking to prod a sluggish world with ridicule or with scorn; but if he be really great, he will patiently set about creating the beauty of which he has dreamed. In the case of Whitman's second volume, as in the first, we have a very human mixture of the two.

In one poem, afterwards dropped, Whitman sends over the roofs of the world a "barbaric yawp" of scornful irony. "Respondez! Respondez!" he cries to the people, in the French he had imperfectly picked up in New Orleans.

Let the crust of hell be neared and trod on! Let the days be darker than
    the nights! Let slumber bring less slumber than waking-time brings!
Let the world never appear to him or her for whom it was all made!
Let the heart of the young man still exile itself from the heart of the old
    man! and let the heart of the old man be exiled from the heart of the
    young man!
Let the sun and moon go! Let scenery take the applause of the audience!
    Let there be apathy under the stars!
Let the eminence of meanness, treachery, sarcasm, hate, greed, indecency,
    impotence, lust, be taken for granted above all!
Let writers, judges, governments, households, religions, philosophies, take
    such for granted above all!
Let the worst men beget children of the worst women!
Let priests still play at immortality!
Let Death be inaugurated!
Let nothing remain upon the earth except the ashes of teachers, artists,
    moralists, lawyers, and learned and polite persons!

Then, dropping the irony for a single line, he explodes his real feeling,

Let him who is without my poems be assassinated!

Then he continues:

Let marriage slip down among fools, and be for none but fools!
Let men among themselves talk and think obscenely of women! and let
women among themselves talk and think obscenely of men!
Let every man doubt every woman! and let every woman trick every man!
Let the earth desert God, nor let there ever henceforth be mentioned the
name of God!
Let there be no God!
Let there be no unfashionable wisdom! Let such be scorned and derided
off from the earth!
Let there be wealthy and immense cities—but through any of them, not a
single poet, saviour, knower, lover!
Let the infidels of These States laugh all faith away! If one be found who
has faith, let the rest set upon him! Let them affright faith! Let them
destroy the power of breeding faith!
Let the she-harlots and the he-harlots be prudent! Let them dance on,
while seeming lasts! (O seeming! seeming! seeming!)

This is the edition that Emerson should have sent to Carlyle,
with this outburst marked. Of course, for all its indictment of
an age not wholly frank with itself, such a jeremiad could accomplish no good, and was not really characteristic of Whitman; but it reveals the strength of his devotion to his cause, and
it betrays the agony of his disappointment. Yet, except perhaps as involuntary autobiography, it had no proper place in
his book. For by his own cardinal evolutionary theory, one
age deserves to be blamed no more than another.

There will never be any more perfection than there is now,
Nor any more heaven or hell than there is now.

The same satire besprinkles some of the other poems, even the
most cheerful of them. But on the whole, the book is not only
full of creative inspiration, but it was slowly evolving a form.

In the first poem, "Salut au Monde!" this form is artificially
superimposed. The lines are mechanically, not to say unmu-
sically, wrought. Each section of the poem begins with a question, "What do you see, Walt Whitman?" "What do you hear,

Walt Whitman?" etc. Numerous parallel lines then answer each question, often, it is true, with the bare names of pictures rather than with the pictures themselves. But even though these lines may not evoke emotional images in the mind of the reader, it does not follow that they had no such value to the author. For Whitman had begun a rigorous course of self-education for his poetic career, reading widely and making countless notes; so that when he says, "I see the electric telegraphs of the earth," he is thinking, though the reader is not, of "the filaments of the news of the wars, deaths, gains, passions, of my race." It is true that he sometimes made the fundamental poetic mistake of supposing that he could write emotional poetry concerning what had not deeply stirred his own emotions; but it is interesting to note that, basing his democracy on the essential equality of mankind, he should so soon have lifted his horizon to include the whole world.

My spirit has passed in compassion and determination around the whole earth;
I have looked for equals and lovers, and found them ready for me in all lands;
I think some divine rapport has equalized me with them.

A very similar poem is the "Song of the Broad-Axe," in which, though his mind roams over history very freely, he has limited his imagination to those events, occupations, institutions that have had some connection with the axe, the symbol of man's domination of the earth. The overture is in rhymed trochees and the interminable catalogues of "Salut au Monde!" are here broken up by passages of poetry, or rhythmical epigrams. Imbedded in one section is a beautiful description of the great city, the ultimate handiwork of the pioneer's axe. Then, foreshadowing the method of his greatest poetry, the real gives way to eidolons, dim shapes of the ideal which alone endures.

In "As I Sat Alone By Blue Ontario's Shore" is further evidence that the mystic is working toward form and beauty. The theme is that of the prose preface to the first edition, but the form has now an added prologue and epilogue, while all the exposition appears as personal experience and avowal. No longer is he merely writing a preface to express the hope for a literature new in America. He definitely assumes the task of creating that literature.

> Fall behind me, States!
> A man before all—myself, typical before all.

The poem is the story of his original commission from the Muse, when

> by Ontario's shore,
> While the winds fann'd me, and the waves came tripping toward me,
> I thrill'd with the Power's pulsations—and the charm of my theme was upon me,
> Till the tissues that held me, parted their ties upon me.
> And I saw the free Soul of poets;
> The loftiest bards of past ages strode before me,
> Strange, large men, long unwaked, undisclosed, were disclosed to me.

Likewise in "This Compost" we have a unifying subject, and a compressed well-balanced poem, with a theme not unlike that of "Thanatopsis." And in "To You" Whitman achieves unity and a fitting form by making the poem a versified letter to the reader, asking friendship and inviting him to start out, with the poet, on the Open Road of individual liberty and joy. The long poem on this theme, "Poem of the Road" (later "Song of the Open Road"), is one of the most buoyant, courageous, stimulating challenges in the whole English language.

> I will scatter myself among men and women as I go;
> I will toss a new gladness and roughness among them;
> Whoever denies me, it shall not trouble me;
> Whoever accepts me, he or she shall be blessed, and shall bless me.

The very symbolism confesses the poet's inability to deal with so broad and elusive a theme except by suggestion.

I swear to you there are divine things more beautiful than words can tell.
And the divinest is the society of the Great Companions, "the swift and majestic men," the greatest women.

He concludes, like some modern David Grayson or Sherwood Anderson, or some classic Emerson:

Allons! be not detain'd!
Let the paper remain on the desk unwritten, and the book on the shelf unopen'd!
Let the tools remain in the workshop! let the money remain unearned!
Let the school stand! mind not the cry of the teacher!
Let the preacher preach in his pulpit! let the lawyer plead in the court, and the judge expound the law.

But doubtless the most beautiful, and at the same time most powerful, poem in the edition was the one which Thoreau lingered over, the "Sun-Down Poem" (now "Crossing Brooklyn Ferry"). Here is the very assurance of eternity, and the equal tone of art; yet there is no monotony in the rising and falling cadences. Nature is beautiful and accurately portrayed, an actual scene; and yet she is caught up into higher poetry than that—she becomes the messenger of one generation to another, not so much to be loved in herself as to be associated with the unending stream of life. Bryant, in his "Flood of Years" was to brood upon the procession of man as an epic panorama; Whitman makes friends with every man in the procession who has shared or will share his experiences—for has he too not stepped from that crowd for a brief moment to pin his message on a faithful tree where all may read? And to make sure that none will feel unworthy of his friendship he avows the evil within him as well as the good.

Nor is it you alone who know what it is to be evil;
I am he who knew what it was to be evil;
I too knitted the old knot of contrariety,
Blabb'd, blush'd, resented, lied, stole, grudg'd,
Had guile, anger, lust, hot wishes I dared not speak,
Was wayward, vain, greedy, shallow, sly, cowardly, malignant;
The wolf, the snake, the hog, not wanting in me,

The cheating look, the frivolous word, the adulterous wish, not wanting,
Refusals, hates, postponements, meanness, laziness, none of these wanting,
Was one with the rest, the days and haps of the rest,
But I was a Manhattanese, free, friendly and proud!

Making careful use of repetition, marvelously blending homely terms and sights in the most harmonious tone, he has written a poem with lasting and human charm.

In such a poem one senses not merely the feeling of immortality which Hazlitt attributed to youthful inexperience, but a feeling of immortality which has no reference to youth or age, a feeling which deals a blow to the tyranny of time. No wonder he complained of the preachers' lack of imagination, they who professed to hold sacred the miracles but who could not see the all-inclusive miracle of creation. Whitman seldom wrote a poem more perfectly suited to what he had to say than "Miracles." To appreciate its real faith we shall have to think of it, not in connection with Emerson's essays, but in connection with churches who considered Beecher and Phillips radicals and who would have been comfortable in the religious atmosphere of modern Daytons.

The only new poems in this edition to enlarge upon his treatment of sex are "Poem of Procreation" (now "A Woman Waits for Me") and "Spontaneous Me." In a few lines of these there was, in comparison with the first edition, less poetic masking of sexual experience; but we shall mention them again, in connection with an entire group of which they formed a part in the third edition and afterwards.

In the last poem in the new edition, Whitman sought to assure the reader that, despite his best effort, the poet had been unable fully to communicate himself through written words.

The truths of the earth continually wait, they are not so conceal'd either;
They are calm, subtle, untransmissible by print;
They are imbued through all things, conveying themselves willingly,
Conveying a sentiment and invitation of the earth—I utter and utter,
I speak not, yet if you hear me not, of what avail am I to you?
The best of the earth cannot be told anyhow.

For to Whitman, borrowing nothing, language is but an understood hint of experience, and men must live fully before they can comprehend the language of a full life.

I swear the earth remains jagged and broken only to him or her who remains jagged and broken!

Likewise the words a poet must utter are those cast up by the experience of his race, his time. Any word in its place is good, if only it do justice to the life for which it stands; borrowed words are lying echoes.

Yet, for all the evidences which the book offered that its author was saner than his age, there was something in it which betrayed, also, that he was not quite master of himself. On the backstrip of the book his publisher had printed in gold a sentence from Emerson's letter; "I greet you at the beginning of a great career," over Emerson's signature. Of course, this was done with Whitman's consent, if not at his suggestion. Whatever may have been his conception of the purpose of the letter, it is hard to see how he could excuse himself for thus making Emerson seem to endorse the new poems which he had never read. It was more than bad taste; it was not playing fair. The letter had never been answered in writing, but it was printed in full in the appendix, together with the press notices, and in reply to it appeared a long and fulsome letter from Whitman. A new volume of poems, he said, was the only adequate reply to such a missive. There was an element of affectation in this, which could have given Emerson no satisfaction; for Emerson had called on Whitman in the meantime, and had, of course, received a personal reply to his letter. The author's lack of perfect self-poise appears further in a passage in which, with what he thought was generosity, he addressed Emerson as "master" and declared that the Concord sage had first discovered America as a literary realm. In his enthusiasm he went on to declare that the first edition of a thousand copies had "readily sold," a statement which was about as far from the facts as it could be, whatever may have been the twist of mind which permitted Whitman to make it. Unless he was merely bluffing, the open road of his literary career was smooth before him. "I keep on till I make a hundred [poems], and then several hundred—perhaps a thousand. The way is clear to me. A few years, and the average annual call for my Poems is ten or twenty thousand copies— more, quite likely. Why should I hurry or compromise? In poems or speeches I say the word or two that has got to be said, adhere to the body, step with the countless common footsteps, and remind every man or woman of something. Master, I am a man who has perfect faith."

"In poems or speeches," he had said. Both before and after his poetic experiment Whitman thought of indulging in the lecturing so popular in the 1850's. Emerson, Thackeray, Curtis, Phillips, and Beecher were doing it with success; why could not he? In some respects it would be more satisfying to "quell America with a great tongue," hearing

> The cry of an applauding multitude,
> Swayed by some loud-voiced orator who wields
> The living mass as if he were its soul,

than to cram himself into print and paper in silent little words so seldom fashioned to his purpose. On the platform he might not only display the persuasiveness of his musical voice, the dignity of his impressive if not majestic frame, but might also find inspiration in the personal presence of those to whom he spoke. He had in the early fifties written many of these lectures—"barrels of them," Mrs. Whitman said; and now, when fear of prosecution for issuing an "obscene" book caused his publishers to stop selling the second edition, he revived his plan of making himself not only the poet of the nation but also its great orator, speaking by word of mouth as did all the ancient prophets. This would have the additional purpose of advertising both himself and his book; it would be a personal introduction to the masses of what had seemed too esoteric for them in print. But it would not be done for personal gain. At most he would charge fifteen cents admission, or ten dollars a lecture. Some lectures would be on religion, some on democracy, others on art and psychology; but he would take care not to allow any fame he might win thereby to entangle him in politics. He would not run for office, as famous orators have commonly done. It was characteristic of him to plan his announcement before he was ready to begin lecturing. Here is a rough draft of it, evidently meant for posting or publication.

"Notice.—Random Intentions.—Two branches.

"Henceforth two co-expressions.—They expand, amicable, from common sources, but each with individual stamp by itself.—

"First, Poems, Leaves of Grass, as of Institutions, the Soul, the Body, (a man, a woman) descending below laws, social routine, creeds, literature, to celebrate a human being, the inherent, the red blood, one male in himself, or one female in herself.—Songs of thoughts and wants hitherto repressed by writers.—Or, it may as well be avowed, to give the personality of Walt Whitman out and out, evil and good—whatever he is or thinks, that sharply set down in a book. The Spirit commanding it; if certain outsiders stop, puzzled, or dispute or laugh, very well.—

"Second, Lectures, as of Reasoning, Reminiscences, Comparison, the Intellectual, the Esthetic, the desire for Knowledge, the sense of richness, refinement and beauty in the mind, as an art, a sensation from an American point of view.—Also, in Lectures, the meaning of Religion, as a statement.—

"Of the above two, both would increase themselves, not at any time finished, any more than any live operation of Nature is—but unfolding, urging onward and outward.—By degrees to fashion for these States two athletic volumes, the first to speak for the permanent Soul (which speaks for all, materials too, but can be understood only by the like of itself—the same being the reason that what is wisdom to one is gibberish to another). But the second, temporary, shall be the speech of the attempt at Argumentation, Art. Both to illustrate America, illustrate the whole, not merely sections, members,—throbbing from the heart

inland, the West, around the great Lakes, or along the flowing
Ohio, or Missouri, or Mississippi.—

"Curious, much advertising his own appearance and views,
(it cannot be helped), offensive to many, too free, too savage
and natural, candidly owning that he has neither virtue or knowledge—such, an account of Walt Whitman, going his own way to
his own work—because that with the rest, is needed—because
in less terms how can he get what he is resolved to have, to himself, and to America?"

It is not recorded that Whitman made an attempt to give a
single lecture at this period, though some of the manuscript notes
are extant. Possibly his courage failed him. For after all,
while a man like Emerson could hold an audience by calmly reading a manuscript, it was because of the art in his carefully chosen
words, and also because of the fact that he was, personally, not
an average man, but the representative of the popular ideal, a
Brahmin. The art of lecturing as Beecher could lecture or, later,
Robert Ingersoll was in some ways more exacting than writing
poetry. It demanded the same inspiration, the same flaming
words, but it also required that this inspiration be under perfect
control, and obedient to time. The orator needs, not only a
perfect body, but an expressive, an acting body; and act Whitman could not. As for controlling the mass he thought he
loved, he should have been merely wounded in his affection had
that mass proved cold to his overtures of friendship, his offers
of leadership. Furthermore, in oratory the whole man actually
speaks; and if readers as sympathetic as Emerson and Thoreau
found in Whitman's book here and there repellent traits, would
not a miscellaneous audience find still more to dislike in the person himself? As Mr. H. B. Binns puts it, he was too "loose
in the knees" to be a commanding platform figure. In any case,
Whitman soon abandoned the idea as impracticable and began
looking around for a way to make a living, now that his dream
of royalties had dissolved. An offer being made, he took charge
of Bennett's Williamsburg newspaper, the *Times*. Inglorious,
no doubt, but sensible. He remained in charge for some two

years, or till it was time to set about publishing his third edition.
Altogether his instinct was more literary than he knew, yet literary only in proportion as he thought of it as religious. In a
private memorandum, such as men set down when they seek to
lay down the law to their wayward wills, he wrote in June, 1857:
"The Great Construction of the New Bible. Not to be di-
verted from the principal object—the main life—the three hundred and sixty-five.—It ought to be ready in 1859." And in
1859 it was.

But to give a true insight into these years we must remember
what that "bible" was, and whence its inspiration came. Whitman was never a recluse, except when he refreshed himself with
nature; and in this period he was giving free reign to his impulses
for mixing with all classes of people that could understand him.
Emerson had sent to Brooklyn other visitors, Thoreau and Alcott; Beecher and Bryant, Whitman's neighbors, came to see him,
and Lord Houghton from overseas, whither his book had
reached a friendly hand. In Thoreau he found what he found in
Carlyle, a distrust, not of the individual, but of the average man;
and they made little progress in conversation. Thoreau's query
as to whether Whitman had read the oriental writers, however,
gave a new interest to his reading. When, long after Whitman's death, Tagore visited America, he declared that no American had caught the Oriental spirit of mysticism so well as he.
Thoreau was repelled by the book rather than by the man. "It
is as if the beasts spake," he said, in an infelicitous phrase; for it
was rather as if a man, discovering that he was an animal, determined, for the moment, to be nothing else, only to find that
civilization cannot be laid aside as can one's garments when one
disports like a fish in the surf. Nevertheless, Thoreau was
magnetized by the man, and asked him, a little patronizingly:
"Whitman, do you have any idea that you are rather bigger
and outside the average—may perhaps have immense significance?"
Whitman did not answer. He knew the dignity and power

that lie in simplicity. When Lord Houghton called, he was not taken to a hotel, but invited to share the Whitmans' simple meal of potatoes.

As to the egotism of his "Leaves," Thoreau was relieved when he had seen the man—Thoreau who might have been expected to feel the egotist's jealousy of other self-centered men. "He may turn out the least braggart of all," he wrote a friend, "having a better right to be confident." Whitman himself appealed for judgment to the future, where there could be no jealousy; and the future has rendered a verdict that, though he may have lacked taste in his selection of reflectors, it would have been false modesty for such a man to have hidden his light under a bushel.

Distinguished visitors were, of course, the exception; Whitman's daily companions were his cronies on bus or boat, and a group of Bohemians who were beginning to frequent a beer cellar on Broadway, just above Bleecker. Pfaff's was the Greenwich Village of that day, the best New York could do for a *Quartier Latin*. The German food was good, the beer and champagne excellent, and the stout host silent but jovial. An ideal place for Whitman, when indisposed to ride a bus or to tramp the "trottoirs," as he called the streets; here he might sit and watch the world go by. In the evenings, when he had finished his day's work on the *Times,* and perhaps had gone to a ball game or a prayer meeting afterwards, he would here find William Winter, the brilliant Fitz-James O'Brien, Henry Clapp and George Arnold of the *Saturday Press,* a new weekly which was quick to print Whitman's poems and to champion his cause, and Ada Claire, "Queen of Bohemia," a queen with a sad life but a brilliant mind, who strongly appealed to Whitman, both personally and as an example of the new woman. As in all such places, there were plentiful arguments over the beer, and much wit. Not infrequently this was at the expense of that hub of the universe where Dr. Holmes was so much at ease, and Longfellow the last word in poets. Sometimes Whitman would go to Pfaff's with the young doctors in Bellevue, after having visited some sick friend of his. And often he would make new acquaintances. One of these, William Dean Howells, remembered him for his jovian largeness and ease, his personal purity and friendliness. Howells too was to try to do a picture of life in America, a realistic picture, and, like Whitman, would sometimes put himself into a character of his story; but—perhaps too well—Howells would know how to avoid arousing the ire of his readers. He would select only life's more cheerful aspects, and depend more on art than on inspiration in presenting them.

Whitman had learned, even in New Orleans, that it was impossible for him long to lose himself in mere sensation or good fellowship and high spirits. Ever and anon came his brooding spirit with the "terrible doubt of appearances," the hint of elusive but eternal realities. One evening, after receiving the welcome with which he was commonly greeted at Pfaff's, he grew melancholy, and set down the following lines:

The vault at Pfaff's where the drinkers and laughers meet to eat and drink
    and carouse,
While on the walk immediately overhead pass the myriad feet of Broadway,
As the dead in their graves are underfoot hidden,
And the living pass over them, recking not of them.
Laugh on Laughers!
Drink on Drinkers!
Bandy the jest! Toss the theme from one to another!
Beam up—Brighten up, bright eyes of beautiful young men!
Eat what you, having ordered, are pleased to see placed before you—after
    the work of the day, now, with appetite, eat,
Drink wine—drink beer—raise your voice,
Behold! your friend as he arrives—welcome him, when, from the upper-
    step, he looks down upon you with a cheerful look.
Overhead rolls Broadway, the myriad rushing Broadway,
The lamps are lit—the shops blaze—the fabrics vividly are seen through
    the plate-glass window,
The strong lights from above pour down upon them and are shed outside,
The thick crowds, well-dressed—the continual crowds as they walk and
    never end.

The curious appearance of the faces—the glimpse of the eyes and expressions as they flit along,
(O you phantoms! oft I pause, yearning to arrest some one of you!
Oft I doubt your reality whether you are real—I suspect all is but a pageant.)

Though Whitman never cared much for polite society as such, he was now moving in the parlors of a few excellent families who looked upon him with the greatest respect and treated him with the greatest consideration.   Mrs. Abby Price was one of these, and she took pains to invite people of importance to meet Whitman, generals, scholars and women who were doing significant things.   Whitman did not care for lionizing; he could often romp with the children better than he could unbosom himself to persons who had come in the hope of provoking him to do so.   Mrs. Price and her daughters were quick to perceive in Whitman what he had perhaps not yet realized in himself, a certain intuitiveness which is more commonly found in, and trusted by, women than by men.   They saw, too, that he was living an inward life of joy which occasionally made his face translucent with something more than a smile.   As Helen Price said, his religion was "that habitual state of feeling in which the person regards everything in God's universe with wonder, reverence, perfect acceptance, and love."   Of course, no good woman who saw this in him could dislike the man or distrust the goodness of what he wrote.

But Whitman was never too engrossed in his wonder and reverence of things mystical to perform acts of practical kindness when occasion arose.   Memoranda like this are to be found in his notebooks:

"Dec. 28 [1861] Saturday night.   Mike Ellis—wandering at the cor of Lexington av & 3rd st.   Took him home to 150 37th Street—4th story back room—bitter cold night—works in Stevenson's carriage factory."

It is interesting to turn through the pages of the Brooklyn Times for 1857–9 and to note how much the editor has grown in the ten years since we made his acquaintance in the editorial rooms of the *Eagle*. Then he was an ardent advocate of particular reforms; now he is impatient with those who in their conceit offer mere panaceas.

"With your farthing rush-light you seek to illumine the illimitable caverns of the infinite. With your favorite (pint) measure, you would ladle out the ocean. It is pitiful. These problems lie so deep, and you approach them so superficially—these qualities are so momentous, and you talk of them so childishly! Heaven is so high, and yet you play before it such fantastic tricks! Nature is so calm, so serene, so certain in her workings, and yet you cannot perceive the beauty and grandeur of the lesson she inculcates. You can accept nothing unquestioned. You place the blatant enthusiast before the reverent philosopher. Fanaticism stands with you in the place of Faith."

The cliques of society and the schisms of the church he deplores because, due to them, "the life-blood of society does not circulate with vigor and freedom." "The churches are one vast lie," Whitman had written Emerson; but he was to feel the power of the churches when his editorials exposed their unfairness in churching one Judge Culver, a Free-soiler. The columns of an independent paper were expected to be open to both sides in a public controversy, but it was suggested to the editor that he had better not take sides. He, however, was not lacking in courage as a journalist. "Those of our readers who have watched the course of the journal during the years that are passed well know that we have never hesitated to assume an independent position and to comment on passing events freely and boldly when we considered it necessary and proper to do so." But in a few months he was deprived of his last editorial position. Doubtless he lost no sleep over it, for it meant that he was now free to bring out his third edition.

We may not look at the increment of poems in that edition, however, until we have turned a few more pages of the old Brooklyn *Times*. We observe less politics, but when the question of free-soil comes up, he is outspoken in sympathy with its champions, Greeley and Phillips, though he demurs to Phillips's invectives against the Constitution. Lincoln has not yet caught his eye, but he admires Douglas's winning fight with the Illinois bosses. "Who would not rather now be Douglas than to be President?" He reads such magazines as the "Westminster" and "Harper's" and writes many editorials suggested by what he finds in them. He even turns the pages of the yellow press and smiles at the sensation stories which Bonner's *Ledger* had popularized as a type. Such stories he had once written himself, and even now he suggests that they cannot be suddenly replaced by the *Christian Standard,* since the masses can respond to no higher form of intellectual stimulation than they afford. He loafs about the factories, in the beer gardens, at the ball games. He attends the firemen's balls and meets many friends there. He inspects the schools as in the *Eagle* days, and drops in on the police courts as he had done in New Orleans; but now his report is less cynical, more filled with compassion for the unfortunate. When the unhappy home life of his one-time idol, Charles Dickens, comes to light, he expresses only a comprehending sympathy. "Not always do the happy sentiment, genial philosophy, the felicitous diction of the novelist spring from an inward perennial fountain of peace—not always are the tragedies of the fictionists drawn from the vivid imagination alone. . . . Of all the calamities of authors—of all the infelicities of genius—it strikes us that their domestic difficulties are the worst. Take all else from a man and leave him a good and faithful wife and he can never be called unhappy, no matter what may be the fluctuations of fortune. But take that comfort, consolation and safeguard away and he becomes 'poor' indeed—a vessel without a rudder, beaten here and there, at the mercy of the wind and waves."

Do we not here strike the unmistakable note of personal experience, even though we cannot know the details of that private pain? For at this very time Whitman hinted to the Prices that he had just composed a new piece, which seems to bear upon the matter. He was urged to bring it over and read it. A visiting friend read it, at Whitman's suggestion, then Mrs. Price, and then, after urging, Whitman himself. There was a note of pathos in it which Helen Price could never forget. Henry Clapp took it at once for the *Saturday Press,* where it caught the eye of John Burroughs, who was to be a staunch but sane admirer of the poet through life. It was "A Word out of the Sea" (now "Out of the Cradle Endlessly Rocking"), based, as Whitman told the Prices, on a real incident. The ballad recounts how a boy stole from his farm-house home at night to listen to the mournful call of a mocking-bird by the sea, as it sat on a nest to which its mate would never return. But the bird evidently symbolizes the poet's own soul, learning in sorrow the sweet mystery of death and separation. Had his lover died? Surely some lover had died, and he could find solace only in song. It is hard to believe that any man could more tenderly have cherished a wife and a home than the author of that immortal lyric.

> O past! O life! O songs of joy!
> In the air—in the woods—over fields;
> Loved! loved! loved! loved! loved!
> But my love no more, no more with me!
> We two together no more.

Happily Whitman had found how to turn his private sorrows to public account. Perhaps all his public spirit, all his poetry, was no more the lyric outburst of a bird which cannot choose but sing than it was a salutary sublimation of frustrated personal emotions. He was thinking more and more of Woman, the woman that might be. No more does he pick out the pretty faces on the street for an editorial tribute; he looks at the average. And what he sees gives him little hope for the future of the race. How different from the magnficent women he had seen and known in the Crescent City! How unlike his own "perfect mother"! "Wherever we go we see hundreds of sickly, feeble girls who can hardly muster courage to perform the ordinary avocations of life. Tell them about early rising,

fresh air and healthy exercise and they heave a lamentable sigh
and are ready to faint away." And the cause? "Listless idleness, inactivity, thin shoes, late hours, muslin dresses, horror
of fresh morning air, and that detestable stuff stitched in pink
and yellow covers, which is flooding the country over." His own
ideal for the modern woman had been described in the 1856 edition:

They are not one jot less than I am,
They are tanned in the face by shining suns and blowing winds,
Their flesh has the old divine suppleness and strength,
They know how to swim, row, ride, wrestle, shoot, run, strike, retreat,
    advance, resist, defend themselves,
They are ultimate in their own right—they are calm, clear, well-possessed
    of themselves.

To call forth such a race—which, fortunately for us, has been
called forth—it would be necessary to begin with a saner, prouder
paternity, and a youth prepared in health of body and mind for
that paternity.

And what of the young men he saw? Was he content with
the self-realization of the young men whose society he so affected? Far from it. Speaking more from observation than
personal experience, he declared that "long before they have
reached physical maturity most of our young men are old in
life, with all its experiences and dissipations. We may well realize the fact that there is amazingly little moral restraint—almost none at all. . . . As a general thing, the masses (probably
two thirds) of city young men, in common life, hold themselves
aloof from the influences of the various benevolent, the pious,
and the reformatory leaders whose movements figure in the papers. With any literature except the lowest and most superficial the masses in question are not conversant at all. Lectures,
Churches, scientific expositions, &c., they never attend. . . . All
the amusements of the majority of nearly grown and just grown
lads, about Brooklyn and New York, are injurious. They soon
get used to drink, and to feel perfectly at home in the most in-

famous places—and to look for their pleasure mostly there. Many of them, by the time they become thirty years of age, are old men, with ruined constitutions."

In the summer of 1859 Whitman was out of a job, and none was in sight. He had enough new poems to enlarge his book by half, but he had no publisher, nor was he likely to have one. As a poet he had largely dropped out of the public view. On June 26 he wrote in his notebook an emphatic injunction to himself: "It is now time to stir first for money enough to live and provide for M——. To stir—first write stories and get out of this slough." Then followed directions for writing the projected stories. One of these narratives he crudely outlines, a melodramatic affair which grows so hazy and formless that he drops it in disgust. Who was the "M——" to whom he alludes? Probably neither his mother nor his sister Mary, for their names would have been written out. Possibly his New Orleans lover was in need, or sick. For the mocking-bird poem was published a few weeks after this. We know nothing of Whitman's movements for the rest of this year, but he was probably whipping into shape a third edition of his poems. By the first of the year Thayer and Eldridge, a publishing firm of Boston, was willing to bring it out and push its sale. In March Whitman took his manuscript and went to Boston for three months to see it through the press. It was to be an odd book, typographically, and with a printer's meticulousness he wanted to keep an eye on it.

In Boston he made new friends. Thayer and Eldridge were also bringing out an Abolitionist novel, "Harrington" and Whitman struck a friendship with its author, William Douglas O'Connor. One day Walt appeared in the court-room where a young man, Frank Sanborn, was trying to convince the judge why he should not be turned over to the Federal authorities to answer the charge of having participated in the John Brown raid at Harper's Ferry. Whitman had never grown so enthusiastic over John Brown as had Emerson and Thoreau, for he did not believe, like Beecher, that the cause of freedom should be fought with "Bibles and Winchesters."   Sanborn noticed the distinguished-looking man in the strange garb, standing near the door, but did not meet him till later.   Then Whitman told him he was there to see that justice was done Sanborn in case the judge did not release him.   The underground railroad, thanks to "Uncle Tom's Cabin," was looked upon in sections of the North as a religious institution; and there was in Boston a plan on foot to rescue Sanborn if necessary.   Whitman would write no more "Boston Ballads"; he would take a hand himself.

A few years later, O'Connor, seeking to praise his friend, published the story of a chance encounter Whitman had during this visit to Boston.   "I remember the anecdote told me by a witness, of his meeting in a by-street in Boston a poor ruffian, one whom he had known well as an innocent child, now a full-grown youth, vicious far beyond his years, flying to Canada from the pursuit of the police, his sin-trampled features bearing marks of the recent bloody brawl in New York in which, as he supposed, he had killed some one; and having heard his hurried story, freely confided to him, Walt Whitman, separated not from the bad even by his own goodness, with well I know what tender and tranquil feeling for the ruined being, and with a love which makes me think of that God which deserts not any creature, quietly at parting, after assisting him from his means, held him for a moment, with his arm around his neck, and, bending to the face, horrible and battered and prematurely old, kissed him on the cheek, and the poor hunted wretch, perhaps for the first time in his low life, receiving a token of love and compassion like a touch from beyond the sun, hastened away in deep dejection, sobbing and in tears."

His most significant meeting, however, was with Emerson. By this time they knew each other well enough for wholesome criticism not to endanger a friendship—even with Whitman, who never took advice.   "In Boston when one wants to talk he goes to the Common," said Emerson; and thither they went, pacing back and forth for two hours under the great elms.   What Emerson wanted to talk to his friend about was the advisability of Whitman's leaving out of his new edition the open treatment of sex which had hitherto kept Whitman's poetry from any popular acceptance. But Whitman had not only written more and franker poems of this sort for the new edition but had brought them together in a section of his book, called *"Enfans d'Adam,"* where they stood, in a way, conspicuously alone. Yet he was willing to listen to Emerson's arguments respectfully. If they could not shake his purpose then he would be unmoved by anything and would, on this point, henceforth be at peace. While writing the poems he had not been without qualms on the point. Emerson's argument has not been recorded, except his emphasis that this was a case in which half a loaf was better than none, that to include the poems in question would mean that none of the poems would get to the people who so much needed the tonic of Whitman's religious individualism. He did not argue that they were impure in intent, he was willing to take Whitman's word for that; though personally, as we know, he found them unnecessarily indelicate in expression. But intent does not determine probable reaction, as Emerson accurately foresaw. Looking up to see why such good Yankee arguments, so skillfully and so sympathetically put, were not eliciting any reply from his big companion, Emerson asked, "What have you to say to such things?"

"Only that," Whitman replied, "while I can't answer them at all, I feel more settled than ever to adhere to my own theory, and exemplify it."

That was the tactical reply to make to an Emerson who had once said to the deacons arguing that he might be mistaken in his own intuitions, "I cannot argue—I only know." So they went to the American House and had a good dinner. The real motives at work under the surface of Whitman's psychology might have come to the surface, for our enlightenment if not his, had he attempted to argue at all. But it seemed to be a case of realizing that to argue would be to yield, and he had made up his stubborn mind not to yield; he had no willingness to believe that Emerson was right. Accord-

ingly he called the Emersonian argument a worldly one and
dismissed it. This was the more easily said, no doubt, because
there was a half-truth in it. But what was it he was being asked
to yield—this theory? Was it merely a plan for his life work
he was being asked to trim? Yes, and all that plan implied
of satisfaction to himself, of service to others. As we have
seen, the impulse to autobiography was compelling in Whitman,
an impulse which was capable of disguising itself as a humanitarian or literary motive, if thus it might the more easily have
its way. His theory was that a man might be absolutely candid
in print, might put himself entirely on record, might make a
complete confession. He had a certain pride in himself when
he looked at his body reflected in water; he had an equal pride
in himself when he looked at his Soul on paper. After all,
he was writing chiefly for himself; if others were provoked into
thinking the more highly of themselves, so much the better,
but he would not make himself over in his natural impulses,
any more than in his poetic diction, to meet current standards
of acceptability. He appealed to the future, not to the Boston
bookstores. And in part that future has agreed with him, that
the American of 1860 was too prudish, that a frank and natural
treatment is more desirable than a furtive and suggestive one.
But the future has had "qualms" too, and always will have till
the argument comes into the open, is clarified as Whitman failed
to clarify it under the elms of Boston Common. It is only
fair that, holding his self-justifying "theory" too closely, he
should be judged out of his own mouth. May it not be that the
reason why readers, too, sometimes feel qualms is that he is
not "whole" enough, that he gives love a fragmentary treatment,
having known only a fragmentary love? For, from either the
individual or the social point of view, half a love is not better
than none.

Discovering in the random outbursts of the first edition much
obvious contradiction, Whitman was complacent, feeling that
they all came from an inscrutable source. But a paradox has
no place in art unless it hints a truth which cannot be stated

explicitly. One who takes literally Emerson's dictum that "a foolish consistency is the hobgoblin of little minds," is likely to find, too late, that his inconsistency lies, not in men's partial views of his great purpose, but between his personal desires and his saner judgment. Whitman professed to include some record of his sexual experiences and his sex emotions because they were an important part of the poet's life, as of any man's life; but by the same token he should have let stand in his first edition some of the "stock poetical touches" which he eliminated with such difficulty. For at the time he was not so unconventional as his book would make him appear, and it was his hard riding of his theory of composition, if not a false pride, that caused him to seek to be so entirely different from other poets. Making great display of candor, he nevertheless had less of it, in certain directions, than he suspected. His responsibility does not extend, of course, to the area of his subconsciousness, and of all this Whitman may have been blissfully unaware, save for the occasional qualms which Emerson, so ironically, put to rest.

Psychologists tell us that the emotions of early childhood are for the most part undifferentiated; certainly they are not consciously classified. For instance, the sense of touch, later to express itself most completely in sex, and the sense of hunger blend in a feeling larger than either. In childhood a certain amount of exhibitionism is normally expressed in a total bodily impulse in which appears a strong desire for athletic exercise. But as the normal child advances toward manhood he learns gradually to classify and to conserve his emotions, cultivating some, repressing others except on occasions recognized as proper. Men of genius are such because some capacity is unusually large, often at the expense of other faculties, which remain in a state of more or less arrested development. Hence, frequently the bold achievements of the imagination, or the religion-founding display of affection, is coupled with the impracticality or the moral obtuseness of a child. In Whitman's case it would seem that he retained in maturity much of the undifferentiated emotionalism of childhood, even while accomplishing with his poetic imagination what can only be ascribed to genius. For instance, he did not carefully distinguish between the athletic approach to nature and the affectionate approach to a person, or between the sort of affection which most men have for particular women and that which they experience toward members of their own sex. Emerson's essays on "Love" and "Friendship," for all their emphasis on transcendental idealism, when placed beside Whitman's love poems ("*Enfans d'Adam*") and his poems of friendship ("Calamus"), reveal how much more normally mature in his emotions the former was than was this unreflecting "caresser of life." Whitman's treatment of sex is further complicated by the fact that, while his "Leaves of Grass" was chiefly autobiographic, he presented much of it as though it were not, so that biographers have always been very cautious in treating many of the poems as the expression of purely personal emotion. Perhaps without realizing it, he confused the lyric and the epic treatment. This tended to distort his own judgment as to both the real intent and the effect of some of his confessions. There can be no doubt, for example, that he succeeded in persuading himself that he was religiously socializing his "egotism" by identifying himself with the average reader. But the prior question remains: Was his, in every respect, a proper "ego" to socialize in this way?

In attempting to analyze what, in his talk with Emerson, Whitman was unwilling or unable to analyze, note should first be made that he wrote three distinct types of poems on the subject of sex, and that he never blended the three into one. Sentimental lyrics born of an ideal romance, like "Out of the Rolling Ocean the Crowd," "I Heard You Solemn Sweet Pipes of the Organ," and "Out of the Cradle Endlessly Rocking," have never given, could never give, offense. They are morally complete as a human experience, so far as we know, even though love here ends, not in fulfillment, but in separation. Then there are "poems of procreation" in which the poet, like a second Adam beginning a new race of men, calls for a healthy and proud breed of parents. This too has vista and is proper material for the poet as well as for the eugenist. But when, in the third small group of poems, Whitman attempts to do justice to the emotions which accompany the initial act of paternity, he falls back not upon the creative imagination but upon the memories of his limited experience. Sex itself is clean and sweet, of course —it has not taken the race, always wiser than the individual man in such matters, so long a time tc discover this elementary fact, though the Puritan degradation of sex to purely utilitarian ends gave Whitman an excellent excuse for emphasizing the fact anew. But the expression of sex may be good or bad according to circumstances. If it involve a disavowal of responsibility to the individual and to society, it is itself marred by the injury it inflicts on the moral nature. For among cultivated individuals sex can never be complete, or completely celebrated, except as a link in the evolution of the race, moral as well as biological. Thinking too precisely on the teleological event, to be sure, inhibits the very emotion through which Nature achieves her hidden purpose; yet to indulge in emotion to the disregard of all responsibility for the future is to eliminate from what should be an integrating experience that moral element which alone gives it permanence and human dignity. "Sex contains all," as Whitman said, but only when all is given to it. Doubtless Whitman's repeated insistence on "identity" as the one constant fact in his universe would have grown less self-conscious had he through normal experiences found a way to such realization of the harmonious wholeness of his nature. For perfect physical, esthetic, and spiritual mating—such as he, being a mixture of bohemian and puritan, probably never had—is a poem in itself, too perfectly satisfying to every emotion to beget any impulse to tell of it in print. That were an offense, for words are not the proper language for such mysteries. If memorial poems must be written, they will deal with those ideal elements in the experience which alone can have significance for others. Had Whitman known more of love he would have realized that those who are worthy to speak of its holy of holies

have no impulse to do so "over the roofs of the world." This is
not prudery; it is the silence of satisfied power.

We must therefore set down Whitman's poems of abandon
to his own fragmentary *affaires de cœur,* and to his longings for
such an experience as would bring him the peace he never found.
He may have had enough of the Latin temperament to cause him
to judge an attachment on its own merits rather than to refer
it to a code; but he had too much of the Anglo-Saxon in him
ever to be a contented dilettante, a gay Lothario. "Why is it,"
runs his notebook quotation of Dickens, "that a sense comes always crushing on me, as of one happiness I have missed in life
and one friend and companion I have never made?"

We can never know what were the barriers to Whitman's ever
marrying. Surely he could have found more than one woman
who was willing. Indeed, as we shall see, one of the finest
of women let him know as much, though this particular avowal,
it is true, came too late. When he chose to give his questioners
on the point any answer, it was that he was inordinately jealous
of his own freedom. How American he was—fearful of restraint, yet by that fear restrained! Had he married a woman
fit to match his high spirit, and able through his love for her to
humble it a little, he might have had to learn adaptability, might
even have had to restrain his muse somewhat; but would he not
have learned also to speak with more authority on all those
themes that were dearest to his pen? He might then have given
us, not indeed that fireside sentiment devoid of any original
thought which his country found so satisfying in Longfellow, but
stimulating, modern songs of the first and last of societies, the
family, without which there can be no sane paternity, no solid
state. One may pity him for his limitations, then, without making a virtue out of them. In many ways he succeeded in loving his art and his fellow men the more as he had no family of
his own to love. Pity is appropriate, indeed, for with a happy
home life Whitman would have discovered attendant blessings.
His friendship for men would have been purified, relieved of that
peculiar sentimentality which expressed itself in caresses, and

which sharply distinguished it from the gospel of the religious leaders he aspired to supplant. Friendship might then have developed into a useful, wholesome comradeship in work, something about which he knew little, rather than perpetual indulgence in loafing on the Open Road. Moreover, it would have given him a second great purpose in life, to complement and relieve his poetic work and to make it the more evenly balanced. He had Nature to go to, fortunately, as did Thoreau; but while Nature is a most comforting mistress, she is no wife at all. She commonly spoils those who have no other love.

Whitman's determination to publish a complete confession of his inward life led him, in this Boston edition, to set forth a group of poems on friendship, or comradeship, or love for men, which is still more pathetic than his futile reaching forth for the love of woman. Whitman, it must be obvious, had one of the most powerful emotional natures that have been exposed to the gaze of the world; and emotion, no less than matter, is indestructible—if not starved it will express itself in one way or another. The emotion here venting itself was so great as to carry with it, for a time, Walt's every ambition. The book was published when his craving for affection was at its height.

Long I thought that knowledge alone would suffice me—Oh if I could but obtain knowledge!

Then my lands engrossed me—Lands of the prairies, Ohio's land, the southern savannahs, engrossed me—

For them I would live—I would be their orator;

Then I met the examples of old and new heroes—I heard of warriors, sailors, and all dauntless persons—And it seemed to me that I too had it in me to be as dauntless as any—and would be so;

And then, to enclose all, it came to me to strike up the songs of the New World—And then I believed my life must be spent in singing;

But now take notice, land of the prairies, land of the south savannahs, Ohio's land,

Take notice, you Kanuck woods—and you Lake Huron—and all that with you roll toward Niagara—and you Niagara also,

And you, California mountains—That you each and all find somebody
else to be your singer of songs,
For I can be your singer of songs no longer—One who loves me is jealous
of me, and withdraws me from all but love,
With the rest I dispense—I sever from what I thought would suffice me,
for it does not—it is now empty and tasteless to me,
I heed knowledge, and the grandeur of The States, and the example of
heroes, no more,
I am indifferent to my own songs—I will go with him I love,
It is to be enough for us that we are together—We never separate again.

Of course, this is a poem born of a mood, and must not be
unduly exaggerated; but it is an unhealthy mood, that leads the
man away from the work of his life to accomplish nothing for
himself or others. And it is the mood which predominates in
these thirty-eight pages. The glory of romantic love for a
wife lies not only in its own satisfactions but in that it stimulates man to perform nobly his share of the work of the world.
But here, on the contrary, a man yields to an impulse which,
were it common, would soon reduce the world to chaos. It is
true that Whitman for a time soothed himself with the dream
that he was doing a high public service by encouraging a sort of
friendship between men—equal in power to the romantic love—
which would unite the nation by ties more real than laws or customs or institutions. But he should have realized from his own
experience, as expressed in the poem just quoted, that when
friendship becomes a jealous emotion rather than a shared ideal,
a comradeship in work, it encounters pschological barriers to
its socialization. Many readers have found comfort in these
poems, no doubt, and have for a time acted toward each other
as though there were some mystic religious tie between them;
but this is due to the effort which Whitman made to spiritualize
the whole conception.

I think it is not for life I am chanting here my chant of lovers—I think
it must be for Death,

For how calm, how solemn it grows, to ascend to the atmosphere of lovers,
Death or life I am then indifferent.

Here Whitman runs counter to his own early doctrine that happiness is to be sought in the present, that death is but a fulfilling of life. Like the early colonizing Puritans, he dreams of a heaven after death because he has no hope of realizing it fully under the conditions of life. But why not? Is it because these dreams will get mixed up with reality, because the body limits the soul as much as the soul lifts the body? Here too he was not without his qualms. He has the "terrible doubt of appearances." The erstwhile self-sufficient man, proud of his physical health, must now acknowledge that his soul is often sick.

Hours discouraged, distracted—for the one I cannot content myself without, soon I saw him content himself without me;
Hours when I am forgotten, (O weeks and months are passing, but I believe I am never to forget!)
Sullen and suffering hours! (I am ashamed—but it is useless—I am what I am;)
Hours of my torment—I wonder if other men ever have the like, out of the like feelings?

He is suspicious of the whole experience, at least the degree to which it seeks to master him.

Earth! my likeness!
Though you look so impassive, ample and spheric there,
I now suspect that is not all;
I now suspect there is something fierce in you, eligible to burst forth;
For an athlete is enamoured of me—and I of him,
But toward him there is something fierce and terrible in me, eligible to burst forth,
I dare not tell it in words—not even in these songs.

Throughout, the treatment is esoteric, furtive, symbolical. Only a few are expected to understand this gospel which is advanced as a solution for the ills of the state, this dream of the "new City of Friends." Others are warned to leave it alone.

Nor will the candidates for my love, (unless at most a very few,) prove
    victorious,
Nor will my poems do good only—they will do just as much evil, perhaps
    more,
For all is useless without that which you may guess at many times and
    not hit—that which I hinted at,
Therefore release me, and depart on your way.

How different are these hard conditions from those which
Jesus laid down for entering the kingdom of heaven; and yet
Whitman's conception of himself as a religious leader may well
have persuaded him that they were essentially the same. We
need not dwell longer on the poems in which the poet wrestles
with a passion so tragically powerful. They colored his world,
now transfiguring it with a Platonic dream of immortal friendship, now giving it a hue more lurid.

Saturate them with yourself, all ashamed and wet,
Glow upon all I have written or shall write, bleeding drops,
Let all be seen in your light, blushing drops.

It is a relief to turn to some of the other poems added in this
edition, notably to the "Song of Joys," to the poem in which he
claims Christ as comrade and brother in the name of a common
Promethean spirit, and to the poem which, paraphrasing the
story of Jesus' sympathy for the outcast, Whitman professes
a charity as impartial as the sunlight. "With Antecedents," developing the idea that man is "an acme of things accomplished,
an encloser of things to be," may have been suggested by Dar-
win's epoch-making book published the year before. The "Song
at Sunset" strikes the old note of faith in God's creation, while
the concluding piece, "So Long" (always kept at the end of
Whitman editions), is a swan song, as if Whitman felt this to
be the last book he should write. But his country was collabo-
rator with him always, and her hour of trial would yet call from
him a wholesomer aspiration, a sublimer art.

BOOK V

''A GLIMPSE OF WAR'S HELL-SCENES''

ESPITE Emerson's fears, the new edition of "Leaves of Grass" sold well. It made Whitman known to a large number of readers, not a few of whom were willing to show their appreciation in the troubled times to follow. To stimulate the sale of the book, Thayer and Eldridge issued a booklet of reviews for free distribution, thus clearing the volume itself of all appendices. On Whitman's return to Boston in June he resumed his life of loafing, well satisfied at the new turn of events. At last he had a regular publisher, and it seemed as if he might find, after all, that a life devoted to writing would harmonize his errant desires. He continued to frequent Pfaff's in the evening, to ride with the stage drivers in the afternoons. But he also took time to attend his sick friends in the hospitals, where the doctors referred to him as "the saint." At home his brother Andrew had married and moved to a house of his own. Jeff too had married, and had named his first daughter Mannahatta, in compliment to her Uncle Walt's poems. The Jefferson Whitmans lived on Portland Avenue with Walt and the family. Jeff was steady, and though sometimes given to moodiness, he was ordinarily the most cheerful member of the group. The monthly salary of ninety dollars he earned as assistant to the chief engineer of the city water works was, when the war left him to be the only breadwinner at home, the main reliance of the whole family. George too had married, but soon he was to be drawn into the maelstrom of war, his wife remaining with the family on Portland Avenue. These increasing family relationships made demands upon Walt's cheer and advice, and he found a sort of vicarious parenthood in his relation to his brother's children. The family had many sorrows, and some friction, conspicuously in

179

the unhappy marriage of Walt's favorite sister, Hannah, who moved to Burlington, Vermont, with her husband, a painter. But to one and all Whitman preached cheerfulness and resignation, self-respect and tolerance.

Affairs in the nation had been growing so ominous that, despite Whitman's withdrawal from politics and political editing, he could not but be conscious that he was treading upon a volcano. The fight for free-soil in "bloody Kansas" seemed but the prelude to the terrible diapason of civil war. And when John Brown sought to free the soil even of the South, it was obvious that unless such an attitude were repudiated in the North, a wall of suspicion, hatred, conflicting interests and theories of government would divide the country into belligerent camps. Instead of being repudiated in the North, John Brown was by even Emerson and Thoreau treated as a martyr to his convictions. They did not flinch from his *reductio ad absurdum* of their transcendental doctrines. Whitman too sympathized with the old fanatic in his courage and unselfishness, though he did not approve of his methods.

I would sing how an old man, tall, with white hair, mounted the scaffold in Virginia,
(I was at hand, silent I stood with teeth shut close, I watch'd,)
I stood very near you old man when cool and indifferent, but trembling with age and your unheal'd wounds, you mounted the scaffold;)

The year 1859–60 seemed to the poet a "year of meteors," portents, "all mottled with evil and good—year of forebodings." And the ship of state was to be guided through these troubled waters by an almost unknown hand, that of the newly elected Abraham Lincoln. Whitman, as a Republican, had voted for him, though New York was far from unanimous in doing so. Lincoln, like himself, put the preservation of the Union above all other questions. But as yet Whitman knew little of the homely, melancholy man. Learning that the President-elect was to pass through New York on his way to Washington, and would stop at the Astor House, Walt determined to see him. In his judgment the presidency had for twelve years been in the hands of "deform'd, mediocre, snivelling, unreliable, false-hearted men," but here was a man from the West; would he have the look of the future in his eyes, and the look of freedom?

Making sure of a good vantage point by climbing to the driver's box on one of the buses that had been turned out of Broadway, Whitman looked over the sullen and silent crowds to catch a first sight of Lincoln. How different from the time he had seen Lafayette on the same spot, or Jackson, Webster, Kossuth, Clay, or, a year before, the Prince of Wales, occasions when he had thrilled to "all that indescribable human roar and magnetism, unlike any other sound in the universe—the glad exulting thunder-shouts of countless unloos'd throats of men. But on this occasion, not a voice—not a sound." Plainly New York did not trust Abraham Lincoln. He was not city-bred. But it had been tacitly agreed that if his supporters would refrain from demonstration, his more numerous enemies would do likewise, though both had come armed for the worst. Ominous indeed, like the false peace and prosperity of the whole nation at the time.

"Presently,"—so Whitman recalled the experience,—"two or three shabby hack barouches made their way with some difficulty through the crowd, and drew up at the Astor House entrance. A tall figure stepp'd out of the center of these barouches, paused leisurely on the sidewalk, look'd up at the granite walls and looming architecture of the grand old hotel—and then, after a relieving stretch of arms and legs, turned round for over a minute to slowly and good-humoredly scan the appearance of the vast and silent crowds. There were no speeches—no compliments—no welcome—as far as I could hear, not a word said. . . . He look'd with curiosity upon that immense sea of faces, and the sea of faces return'd the look with similar curiosity. In both there was a dash of comedy, almost farce, such as Shakespeare puts in his blackest tragedies." The President-elect looked fit for his great task. The sharp observing eyes of Whitman noted his "perfect composure and coolness—his unusual and uncouth height, his dress of complete black, stove-pipe hat pushed back on the head, dark-brown complexion, seam'd and wrinkled yet canny-looking face, black, bushy head of hair, disproportionately long neck, and his hands held behind as he stood observing the people." To do justice to that strange figure, the journalist thought, would be needed "the eyes and brains and finger-touch of Plutarch and Eschylus and Michael Angelo, assisted by Rabelais."

To Lincoln, as to any informed person, it must have seemed that the nation would be out of hand even before he could take up the reins of power. Immediately on his election the South, mistakenly interpreting his victory as the elevation of the hated Abolitionists to power, had issued a manifesto calling for secession, and within a week after his inauguration on March 4, 1861, the Confederacy had framed its own constitution at Montgomery, Alabama. But Whitman, with true bohemian detachment and Quaker passivity, saw nothing that he could do about it, and went on his way without marked change of habit. He was, as always, fond of the opera, which he would attend when he could, sometimes taking a friend, or his brother Jeff with him, or Martha, Jeff's wife, whom he loved dearly. On the 12th of April he had gone alone to the opera in Fourteenth Street. Coming out after the performance about midnight, he heard, as he walked down Broadway toward the ferry, the wild shouts of newsboys darting back and forth crying extras. Walt bought one, but it was too dark to see what the commotion was about. So he crossed to the Metropolitan Hotel to read under a lamp. What his eye caught was a brief dispatch stating that the South had begun war by firing upon the flag at Fort Sumter. A crowd gathered, many having no papers. Some one, perhaps Whitman, read the news aloud to them. Too staggered by the sudden, insolent blow of war to speak, they separated to meditate its significance alone.

As for Whitman, who had long trained himself to look toward the future and who had seen many of his shrewd prophecies come to pass, perhaps the news was a surprise only in the sense that bad news, violent shakings of our easy-going lives, always seem to come suddenly, if only by contrast. For in his last edition of poems he had prophesied this very thing. A poem called, with satirical burlesque, "To the States—to identify the 16, 17th, or 18th Presidentiad" (administrations of Fillmore, Pierce, and Buchanan), reveals Whitman's fear lest politics, in such incompetent hands, would bring the country to grief.

Why reclining, interrogating? Why myself and all drowsing?
What deepening twilight! scum floating atop of the waters!
Who are they, as bats and night-dogs, askant in the Capitol?
What a filthy Presidentiad! (O south, your torrid suns! O north, your arctic freezings!)
Are those really Congressmen? are those the great Judges? is that the President?
Then I will sleep awhile yet—for I see that These States sleep, for reasons;
(With gathering murk—with muttering thunder and lambent shoots, we all duly awake,
South, north, east, west, inland and seaboard, we will surely awake.)

In prose Whitman made more definite his criticism of the party politics of the period. In the following vitriolitic description he perhaps has the Buffalo convention in mind.

"One of these conventions, from 1840 to '60, exhibited a spectacle such as could never be seen except in our own age and in these States. The members who composed it were, seven-eighths of them, the meanest kind of bawling and blowing office-holders, office-seekers, pimps, malignants, conspirators, murderers, fancy-men, custom-house clerks, contractors, kept-editors, spaniels well-train'd to carry and fetch, jobbers, infidels, disunionists, terrorists, mail-riflers, slave-catchers, pushers of slavery, creatures of the President, creatures of would-be Presidents, spies, bribers, compromisers, lobbyers, sponges, ruin'd sports, expell'd gamblers, policy-backers, monte-dealers, duellists, carriers of conceal'd weapons, deaf men, pimpled men, scarr'd inside with vile disease, gaudy outside with gold chains made from the people's money and harlots' money twisted together; crawling, serpentine men, the lousy combings and born freedom-sellers of the earth. And whence came they? From back-yards and bar-rooms; from out of the custom-houses, marshals' offices, post-offices, and gambling-hells; from the President's house, the jail, the station-house; from unnamed by-places, where devilish disunion was hatch'd at midnight; from political hearses, and from the coffins inside, and from the shrouds inside of the coffins; from the tumors and abscesses of the land; from the skeletons and skulls in the vaults of the federal almshouses; and from the running sores of the great cities. Such, I say, form'd, or absolutely controll'd the forming of, the entire personnel, the atmosphere, nutriment and chyle, of our municipal, State, and National politics—substantially permeating, handling, deciding, and welding everything—legislation, nominations, elections, 'public sentiment,' &c.—while the great masses of the people, farmers, mechanics, and traders, were helpless in their gripe. These conditions were mostly prevalent in the north and west, and especially in New York and Philadelphia cities; and the southern leaders, (bad enough, but of a far higher order,) struck hands and affiliated with, and used them. Is it strange that a thunder-storm follow'd such morbid and stifling cloud-strata?"

But the populace are awakened now, at midnight:

Forty years had I in my city seen soldiers parading;
Forty years as a pageant—till unawares, the Lady of this teeming and turbulent city,
Sleepless amid her ships, her houses, her incalculable wealth,
With her million children around her—suddenly,
At dead of night, at news from the south,
Incens'd, struck with clench'd hand the pavement.

A shock electric—the night sustain'd it;
Till with ominous hum, our hive at day-break pour'd forth its myriads.

From the houses then, and the workshops, and through all the doorways,
Leapt they tumultuous—and lo! Manhattan arming.

Three days later Lincoln answered the challenge of Carolina

by calling for seventy-five thousand volunteers to put down the rebellion in three months.   He knew as little as did the rest of the country about the proportions of the war then beginning. But though Douglas, the champion of "squatter sovereignty," had polled almost as many votes in the North as Lincoln, neither receiving a majority throughout the country, at the call for volunteers there was the natural rush to the colors by men of all factions.   George Whitman, though married, was one of the first to go, enlisting as a private in the 51st New York Volunteers.   Perhaps Walt felt the impulse to go also, for, though his gray hair would make him appear too old to enlist, he knew his health was perfect.   In any case, the war was but a few days old when he vowed a vow unto himself as if in preparation for withstanding whatever hardships the war might bring him, on the field or elswhere: "Thursday, April 18, 1861.   I have this hour, this day resolved to inaugurate a sweet, clean-blooded body by ignoring all drinks but water and pure milk—and all fat meats, late suppers—a great body—a purged, cleansed, spiritualized invigorated body."   At once he began to "absorb" the war, to allow it to have over his personal habits and indulgences the cleansing, ennobling effect of an unselfish purpose.   Whether from this cause or from motives of patriotic economy, we shall see that for years he lived very frugally even though performing the most enervating tasks.   Whitman could enjoy, as few others, lassitude and loafing; but when deeply stirred he showed that there was firmness too in his character.   What Emerson saw, Whitman felt:

> In an age of fops and toys,
> Wanting wisdom, void of right,
> Who shall nerve heroic boys
> To hazard all in Freedom's fight—
> Break sharply off their jolly games,
> Forsake their comrades gay
> And quit proud homes and youthful dames
> For famine, toil and fray?
> Yet on the air benign

Speed nimbler messages,
That waft the breath of grace divine
To hearts in sloth and ease.
So nigh is grandeur to our dust,
So near is God to man,
When Duty whispers low, *Thou must,*
The youth replies, *I can.*

It is a moment which seldom comes more than once in a lifetime. The flag never seems more beautiful than when every
drum is beating to muster in its defense. It is the poet's hour,
and he must make clear the claims of the ideal "Mother of all"
over each man's private loves or hates. While Bret Harte was
writing his "Reveille" and thereby making sure that California
would remain in the Union, Whitman caught up the same strain
in Manhattan. The indifference of the electorate might have
long expressed itself in the sordidness and inefficiency of politics,
but he would show that the grandeur of a great sacrifice was yet
nigh our democratic dust. Through these summoning drums
the call of the nation, the hope of the future, becomes audible.
And we who have seen modern warfare enlisting every man and
woman and child in the nation, revealing the little suspected relation of each to all, can respond to this poem even more uni-
versally than our Civil War ancestors could.

Beat! beat! drums!—Blow! bugles! blow!
Through the windows—through doors—burst like a ruthless force,
Into the solemn church, and scatter the congregation,
Into the school where the scholar is studying;
Leave not the bridegroom quiet—no happiness must he have now with his
    bride,
Nor the peaceful farmer any peace, plowing his field or gathering his
    grain,
So fierce you whirr and pound, you drums—so shrill you bugles blow.

Beat! beat! drums!—Blow! bugles! blow!
Over the traffic of cities—over the rumble of wheels in the streets;
Are beds prepared for sleepers at night in the houses? no sleepers must
    sleep in those beds,

No bargainers' bargains by day—no brokers or speculators—would they continue?
Would the talkers be talking? would the singer attempt to sing?
Would the lawyer rise in the court to state his case before the judge?
Then rattle quicker, heavier drums—you bugles wilder blow.

Beat! beat! drums!—blow! bugles! blow!
Make no parley—stop for no expostulation,
Mind not the timid—mind not the weeper or prayer,
Mind not the old man beseeching the young man,
Let not the child's voice be heard, nor the mother's entreaties,
Make even the trestles to shake the dead where they lie awaiting the hearses,
So strong you thump O terrible drums, so loud you bugles blow.

When the emotion is so strong in Whitman, and the desire to reach his audience so compelling, his form approximates regular meter, the freedom that remains being retained, not for its own sake, but as itself expressive of variations in the matter. But especially in the martial spirit of the man—as of the nation—appears something unsuspected and grand. It was painful to see his city go forth to war—Whitman's own family had sent forth the best soldier it had—yet it would have been worse not to go.

Spring up O city—not for peace alone, but be indeed yourself, warlike!
Fear not—submit to no models but your own O city!
Behold me—incarnate me as I have incarnated you!
I have rejected nothing you offer'd me—whom you adopted I have adopted,
Good or bad I never question you—I love all—I do not condemn anything,
I chant and celebrate all that is yours—yet peace no more,
In peace I chanted peace, but now the drum of war is mine,
War, red war is my song through your streets, O city!

And the city responded, as cities do, with spontaneous enthusiasm. One regiment marched forth from Brooklyn with pieces of rope dangling from their rifle barrels, with which each man expected to bring back his contemptible prisoner. But when the Fifty-first began its many hard campaigns, its many decimating battles, Walt was left behind. Why had he not marched forth too? Was it that he was eager to urge others to battle, like Bryant in "Our Country's Call," but, without Bryant's age as an excuse, willing to remain behind when the danger neared? In making decision on such a point it was characteristic of Whitman to feel safest when he followed his own deep impulses, rather than the cold suggestions of his reason. These would have told him that, though forty-two years old, he was strong enough to fight, and he was practically unencumbered. But though he did not go so far as the Quaker Whittier in protesting against all war, he did have the Quaker's and the poet's natural shrinking from anything so coarse and cruel in its methods. It was for him to save life rather than to take it, and to save it he would gladly risk his own. Besides, he was the virtual head of the family, now that his father was dead and his older brother Jesse was mentally unfit. His uncommon love for his mother, moreover, would prompt him to remain as her comfort and provider while George was away. It was by no means sure that any great army would be needed, in any case; and if not, of course the younger men should go first. Then, too, he remembered his own lines in 1855, concerning the great poet: "In war he is the most deadly force of the war. Who recruits him recruits horse and foot . . . he can make every word he speaks draw blood." Just as it was the duty of the nation's President to remain at Washington, perhaps it was the duty of the nation's poet to sing the needful song, provided only he do it from duty and not from fear.

Already in Whitman's mind a new book was taking form, or rather an addition of his life-book, the "Leaves," to record his reactions to this new act in the national drama. He would call it "Drum-Taps." But he might have to wait for some time to get it published, and these poems, to have practical value in the war, should reach the people now. The *Atlantic* had welcomed his "Bardic Symbols" when he was in Boston; and, proud of hav-

ing appeared in such a magazine, Whitman determined to send
to it three of his early war poems.   But the magazine, finding
that it would be crowded for space till these poems would have
lost their timely interest, had to return them.   About this time,
however, a new paper was being started in Brooklyn, the *Standard,* and in June Whitman was employed to write for it a series
of special articles on the history of the city.   When these
"Brooklyniana" sketches had only begun, however, something
caused them suddenly to cease.   It may have been the disastrous
revelations of the first Bull Run, making it clear, to North and
South alike, that this war would be no summer holiday, but a
struggle to the death.   What might it not involve?   Whitman
would have to think it over.   So he betook himself to nature
again, going in the fall to visit his sister Mary at Greenport.
Since the Bull Run fiasco the contestants, who were more evenly
matched, all things considered, than might appear, were taking
time to prepare themselves for a great struggle.   Accordingly
little significant fighting took place during the first year.
George was well, and the war was too undramatic to harry the
emotions of those at a distance.   Whitman was feeling, too,
a natural reaction to that impulse which had beat the mustering
drums.   "If nations stopped long enough when they are mad
to ask themselves that question [what they are quarreling
about] we would have no wars," he said with deliberation
long afterwards.   That was what the Constitutional Union
Party had said in the 1860 campaign.   Were history not always
prejudiced in favor of the accomplished fact, it might appear
that that party, though it polled only a handful of votes, had
been nearest right after all.   In any case, it was nearest what
was most fundamental in Whitman's temperament.   He resented any attack on his beloved Union; yes, but what was that
Union?   Did it not include his "magnet South" to which he was
bound by all that was Southern and Latin in his nature?   But the
war was on, and this was no time for thinking so precisely of the
event.   At any time he might be summoned to the colors himself.   Nevertheless, he would take a farewell of the woods and

shores of Paumanok while he could, a brief vacation before becoming involved personally in the struggle.

Let us catch one more glimpse of him before scenes of war have altered forever the spirit of the faun. It is the day before Waterloo, but he spends it in outdoor sport, not in wild and wicked revel. Whitman had just hauled up a big black fish at the end of the dock at Greenport, and was casting in again when he heard a voice from a sloop that was making for the pier.

"Ease away your lines for a moment," requested the young sailor who was manning her, "till we shove along the pier."

"Where are you bound for?" asked Whitman, as he complied.

"To Montauk Point," said the young man—adding with sailor-like hospitality, "won't you go along?"

Whitman would, in fisherman's garb though he was. Sending his fish to his sister, he entered the sloop—not, however, by using the sailor's proffered shoulder for a step. Whitman weighed over two hundred.

In the little boat were a party of lively girls, a chaperoning cleric, and one or two younger boys. The only misgiving Whitman had so far as the party was concerned, was caused by the country clergyman. But discovering him to be exceptional among his kind in that he "laughed and told stories and ate luncheons, just like a common man," Whitman made room on the Open Road for him too. High spirits reigned, and Whitman contributed his share. But he did not need this for pleasure. "As for me, I blessed my lucky stars; for merely to sail—to lie on my back and gaze by the half-hour at the passing clouds overhead—merely to *breathe and live* in the sweet air and clear sunlight—to hear the musical chatter of the girls, as they pursued their own glee—was happiness enough for one day. You may laugh at me, if you like," he told the readers of the *Standard,* "but there is an ecstatic satisfaction in such *lazy philosophy,* such passive yielding up of one's self to the pure emanation of Nature, better than the most exciting pleasures."

Landing at length on Montauk Point, they proceeded to give vent to their pent-up emotions. Man is always a little wilder,

even in his recreations, in war time.   It is Whitman's voice that
is lifted loudest in declamation and merriment.

"We rambled up the hills to the top of the highest, we ran
races down, we scampered along the shore, jumping from rock
to rock we declaimed all the violent appeals and defiances we
could remember, commencing with:

'Celestial states, immortal powers, give ear!'

away on to the ending which announced that Richard had almost
lost his wind by dint of calling Richmond to arms.   I doubt
whether these terrible echoes ever before vibrated with such terrible ado.   Then we pranced forth again, like mad kine, we
threw our hats in the air, aimed stones at the shrieking sea-gulls,
mocked the wind, and imitated the cries of various animals in a
style that beat nature all out!

"We challenged each other to the most deadly combats—we
tore various past passions into tatters—made love to the girls
in the divine words of Shakespeare and other poets, whereat the
said girls had the rudeness to laugh till the tears ran down their
cheeks in torrents.   We indulged in some impromptu quadrilles,
of which the 'chassez' took each participant couple so far away
from the other that they were like never to get back.   We
hopped like crows; we pivoted like Indian dervishes; we went
through the trial dance of *La Bayadere* with wonderful vigor;
and some one of our party came nigh dislocating his neck through
volunteering to turn somersaults like a circus fellow.   Everybody caught the contagion, and there was not a sensible behaved
creature among us, to rebuke our mad antics by comparison."

Not far behind such a man is his childhood, and by dropping
into its moods he regains the elasticity of spirit which he needs.
Throughout the day the riot of joy was unconstrained.   But
going home, the sailors miscalculated the tide, so that they had
to spend the night on board the sloop.   At this Whitman was
at home.   Spreading a huge bearskin on the deck, he threw himself upon it, and while others sang ditties and told ghost stories,
he looked silently at the stars.   When quiet ensued he made his

bed in the furled sail like an old salt; but he could scarcely
sleep for watching the constellations—"the countless armies of
heaven marching stilly and slowly on, and others coming out of
the east to take their places." They reminded one of those
other countless armies marching to death throughout the land.
They brought the solitary muser back to reality. He would
never be the same care-free spirit again. Poets sometimes have
premonitions of such things, and it was with no little reluctance
that Whitman ended so happy an outing. "We landed at the
dock, and went up to the village, and felt the tameness of respectable society settling around us again. Doubtless it was
all right; but as for me, I fancied the mercury dwindling down,
down, down into the very calves of my legs."

Back in Brooklyn and to work. In December he recom-
menced his promised articles for the *Standard,* running them
very irregularly till the next November. Whitman had for
several years been collecting data for such a book, reading old
histories, talking with antiquarians, examining landmarks, exploring the files of old newspapers and his own retentive memory. No one had attempted just that sort of thing in Brooklyn,
and Whitman's rambling, familiar stories full of local gossip
were popular. But it was strange business for the bard of the
future to be about just now. Doubtless it was a pot-boiler,
the only thing he could sell; and doubtless also it, like his outing,
had the effect of affording some relief from the tormenting
anxieties of the day.

If the motives which actuate an individual are mixed, those
behind the acts of a nation are more so, however simple the politicians may try to make them appear; so that after the first war
fever had passed, Whitman, as an intelligent man, must have
tried to weigh in his mind the arguments which, North and
South, were sending millions of men to the field of battle. His
attitude toward life made it easy for him to sympathize with
all points of view, even though he felt compelled to act according to his own. Such temperaments are fitted for anything
better than the sharp, efficient decisions of war time. With

nearly half the North in sympathy with the South, with his own
sympathies divided, though never his loyalties, it was no wonder
that the only thing which seemed to remain fixed in this time of
doubt was the doubter himself.

Quicksand years that whirl me I know not whither,
Your schemes, politics, fail, lines give way, substances mock and elude me,
Only the theme I sing, the great and strong-possess'd soul, eludes not,
One's-self must never give way—that is the final substance—that out of
   all is sure,
Out of politics, triumphs, battles, life, what at last finally remains?
When shows break up what but One's-Self is sure?

But this war was to teach him that there is something more enduring than the individual, something nobler than the aggran-
dizement of one's self.   And when he should see it he would
be free from the torment of uncertainty concerning individual
action or reaction.

The rifts of war disturbed even Bohemia.   One night at
Pfaff's when the war was being discussed by Unionists and
"Copperheads"—as Southern sympathizers were stigmatized
regardless of the honesty of their opinions—George Arnold
arose and, lifting his glass of wine, proposed the toast, "Success
to the Southern Arms."   Whitman, usually deliberate, thereupon burst out into a speech of patriotic indignation.   In the
heat of the violent argument Arnold reached across the table
and took Whitman by the hair.   But when he had said his say,
Whitman took his leave of Pfaff's not to return until twenty
years later, when only Pfaff himself remained of the old merry
group.

The destiny that has our hero in charge has prepared an absolutely new stage for him, and now she gives him his unmistakable cue.   When Burnside failed in his drive toward Richmond, losing to Lee great numbers at Fredericksburg, this fate
listed George Whitman in the New York papers among the
wounded.   Already the family on Portland Avenue had learned,

in reading newspaper accounts of battles, to look first, not for news of victory or defeat, but to see whether the 51st New York Volunteers were engaged, and whether the name of Lieutenant Whitman appeared among the dead or wounded. At last, on December 14th it did; but the dispatch neglected to indicate, with the cruel brevity of such communications, whether the injury were serious or trifling. There was but one thing to do. Walt must go at once to care for George. Hastily packing a carpet bag, drawing fifty dollars out of the bank, and bidding the family good-bye, Walt was off for Philadelphia, where he made a quick change for Washington. As luck would have it, he ran across William Douglas O'Connor, whom he had met in Boston, and the O'Connors would have nothing but that he should stay with them. Eager to see whether his brother were in one of the Washington hospitals, he hastily made the round of them in two days. When he found that George had not been sent up from the front, he then tried to get down to the army on the Rappahannock, and finally succeeded in doing so. Whitman's letter to his distressed mother recounts his first experiences at the seat of war.

"Washington, Monday forenoon,
"Dec. 29, 1862.

"Dear, dear Mother—Friday the 19th inst. I succeeded in reaching the camp of the 51st New York and found George alive and well. In order to make sure that you would get the good news, I sent back by messenger to Washington a telegraphic dispatch (I dare say you did not get it for some time) as well as a letter—and the same to Hannah at Burlington. I have staid in camp with George ever since, till yesterday, when I came back to Washington, about the 24th. George got Jeff's letter of the 20th. Mother, how much you must have suffered, all that week, till George's letter came—and all the rest must too. As to me, I know I put in about three days of the greatest suffering I ever experienced in my life. I wrote to Jeff how I had my pocket picked in a jam and hurry, changing cars, at Philadelphia—so that I landed here without a dime. The next two days I spent hunting through the hospitals, walking day and night, unable to ride, trying to get information—trying to get access to big people, etc.—I could not get the least clue to anything. Odell would not see me at all. But Thursday afternoon, I lit on a way to get down on the Government boat that runs to Aquia creek, and so by railroad to the neighborhood of Falmouth, opposite Fredericksburg—so by degrees I worked my way to Ferrero's brigade, which I found Friday afternoon without much trouble after I got to camp. When I found dear brother George, and found that he was alive and well, O you may imagine how trifling all my little cares and difficulties seemed—they vanished into nothing. And now that I have lived for eight or nine days amid such scenes as camps furnish, and had a practical part in it all, and realize the way that hundreds of thousands of good men are now living, and have had to live for a year or more, not only without any of the comforts, but with death and sickness and hard marching and hard fighting (and no success at that) for their continual experience—really nothing we call trouble seems worth talking about. One of the first things that met my eye in camp was a heap of feet, arms, legs, etc., under a tree in front of a hospital, the Lacy house.

"George is very well in health, has a good appetite—I think he is at times more wearied out and homesick than he shows, but stands it upon the whole very well. Every one of the soldiers, to a man, wants to get home.

"I suppose Jeff got quite a long letter I wrote, from camp, about a week ago. I told you that George had been promoted to captain—his commission arrived while I was there. When you write, address, Capt. George W. Whitman, Co. K., 51st New York Volunteers, Ferrero's brigade, near Falmouth, Va. Jeff must write oftener, and put in a few lines from mother, even if it is only two lines—then in the next letter a few lines from Mat, and so on. You have no idea how letters from home cheer one up in camp, and dissipate homesickness.

"While I was there George still lived in Capt. Francis's tent —there were five of us altogether, to eat, sleep, write, etc., in a space twelve feet square, but we got along very well—the weather all along was very fine—and would have got along to perfection, but Capt. Francis is not a man I could like much—I had very little to say to him. George is about building a place, half hut and half tent, for himself, (he is probably about it this very day,) and then he will be better off, I think. Every captain has a tent, in which he lives, transacts company business, etc., has a cook, (or a man of all work,) and in the same tent mess and sleep his lieutenants, and perhaps the first sergeant. They have a kind of fire-place—and the cook's fire is outside on the open ground. George had very good times while Francis was away—the cook, a young disabled soldier, Tom, is an excellent fellow and a first-rate cook, and the second lieutenant, Pooley, is a tip-top young Pennsylvanian. Tom thinks all the world of George; and when he heard he was wounded, on the day of the battle, he left everything, got across the river, and went hunting for George through the field, through thick and thin. I wrote to Jeff that George was wounded by a shell, a gash in the cheek—you could stick a splint through into the mouth, but it has healed up without difficulty already. Everything is uncertain about the army, whether it moves or stays where it is. There are no furloughs granted at present. I will stay here for the present, at any rate long enough to see if I can get any employment at anything, and shall write what luck I have. Of course I am unsettled at present. Dear mother, my love. WALT.

"If Jeff or any writes, address me, care of Major Hapgood, paymaster, U. S. A. Army, Washington, D. C. I send my love to dear sister Mat, and little Sis—and to Andrew and all my brothers. O Mat, how lucky it was you did not come—together, we could never have got down to see George."

Whitman remained a week or so in this camp. Here he was awakened to a life of self-forgetting action, saw the grim danger face to face, and for a time wondered if the Union were not gone, after all. Any glamour war may have had for him at a

distance disappeared before this cruel reality, as he talked with
men eager for nothing so much as to get back home, as he ate
his monotonous salt pork and hardtack, and as he saw the young
men he loved mutilated and dying with little comfort or assistance in their extremity.   Looking for his wounded brother
on his arrival in camp, he went naturally to the Lacy house, a
Southern mansion which was used as a hospital.   As he approached the house he noted, at the foot of a tree, the heap of
"amputated feet, legs, hands, &c., a full load for a one-horse
cart" to which he had alluded in his letter to his mother.   "Several dead bodies lie near," he added, in his memorandum book,
"each covered with its brown woolen blanket."   In another
notebook, he jotted down this:

"Sight at daybreak in camp of the hospital tent three dead
men lying, each with a blanket spread over him—I lift up one
and look at the young man's face, calm and yellow.   'Tis
strange! (Young man: I think this face of yours the face of
my dead Christ.)"

But to get his emotions, we must wait till the experience
has had time, and the author leisure, to find poetic expression.

A sight in camp in the daybreak gray and dim,
As from my tent I emerge so early sleepless,
As slow I walk in the cool fresh air the path by the hospital tent,
Three forms I see on stretchers lying, brought out there untended lying,
Over each the blanket spread, ample brownish woolen blanket,
Gray and heavy blanket, folding, covering all.

Curious I halt and silent stand,
Then with light fingers I from the face of the nearest just lift the
    blanket;
Who are you elderly man so gaunt and grim, with well-gray'd hair, and
    flesh all sunken about the eyes?
Who are you my dear comrade?

Then to the second I step—and who are you my child and darling?
Who are you sweet boy with cheeks yet blooming?

Then to the third—a face nor child nor old, very calm, as of beautiful
yellow-white ivory;
Young man I think I know you—I think this face is the face of the Christ
himself,
Dead and divine and brother of all, and here again he lies.

The note of Calamus friendship is now sweetly solemnized by
death. Whitman, who two years before had been so tormented
by his hunger for the emotional friendship of men, discovered
on the battlefield not only the meaning of comradeship for men
en masse, but learned the blessedness of those who give rather
than receive. Compared to the boys of sixteen and the young
men of twenty, he seemed in his graying beard and his great
benignity a father rather than a friend. He learned to address
each of these brave youngsters as "dear son and comrade," and
they called him "father." Perhaps this was what he had hun-
gered for so long, not knowing it, the love of a father for a child
on whom to lavish his affection and help. He had dreamed of
the future of his race, his land; but here, marshaled in the
tested power of a great army, he saw that future in its youth,
and he knew that it was safe.

No poet can be unmoved by the sight of a camp asleep. If,
like Whitman, he have the mothering instinct in him, he feels
that he stands guard over an immense family, detached from
and yet tied by invisible bonds to every sleeping form.

By the bivouac's fitful flame,
A procession winding around me, solemn and sweet and slow—but first
I note,
The tents of the sleeping army, the fields' and woods' dim outline,
The darkness lit by spots of kindled fire, the silence,
Like a phantom far or near an occasional figure moving,
The shrubs and trees, (as I lift my eyes they seem to be stealthily watch-
ing me,)
While wind in procession thoughts, O tender and wondrous thoughts,
Of life and death, of home and the past and loved, and of those that are
far away;

WHITMAN AT FIFTY

Photograph by Frank Pearsall

A solemn and slow procession there as I sit on the ground,
By the bivouac's fitful flame.

Whitman went impartially among the wounded, boys in blue
and those in gray. He would speak to them with uniform
solicitude, seeking to be of what service he could to all. He
had no funds, but he wrote letters, read, conversed, or best of
all, laid hold on despairing souls with the magnetism of his
great health and hope. He had to cultivate that intuition which
makes women the best nurses, detecting without words the man
who needed him most and who would respond to his care.
Sometimes a deep friendship sprang up, to last for years.
Those who have known war only through the experiences of
the United States armies in the great war of recent years, with
its highly organized and adequately trained and financed corps
of Red Cross nurses and its welfare workers, can hardly understand how appreciated was such a wholesome and human volunteer as Whitman. Trained to friendship with all classes, skilled
in nursing disabled stage drivers, doing nothing in perfunctory
manner or from mixed motives, he went into the hospital tents
on the Rappahannock, where homesick boys, wounded or suffering from diarrhea, that scourge of camps, lay on the ground
in the winter and grew worse till sent to Washington—often too
late—for better care.

With a detachment of these Whitman returned on a flat-car
train and a government steamer to Washington, doing what he
could to aid them on the way. But what could one man do to
handle a problem which required an organized corps? "On the
boat I had my hands full," he said. "One poor fellow died going up." Every transport welfare worker will understand the
meaning of that.

For a time Whitman lived with the O'Connors; in fact, until
they gave up their apartment. They would accept no money
for board, inasmuch as he was devoting his energies to his
hospital ministrations. For this was one thing he could do, not

only to help win the war, but to save the men. From camp he had sent a number of dispatches to the New York *Times,* which printed them as special correspondence from the front. And now, at intervals, he sent letters to New York and Brooklyn papers recording his observations, and describing his work. Nor did he hesitate to criticize the methods of a feudal military system, or callousness and bad judgment on the part of those entrusted with the wounded. He also did hack work for the local papers and spent a few hours each day copying in the office of Major Hapgood, army paymaster, at a good rate of remuneration. This last opportunity to make expenses he secured, no doubt, through a clerk in Major Hapgood's department, Charles Eldridge, Whitman's erstwhile Boston publisher. But the larger part of his income, even when he had left the O'Connors and had to pay for his meals, he devoted to the sick and wounded.

Whitman wrote regularly to his mother; but, for all his devotion to her, he knew her limitations. Her strong points were natural qualities of sympathy, common sense, health and native dignity; but she was quite unschooled and unliterary, so that Whitman consciously trimmed his letters to fit her powers of comprehension, falling sometimes even into the colloquialisms of the Whitman home. He could be all things to all men—a fact which accounts for the many conflicting reports that have survived of Whitman himself. There were in New York, however, correspondents, boon companions of the Pfaffian days, to whom Whitman could not only unbosom himself, but could indulge in a wider range of reference in exhibiting his feelings. One of the most illuminating letters of this sort was written to Fred Gray and his brother Nat, early in 1863.

"Washington, March 19, 1863.

"Dear Nat and Fred Gray:

"Since I left New York I was down in the Army of the Potomac in front with my brother a good part of the winter, commencing time of the battle of Fredericksburgh—have seen *war-*

life, the real article—folded myself in a blanket, lying down in the mud with composure—relished salt pork and hardtack—have been on the battlefield among the wounded, the faint and the bleeding, to give them nourishment—have gone over with a flag of truce the next day to help direct the burial of the dead—have struck up a tremendous friendship with a young Mississippi captain (about 19) that we took prisoner badly wounded at Fredericksburgh (he has followed me here, is in the Emory hospital here minus a leg—he wears his confederate uniform, proud as the devil—I met him first at Falmouth, in the Lacy house middle of December last, his leg just cut off, and cheered him up—poor boy, he has suffered a great deal, and still suffers—has eyes bright as a hawk, but face pale—our affection is an affair quite romantic—sometimes when I lean over to say I am going, he puts his arms around my neck, draws my face down, etc., quite a scene for the New Bowery). I spent the Christmas holidays on the Rappahannock.—During January came up hither, took a lodging room here. Did the 37th Congress, especially the night sessions the last three weeks, explored the Capitol, meandering the gorgeous painted interminable Senate corridors, getting lost in them (a new sensation, rich and strong, that endless painted interior at night)—got very much interested in some particular cases in Hospitals here—go now steadily to more or less of said Hospitals by day òr night—find always the sick and dying soldiers forthwith begin to cling to me in a way that makes a fellow feel funny enough. These Hospitals, so different from all others—these thousands, and tens and twenties of thousands of American young men, badly wounded, all sorts of wounds, operated on, pallid with diarrhœa, languishing, dying with fever, pneumonia, etc., open a new world somehow to me, giving closer insights, new things, exploring deeper mines, than any yet, showing our humanity (I sometimes put myself in fancy in the cot, with typhoid, or under the knife) tried by terrible, fearfullest tests, probed deepest, the living soul's, the body's tragedies, bursting the petty bonds of art. To these, what are your dramas and poems, even the oldest and the fearfullest? Not old Greek mighty ones; where man contends with fate (and always yields)—not Virgil showing Dante on and on among the agonized and damned, approach what here I see and take part in. For here I see, not at intervals, but quite always, how certain man, our American man—how he holds himself cool and unquestioned master above all pains and bloody mutilations. It is immense, the best thing of all—nourishes me of all men. This then, what frightened us all so long. Why, it is put to flight with ignominy—a mere stuffed scarecrow of the fields. O death, where is thy sting? O grave, where is thy victory?

"In the Patent Office, as I stood there one night, just off the cot-side of a dying soldier, in a large ward that had received the worst cases of Second Bull Run, Antietam, and Fredericksburgh, the surgeon, Dr. Stone (Horatio Stone the Sculptor) told me, of all who had died in that crowded ward the past six months, he had still to find the *first man* or *boy* who had met the approach of death with a single tremor or unmanly fear. But let me change the subject—I have given you screed enough about Death and the Hospitals—and too much—since I got started. Only I have some curious yarns I promise you my darlings and gossips, by word of mouth whene'er we meet.

"Washington and its points I find bear a second and a third perusal, and doubtless many. My first impressions, architectural, etc., were not favorable; but upon the whole, the city, the spaces, buildings, etc., make no unfit emblem of our country, so far, so broadly planned, everything in plenty, money and materials staggering with plenty, but the fruit of the plans, the knit, the combination yet wanting— Determined to express ourselves greatly in a Capitol but no fit Capitol yet here (time, associations, wanting I suppose) many a hiatus yet—many a thing to be taken down and done over again yet—perhaps an entire change of base—maybe a succession of changes.

"Congress does not seize very hard upon me; I studied it and its members with curiosity, and long—much gab, great fear of public opinion, plenty of low business talent, but no masterful man in Congress (probably best so). I think well of the President.   He has a face like a Hoosier Michael Angelo, so awful ugly it becomes beautiful, with its strange mouth, its deep cut, criss-cross lines, and its doughnut complexion.—My notion is too, that underneath his outside smutched mannerism, and stories from third-class county bar-rooms (it is his humor), Mr. Lincoln keeps a fountain of first-class practical telling wisdom. I do not dwell on the supposed failures of his government; he has shown, I sometimes think, an almost supernatural tact in keeping the ship afloat at all, with head steady, not only not going down, and now certain not to, but with proud and resolute spirit, and flag flying in sight of the world, menacing and high as ever.   I say never yet captain, never ruler, had such a perplexing dangerous task as his, the past two years.   I more and more rely upon his idiomatic western genius, careless of court dress or court decorum.

"I am living here without much definite aim (except going to the hospitals)—yet I have quite a good time—I make some money by scribbling for the papers, and as copyist.   I have had (and have) thoughts of trying to get a clerkship or something, but I only try in a listless sort of way, and of course do not succeed.   I have strong letters of introduction from Mr. Emerson to Mr. Seward and Mr. Chase, but I have not presented them.   I have seen Mr. Sumner several times anent my office hunting—he promised fair once—but he does not seem to be finally fascinated.   I hire a bright little 3rd story front room, with service, etc., for $7 a month, dine in the same house (394 L St. a private house)—and remain yet much of the old vagabond that so gracefully becomes me.   I miss you all, my darlings and gossips, Fred Gray, and Bloom and Russell and everybody.   I wish you would all come here in a body—that would be divine (we would drink ale, which is here the best).   My health, strength, personal beauty, etc., are, I am happy to inform you, without diminution, but on the contrary quite the reverse.   I weigh full 220 pounds avoirdupois, yet still retain my usual perfect shape—a regular model.   My beard, neck, etc., are woolier, fleecier, whiteyer than ever.   I wear army boots, with magnificent black morocco tops, the trousers put in, wherein shod and legged, confront I Virginia's deepest mud with supercilious eyes. The scenery around Washington is really fine, the Potomac a lordly river, the hills, woods, etc., all attractive. I poke about quite a good deal. Much of the weather here is from heaven—of late though, a stretch decidedly from the other point. To-night (for it is night about 10) I sit alone writing this epistle (which will doubtless devour you all with envy and admiration) in a room adjoining my own particular. A gentleman and his wife who occupy the two other apartments on this floor have gone to see Heron in 'Medea'—have put their little child in bed and left me in charge. The little one is sleeping soundly there in the back room, and I (plagued with a cold in the head) sit here in the front by a good fire writing as aforesaid to my gossips and darlings. The evening is lonesome and still, I am entirely alone—'Oh, Solitude where are the charms, etc.'

"Now you write to me good long letters, my own boys. You, Bloom, give me your address particular, dear friend. Tell me Charles Russell's address, particular—also write me about Charles Chauncey. Tell me about everybody. For, dearest gossips, as the heart panteth, etc., so my soul after any and all sorts of items about you all. My darling, dearest boys, if I could be with you this hour, long enough to take only just three mild hot rums, before cool weather closes.

"Friday Morning, 20th—I finish my letter in the office of Major Hapgood, a paymaster, and a friend of mine. This is a large building filled with paymasters' offices, some thirty or forty or more. This room is up on the fifth floor (a most noble and broad view from my window) curious scenes around here— a continual stream of soldiers, officers, cripples, etc., some climbing wearily up the stairs. They seek their pay—and every hour, almost every minute, has its incident, its hitch, its romance, farce or tragedy. There are two paymasters in this room. A sentry at the street door, another halfway up the stairs, another at the chief clerk's door, all with muskets and bayonets—sometimes a great swarm, hundreds around the sidewalk in front waiting (everybody is waiting for something here). I take a pause, look up a couple of minutes from my pen and paper—see spread, off there the Potomac, very fine, nothing petty about it—the Washington monument, not half finished—the public grounds around it filled with ten thousand beeves on the hoof—to the left the Smithsonian with its brown turrets—to the right far across, Arlington Heights, the forts, eight or ten of them—then the long bridge, and down a ways but quite plain, the shipping of Alexandria. Opposite me, and in a stone throw, is the Treasury Building, and below the bustle and life of Pennsylvania Avenue. I shall hasten with my letter, and then go forth and take a stroll down 'the avenue' as they call it here.

"Now you boys, don't you think I have done the handsome thing by writing this astoundingly magnificent letter—certainly the longest I ever wrote in my life. Fred, I wish you to present my best respects to your father, Bloom and all; one of these days we will meet, and make up for lost time, my dearest boys.

"WALT.

"Address me, care Major Hapgood, paymaster U. S. Army, Cor. 15th & F. St., Washington. How is Mullen? Give him my respects—How is Ben Knower? How the twinkling and temperate Towle? Remember me to them."

Whitman would sleep rather late, resting well after a night of emotional strain. After leaving the O'Connors he had breakfast in his room. A lady visitor describes what he had to eat—tea without milk, a little sugar in a paper sack, toast, with butter from another paper bag, with sometimes a sweetmeat. Then he would stroll down to Fifteenth and F Streets and climb five stories to the Paymaster's Office. About three in the afternoon he would stop and go to a restaurant for his second and last meal of the day. He seldom spent more than thirty cents for it. Then he would bathe, refresh himself with clean linen and, putting on as cheerful a heart as he could, and slinging his army knapsack over his shoulder, he would fill it at the stores with the articles which experience had taught him would be most welcome to his soldier boys. The money for this came not only from his own pocket but from contributions, amounting to some seven thousand dollars in all, which were sent him by Emerson and Alcott, as well as friends in Providence, New York and Brooklyn who had learned of his work. He went everywhere—to the camps of teamsters where nobody else would go, to the hospitals scattered through the government buildings, to the barrack-like hospitals about the city and even those several miles out of town. But he went most often where he was most needed—to the Armory Square, where were the worst cases and where the Christian Commissioners were least often to be seen, or the fashionable women. Sometimes a friend would accompany him. John Burroughs once met him on the road leading to one of the outlying hospitals and, being permitted to accompany him, began a friendship which had been impossible in the more formal manner. And one night his early friend John Swinton went with him to another. Swinton has described what he saw, a scene which was, with Whitman, a daily occurrence throughout the war, and till the last hospital closed.

"Never shall I forget one night when I accompanied him on his rounds through a hospital, filled with those wounded young Americans whose heroism he has sung in deathless numbers. There were three rows of cots, and each cot bore its man. When he appeared, in passing along, there was a smile of affection and welcome on every face, however wan, and his presence seemed to light up the place as it might be lit by the presence of the Son of Love. From cot to cot they called him, often in tremulous tones or in whispers; they embraced him, they touched his hand, they gazed at him. To one he gave a few words of cheer, for another he wrote a letter home, to others he gave an orange, a few comfits, a cigar, a pipe and tobacco, a sheet of paper or a postage stamp, all of which and many other things were in his capacious haversack. From another he would

receive a dying message for mother, wife, or sweetheart; for
another he would promise to go an errand; to another, some
special friend, very low, he would give a manly farewell kiss.
He did the things for them which no nurse or doctor could do,
and he seemed to leave a benediction at every cot as he passed
along. The lights had gleamed for hours in the hospital that
night before he left it, and as he took his way towards the door,
you could hear the voice of many a stricken hero calling, 'Walt,
Walt, Walt, come again! come again!'

"His basket and stores, filled with all sorts of odds and ends
for the men, had been emptied. He had really little to give,
but it seemed to me as though he gave more than other men."

Sometimes when the wounded were dumped on the wharf, he
would buy all the oyster soup a restaurant had on hand and,
with the assistance of the nurses, feed it to the weak and weary
men. Sometimes he would buy a freezer of ice cream and treat
a whole ward. Sometimes he would gather the men about him
in some hospital where they were not bedfast and read them
declamatory pieces of poetry. If a dying man wished a priest
or minister of some particular denomination, Whitman would
scour the city till he got him. Or if some religiously raised boy
wanted a passage read from the Bible, Whitman was ready
to read that book of consolation. Unlike the professional mis-
sionaries, he had no propaganda to urge; he carried no tracts.
He merely wanted to show his love and gratitude by easing for
these boys the horrors of war. He himself did not smoke, but
that was no reason he should lecture them on the evils of smok-
ing. If a boy declined the proffered tobacco, Whitman would
commend him on his habits; but if he accepted it with that hunger which smokers never feel so much as in an army, he would
give him pipe or cigar, saying, "Take it, my brave boy, and
enjoy it."

In striking contrast to the welfare organizations in the World
War, the Christian Commission distributed no tobacco. The
emphasis they laid on making the boys better rather than happier
is perhaps not inaccurately indicated by their annual report.

Tracts had been distributed to the number of 787,276 pages, while fifteen reams of letter paper were thought sufficient!

But Walt's work did not fall into the impersonal routine which its constancy and its magnitude would have made all too easy for a less sympathetic and courageous man. During the war he ministered, according to his own estimate, to perhaps a hundred thousand soldiers; yet he had time to make diary notes of countless individual cases, which he followed up, sometimes for months at a time, till they had won or lost their fight with death. A Union soldier named Rafferty had been severely wounded above the knee. The surgeons, who seemed to have used the knife more recklessly than modern army men, said he would have to lose the leg or his life. He was frantic, but to no purpose; he was at their mercy. But he decided to appeal to Walt. Listening to his story in silence, Whitman patted the lad on the head reassuringly and said, "Make your mind rest easy, my boy; they shan't take it off." And they didn't. Many years afterwards that veteran, telling the story with a gratitude still warm, slapped his thigh and exclaimed, "This is the leg that man saved for me." And the doctors told Whitman that he often did more than that; he did what in his first edition he said he would do:

I seize the descending man and raise him with resistless will,
O despairer, here is my neck,
By God, you shall not go down! hang your whole weight upon me.

I dilate you with tremendous breath, I buoy you up,
Every room of the house do I fill with an arm'd force,
Lovers of me, bafflers of graves.

Sleep—I and they keep guard all night,
Not doubt, not disease shall dare lay finger upon you,
I have embraced you, and henceforth possess you to myself,
And when you rise in the morning you will find what I tell you is so.

One case will stand for many, and we shall let Whitman tell of it. With him we enter Ward 6 of the Campbell Hospital, situated at the end of the horse-car line on Seventh Avenue. "It contains to-day, I should judge," he wrote at the time, "eighty or a hundred patients, half sick, half wounded. The edifice is nothing but boards, well whitewash'd inside, and the usual slender-framed bedsteads, narrow and plain. You walk down the central passage, with a row on either side, their feet towards you, and their heads to the wall. There are fires in large stoves, and the prevailing white of the walls is reliev'd by some ornaments, stars, circles, &c., made of evergreens. The view of the whole edifice and occupants can be taken at once, for there is no partition. You may hear groans or other sounds of unendurable suffering from two or three of the cots, but in the main there is quiet—almost a painful absence of demonstration; but the pallid face, the dull'd eye, and the moisture of the lip, are demonstration enough. Most of these sick or hurt are evidently young fellows from the country, farmers' sons, and such like. Look at the fine large frames, the bright and broad countenances, and the many yet lingering proofs of strong constitution and physique. Look at the patient and mute manner of our American wounded as they lie in such a sad collection; representatives from all New England, and from New York, and New Jersey, and Pennsylvania—indeed from all the States and all the cities—largely from the West. Most of them are entirely without friends or acquaintances here—no familiar face, and hardly a word of judicious sympathy or cheer, through their sometimes long and tedious sickness, or the pangs of aggravated wounds." Excepting, always, that of the "good gray poet" who before setting pen to paper wrote his war-time poems in unpretentious deeds of love.

His ministrations were entirely personal, as this instance, taken at random from many, will testify. "Take this case in Ward 6, Campbell hospital; a young man from Plymouth county, Massachusetts; a farmer's son, aged about twenty or twenty-one; a soldierly, American young fellow, but with sensitive and tender feelings. Most of December and January last he lay very low, and for quite a while I never suspected he would recover. He had become prostrated with an obstinate diarrhœa: his stomach would hardly keep the least thing down; he was vomiting half the time. But that was hardly the worst of it. Let me tell his story—it is but one of thousands.

"He had been sick some time with his regiment in the field, in front, but did his duty as long as he could; was in the battle of Fredericksburgh; soon after was put in the regimental hospital. He kept getting worse—could not eat anything they had there; the doctor told him nothing could be done for him there. The poor fellow had fever also; received (perhaps it could not be helped) little or no attention; lay on the ground, getting worse. Toward the latter part of December, very much enfeebled, he was sent up from the front, from Falmouth station, in an open platform car (such as hogs are transported upon North), and dumped with a crowd of others on the boat at Aquia creek, falling down like a rag where they deposited him, too weak and sick to sit up or help himself at all. No one spoke to him or assisted him; he had nothing to eat or drink; was used (amid the great crowds of sick) either with perfect indifference, or, as in two or three instances, with heartless brutality.

"On the boat, when night came and when the air grew chilly, he tried a long time to undo the blankets he had in his knapsack, but was too feeble. He asked one of the employees, who was moving around deck, for a moment's assistance to get the blankets. The man asked him back if he could not get them himself. He answered, no, he had been trying for more than half an hour, and found himself too weak. The man rejoined, he might then go without them, and walked off. So H. lay chilled and damp on deck all night, without anything under or over him, while two good blankets were within reach. It caused him a great injury—nearly cost him his life.

"Arrived at Washington, he was brought ashore and again left on the wharf, or above it, amid the great crowds, as before, without any nourishment—not a drink for his parched mouth; no kind hand had offered to cover his face from the forenoon sun. Conveyed at last some two miles by ambulance to the hospital, and assigned a bed . . . he fell down exhausted upon the bed. But the ward-master (he has since been changed) came to him with a growling order to get up: the rules, he said, permitted no man to lie down in that way with his clothes on; he must sit up—must first go to the bath-room, be washed, and have his clothes completely changed. (A very good rule, properly applied.) He was taken to the bath-room and scrubbed well in cold water. The attendants, callous for a while, were soon alarmed, for suddenly the half-frozen and lifeless body fell limpsey in their hands, and they hurried it back to the cot, plainly insensible, perhaps dying.

"Poor boy! the long train of exhaustion, deprivation, rudeness, no food, no friendly word or deed, but all kinds of upstart airs and impudent, unfeeling speeches and deeds, from all kinds of small officials (and some big ones), cutting like razors into that sensitive heart, had at last done the job. He now lay, at times out of his head but quite silent, asking nothing of any one, for some days, with death getting a closer and a surer grip upon him; he cared not, or rather he welcomed death. His heart was broken. He felt the struggle to keep up any longer to be useless. God, the world, humanity—all had abandoned him. It would feel so good to shut his eyes forever on the cruel things around and toward him.

"As luck would have it, at this time I found him. I was passing down Ward No. 6 one day about dusk (4th January, I think), and noticed his glassy eyes, with a look of despair and hopelessness, sunk low in his thin, pallid-brown young face. One learns to divine quickly in the hospital, and as I stopped by him and spoke some commonplace remark (to which he made no reply), I saw as I looked that it was a case for ministering to the affection first, and other nourishment and medicines afterward. I sat down by him without any fuss; talked a little; soon saw that it did him good; led him to talk a little himself; got him somewhat interested; wrote a letter for him to his folks in Massachusetts (to L. H. Campbell, Plymouth county); soothed him down as I saw he was getting a little too much agitated, and tears in his eyes; gave him some small gifts, and told him I should come again soon. (He has told me since that this little visit, at that hour, just saved him; a day more, and it would have been perhaps too late.)

"Of course, I did not forget him, for he was a young fellow to interest any one. He remained very sick—vomiting much every day, infrequent diarrhœa, and also something like bronchitis, the doctor said. For a while I visited him almost every day, cheered him up, took him some little gifts, and gave him small sums of money (he relished a drink of new milk, when it was brought through the ward for sale). For a couple of weeks his condition was uncertain—sometimes I thought there was no chance for him at all; but of late he is doing better—is up and dressed, and goes around more and more (February 21) every day. He will not die, but will recover.

"The other evening, passing through the ward, he called me— he wanted to say a few words, particular. I sat down by his side on the cot in the dimness of the long ward, with the wounded soldiers there in their beds, ranging up and down. H. told me I had saved his life. He was in the deepest earnest about it. It was one of those things that repay a soldiers' hospital missionary a thousandfold—one of the hours he never forgets.

"A benevolent person, with the right qualities and tact, cannot, perhaps, make a better investment of himself, at present, anywhere upon the varied surface of the whole of this big world, than in these military hospitals, among such thousands of most interesting young men."

Of course, the question recurred to Whitman whether he should not have enlisted, displaying the masculine courage to kill and be killed, rather than the feminine courage to suffer that life may endure. When the first draft was applied, though not without protesting riots in New York, Whitman was in fear that Jeff's name would be drawn. He could not endure to think of Jeff's being taken away from his wife and child—Jeff, still the chief support of the family even though his salary had recently

been cut in half.   So he proposed borrowing money and hiring
a substitute.   But for himself it was a question of where he,
with his qualities, would be worth most.   But, as if to assure
himself that his motives were untinged with cowardice, he insisted that his name be put down on the draft list where fate
might do with him as she would.   Yet for all that, it was not in
Whitman to level a rifle or thrust a sword at his brother man.

In Whitman were many qualities so highly developed that any
one might have destroyed his health and his happiness were
it not under the control of a natural instinct for letting other
qualities have their innings; his poise was not that of a simple,
fanatical nature, much less that of a callous one; it was the poise
of powers balanced against each other.   If any one gave way,
the force of its correlative became apparent.   Even his philanthropy in the hospitals was two-sided.   He was learning from
the soldiers, as well as comforting them—learning, for instance,
the human history of the war, learning much of manly endur-
ance and stoical self-restraint, and of the strength of that wide-
spread love of America which he had once thought more or less
peculiar to himself.   But the wounds of war did not fill his
whole horizon.   The life he lived was picturesque, as well, and
exciting; and there was no place to get at the heart of it like
the national capital, near the front.   He sat at his window and
contemplated a cavalry camp opposite; he studied the expression on the faces of Southern prisoners or the Union deserters;
he went freely among the countless teamsters; he thrilled to the
proud march of a regiment passing down the street.   One
day in 1864, when Burnside's army was scheduled to pass
through Washington, Walt stood on the curb scanning the faces
of the captains for a sight of George.   After three hours he
picked him out, marching erect.   Stepping from the curb to
the side of the brother of whose record he was so proud, Whitman marched with him, talking quietly, but so eagerly that
George, to his great chagrin, neglected to salute the President
on a balcony as they passed.   Whitman's sharp eye had picked
him out, but not until it was too late.   Lincoln was a sight famil-

iar to Whitman in these days, passing daily in his open barouche near the poet's rooming place. Each had recognized the unusual caliber of the other, and they saluted each other with a bow.

The summer of 1863 was a trying one. The heat was unusual, and Whitman had never spent a summer so far south. The depressing effect of close contact with the pitiful side of war was not easily shaken off when after each battle fresh thousands of wrecked young bodies were sent to the Washington hospitals. He opened his heart to his mother in his regular letters of filial tenderness. "Every once in a while I feel so horrified and disgusted—it seems to me like a great slaughter-house and the men mutually butchering each other—then I feel how impossible it appears, again, to retire from this contest, until we have carried our points." So every one feels who is close to war itself. Possibly both sides could have retired after Gettysburg had there been any foreign peacemaker; but European governments, fearful of the spread of democracy, were all too hopeful that the South would make good its secession from the Union. Whitman thought such sympathy with the rebellion a poor return for America's national hospitality, yet he blamed not the peoples so much as their governments. Those governments doubtless realized that the world cannot always remain half democratic and half aristocratic. Whitman, at least, realized this, for about this time he wrote a poem of remarkable prophecy, "Years of the Modern," foreseeing, as in a mystic vision, a "civil" war of the world, on this very issue. But America, like himself, was a pioneer, and had to pay the price of loneliness for the privilege of living in the future. These Western youths, willingly dying for freedom, had brought to him afresh his theme.

All the past we leave behind,
We debouch upon a newer mightier world, varied world,
Fresh and strong the world we seize, world of labor and the march,
Pioneers! O pioneers!

By October Whitman felt that he must go home for a time. He had left Brooklyn on a temporary mission, but now he had been away nearly a year. His brother Andrew was approaching death from a throat disease which steadily grew worse. Whitman had never been away from his mother so long before. Moreover, he had a new niece, sister to Mannahatta, whom Walt longed to see. Besides, he needed a change. An army friend, Will Wallace, steward in charge of a hospital in Nashville, had urged him to come to Nashville and live with him in a hotel the former was running for the army, promising him work on a newspaper just being started there. He addressed Whitman as "Prince of Bohemians" and held out as a special inducement the fact that he had a number of beautiful army nurses boarding at his hotel. Doubtless the laxity in morals which accompanies every war was no exception with the armies then; Wallace admitted in a second letter that he had had to dismiss his most beautiful nurse, who was French, in order to save the reputation of the hospital. And his reference to a Whitman letter which has been lost makes it clear that Whitman himself, unknown of course to the O'Connors and the Burroughses, had, to the temporary hurt of his health, yielded to the temptations which had left their mark upon him in New Orleans. The effect of the experience was, however, far more incidental than that of his friendship for the soldier boys. Had Whitman gone to Nashville, he might still have ministered to the wounded and earned the money of which he stood so much in need. Although throughout these years he contemplated a lecture tour to supply him with the funds his hospital work required, nothing came of it.

Doubtless one other reason why he went back to Brooklyn at this time was his hope of persuading some publisher to bring out a little book , "Memoranda of a Year," intended for the Christmas trade and for sale among the army. It was the realistic, yet highly spiritual, diary jottings of his hospital experiences, the like of which had never been written. Later he published them

in "Specimen Days," but in 1863 publishers were wary of inno-
vations, or possibly they feared that such an unmasking of the
horrors of war would discourage enlistments. His chief ambition, however, was to get a publisher for "Drum Taps," which
had now been augmented by many new poems descriptive of
scenes at the front and in the Washington hospitals. He had a
right to be proud of these poems, for they showed a distinct
artistic improvement. The fire of inspiration is still there, but
now it is controlled. The poems are purged of redundancy, increased in lyrical smoothness, carefully constructed, and shot
through with the most exalted patriotism. It was the new chap-
ter in his autobiography, all the more his own for betraying so
little self-consciousness. He had given himself to a great cause;
he had been rewarded in his art. Never again did he write an
egotistical line, or celebrate the matter apart from spirit. In
"Drum-Taps" he achieves his ideal, that of expressing at once
his own spirit and that of his country. Yet a publisher was not
immediately to be found for the book.

In New York old friendships, old sights and pleasures reached
out inviting fingers to draw him back into his former self-
indulgent life; but they were comparatively powerless. He had
become father to the army, and felt not only a father's responsibility but a parent's joy in investing himself in younger life. A
single letter written at the time will clearly reveal his mood.

"Brooklyn, Saturday night, Nov. 21, '63.
Dear son and comrade. I wrote a few lines about five days ago
and sent on to Armory Square, but as I have not heard from
it I suppose you have gone to Michigan. I got your letter of
Nov. 10th and it gave me much comfort. Douglas I shall return to Washington about the 24th so when you write direct to
care of Major Hapgood, paymaster U. S. A., Washington,
D. C.—Dearest comrade I only write this lest the one I wrote
five days ago may not reach you from the hospital. I am still
here at my mother's and feel as if I have had enough of going
around New York—enough of amusements, suppers, drinking,

and what is called *pleasure*.—Dearest son: it would be more
pleasure if we could be together just in quiet, in some plain way
of living, with some good employment and reasonable income,
where I could have you often with me, than all the dissipations
and amusements of this great city—O I hope things may work so
that we can yet have each other's society—for I cannot bear the
thought of being separated from you—I know I am a great fool
about such things but I tell you the truth dear son. I do not
think one night has passed in New York or Brooklyn when I
have been at the theater or opera or afterward to some supper
party or carousal made by the young fellows for me, but what
amid the play or singing I would perhaps suddenly think of
you,—and the same at the gayest supper party of men where all
was fun and noise and laughing and drinking, of a dozen young
men, and I among them would see your face before me in my
thought as I have seen it so often there in Ward G, and my
amusement or drink would all be turned to nothing, and I would
realize how happy it would be if I could leave all the fun and
noise and crowd and be with you—I don't wish to disparage my
dear friends and acquaintances here, there are so many of them
and all so good, many so educated, traveled, &c., some so handsome and witty, some rich &c., some among the literary class—
many young men—all good—many of them educated and polished and brilliant in conversation, &c.—and though I value
their society and friendship—and I do, for it is worth valuing
—but Douglas I will tell you the truth. You are so much closer
to me than any of them that there is no comparison—there has
never passed so much between them and me as we have—besides
there is something that takes down all artificial accomplishments,
and that is a manly and loving soul— My dearest comrade, I
am sitting here writing to you very late at night—I have been
reading—it is indeed after 12, and my mother and all the rest
have gone to bed two hours ago, and I am here above writing to
you and I enjoy it too. Although it is not much yet I know it
will please you dear boy. If you get this you must write and
tell me where and how you are. I hope you are quite well and

with your dear wife, for I know you have long wished to be with her, and I wish you to give her my best respects and love too.

"Douglas I haven't written any news for there is nothing particular I have to write. Well, it is now past midnight, pretty well on to one o'clock, and my sheet is mostly written out—so my dear darling boy, I must bid you good night, or rather good morning, and I hope it may be God's will we shall yet be with each other—but I must indeed bid you good night my dear loving comrade, and the blessing of God on you by night and day my darling boy."

Perhaps hundreds of such Whitman letters exist, revealing how pity has grown into sympathy, and that into personal affection. Comrades or "buddies" grown into a great family through common love for the "Mother of all," separated when the war is over, vainly striving to transmute into friendship that will endure an emotion which after all is spiritual rather than personal. The very multitude of such contacts was the salvation for the author of "Calamus." We note that now he has no demands to make, he suffers from no jealousy. He gives, rather than receives, and submits the course of his attachment, not to his imperious needs, but to the will of God.

Walt had just returned to Washington and reoccupied his little third-story-back room when a letter from Jeff informed him that Andrew was dead. He did not attend the funeral—probably because he could not buy a ticket. He had traveled before on transportation furnished him by John Hay. When George's term of enlistment expired, he longed to be at home to see him, but that pleasure too had to be foregone. There is a touch of pathos in his memory of his recent visit. "When I come home again," he writes his mother, "I shall not go off gallivanting with my companions half as much nor a quarter as much as I used to, but shall spend the time quietly with you while I do stay; it is a great humbug to go spreeing around, and a few choice friends for a man, the real right kind in a quiet way, are enough."

In February, Major Hapgood went down to Culpeper, Virginia, to pay off the army there, taking Eldridge with him. Probably it was in this company that Whitman also went down. He had expressed a wish to see a real battle, partly, no doubt, out of his omnivorous curiosity, partly because he could hardly say he had seen the war without having seen any fighting. Then too, he thought his services to the wounded might be more valuable in a field hospital. He was in the South only about two weeks, but it was worth his while to go. The beautiful country, the tender air, the noble grace of the Confederate mother with whom he boarded—yet there about him the fever of war, the fear of some sudden, terrible attack by Lee. He kept step with the army when on "a march in the ranks hard-pressed and the road unknown," he plowed the "unctuous mud," he kept vigil all night with the body of a fallen comrade.

Vigil wondrous and vigil sweet there in the fragrant silent night,
But not a tear fell, not even a long-drawn sigh, long, long I gazed,
Then on the earth partially reclining sat by your side leaning my chin in
    my hands,
Passing sweet hours, immortal and mystic hours with you dearest comrade—
    not a tear, not a word,
Vigil of silence, love and death, vigil for you my son and my soldier,
As onward silently stars aloft, eastward new ones upward stole,
Vigil final for you brave boy, (I could not save you, swift was your death,
I faithfully loved you and cared for you living, I think we shall surely
    meet again,)
Till at the latest lingering of the night, indeed just as the dawn appear'd,
My comrade I wrapt in his blanket, envelop'd well his form,
Folded the blanket well, tucking it carefully over head and carefully under
    feet,
And there and then and bathed by the rising sun, my son in his grave, in
    his rude-dug grave I deposited,
Ending my vigil strange with that, vigil of night and battle-field dim,
Vigil for boy of responding kisses, (never again on earth responding,)

Vigil for comrade swiftly slain, vigil I never forget, how as day brighten'd,
I rose from the chill ground and folded my soldier well in his blanket,
And buried him where he fell.

Returning to Washington, Whitman resumed his hospital visits. But soon the strain began to tell on even his magnificent physique. For he not only subjected himself to a daily harrowing of his emotions in caring for and comforting the sick; he was wound-dresser as well, combining in his self-imposed service the functions of the Red Triangle and the Red Cross.

Bearing the bandages, water and sponge,
Swift and straight to my wounded I go,
Where they lie on the ground after the battle brought in,
Where the priceless blood reddens the grass the ground,
Or to the rows of the hospital tent, or under the roof'd hospital,
To the long rows of cots up and down each side I return,
To each and all one after another I draw near, not one do I miss,
An attendant follows holding a tray, he carries a refuse pail,
Soon to be fill'd with clotted rags and blood, emptied, and fill'd again.

I onward go, I stop,
With hinged knees and steady hand to dress wounds,
I am firm with each, the pangs are sharp yet unavoidable,
One turns to me his appealing eyes—poor boy, I never knew you,
Yet I think I could not refuse this moment to die for you, if that would
    save you.

But perhaps the hardest of his tasks came when, despite his best efforts, the boy died, and he must write the melancholy news to parent or sister. Even the letter of condolence which Lincoln, under a misapprehension of the facts, wrote to Mrs. Bixby revealed no more compassionate heart than did these letters. Whitman visualized the mother as she read it—seeing in her his own mother reading news of the wounding of George—and always he so tempered the winds of war to the shorn lamb as to make even cruel news a benediction. Often he was rewarded by the gratitude of those to whom he wrote. Instance his letter about the wounding of Cunningham, which inspired his touching poem, "Come Up from the Fields, Father." War is easily made heroic and romantically glamorous when we deal with it in the mass. Whitman felt this in Virginia, as, standing in the darkness, he watched an army passing by, not as individuals temporarily forming a cohort, but as a majestic people *en masse.* "It fell upon me like a great awe," he said. But it was realistic too; and while he believed there were social and political ideals more precious than life, he also believed that a war which destroys the humanity of the warriors can accomplish no commensurate good. Yes, Walt kept close to reality; attendants in a military hospital are lucky if they do not lose their ideals altogether. The hospital malaria, however, and the contact with innumerable gangrenous wounds, gave him an infection and undermined his vitality little by little. The doctors, fearful of the health of so valuable an assistant, warned him; but he who had never known sickness did not appreciate the importance of the warning. In June, 1864, he had to give up entirely, for several months. He was reluctant to do so, however, for he was haunted by the fear that George might one day be brought in and he not there to minister to his own. He went home to recuperate. But as soon as he was able to be about, he again took up his task in the poorly cared-for hospitals in Brooklyn and New York. Then came the news that George was a Confederate prisoner, at the Petersburg camp, in Virginia. At once Walt tried to get through the lines to nurse him and his comrades, but without success. He then sought, through his connections in Washington, to have his brother exchanged, only to learn that all exchanges had been stopped. In his personal anxiety he wrote an indignant letter to the press severely condemning this policy of the administration as unnecessarily brutal, whatever military reasons might be assigned for it. Eventually, however, George was exchanged, and continued his career of bravery in the Union Army.

Meanwhile the energetic O'Connor was trying to get Whitman a clerkship in one of the departments at Washington such as he and Eldridge and Burroughs enjoyed, which letters from Emerson and others had never as yet secured for Whitman. The reputation of the 1860 edition was against him. First O'Connor obtained for Walt a position in the Post Office, but declined to present it to Whitman, as not suited to his way of working. Finally, however, through Hubley Ashton, he found a clerkship in the Department of the Interior, under Secretary Harlan, ex-preacher and ex-senator. His work would require but a few hours a day, he would have ample funds for his needs and his hospital benefactions, he would have an excellent place to prepare his contemplated fourth edition of "Leaves of Grass," incorporating "Drum-Taps," not yet published.

Copying documents and investigating routine cases naturally had little interest for Whitman, but in the Interior Department (Indian Bureau) he had opportunity to observe many Indians themselves, who, coming to Washington to call on the President or to sign treaties, would sit on the floor about the wall in the Bureau Office in the Treasury Building. Whitman had imbibed not a little of Rousseau's passion for the natural man; here he had a chance to see the best that nature, unassisted by civilization and art, could do with humanity. And he was not disappointed. Of course, he knew nothing of Indian life, or Indian psychology, though in his youth he had written the Indian stories then so popular, but judging by what that life had made the chiefs mean to themselves, in pride of personal bearing, he was not so sure the white man had not paid too high a price for his elegance, his mastery and his smartness. "Their feathers, paint —even the empty buffalo skull [which one wore as a headpiece] —did not, to say the least, seem any more ludicrous to me than many of the fashions I have seen in civilized society. I should not apply the word savage (at any rate, in the usual sense) as a leading word in the description of those great aboriginal specimens, of whom I certainly saw many of the best. There were moments, as I look'd at them or studied them, when our own exemplification of personality, dignity, heroic presentation anyhow (as in the conventions of society, or even in the accepted poems and plays,) seem'd sickly, puny, inferior. . . . Occasionally I would go to the hotels where the bands were quarter'd, and spend an hour or two informally. . . . I had the good luck to be invariably receiv'd and treated by all of them in their most cordial manner." Fifteen years later, stopping at Topeka on a trip to Colorado, Whitman accompanied a group of officials to see a number of these Indians in prison. They uniformly refused recognition to any of the impressively introduced government men but, following the lead of one of the old chiefs, each extended to Whitman his hand and voiced a cordial "How." And Whitman, "meeter of saint and savage on equal terms," confessed, "I was not a little set up to find that the critters knew the difference and didn't confound me with the big guns of officialism."

But Whitman's connection with the Indian Bureau was brief, and even that brief connection was broken by a trip to Brooklyn, whither he went to publish "Drum-Taps" at his own expense. In May he had been promoted from a first-class clerkship, paying $1200 a year, to one of the second class paying $1600. There had been no complaint on the score of his competency or his faithfulness. He was the more chagrined, therefore, on June 30th, to find himself dismissed from his office by the Secretary himself, who assigned no reason. Here was a case, as Whitman could see, in which he must wisely make use of his friends. Mr. Ashton, the Assistant Attorney-General, called the next day upon Secretary Harlan to find out the cause of the sudden dismissal. Harlan was perfectly frank to say that he dismissed Whitman because of his authorship of "Leaves of Grass." His impression of Whitman was that he was a free-lover, and advocated free-love principles. The book was out of print, but Harlan had got hold of Whitman's own annotated copy in or on his desk and, turning its pages after office hours, had at once made up his mind to dismiss him. He was not a man of wide outlook, and had that ingrained Puritanism common to Methodist ministers of the West, with little knowledge of literature. It was not a political move on the Secretary's part, for he expected it to be kept quiet. But he was so sincere, whether from bigotry or the same feeling which had inspired so many of the early reviews and some of Emerson's reservation, that he would retreat from his position before no eloquence of Mr. Ashton concerning Whitman's character and manner of life in Washington. Indeed, he declared he would resign his own position first. He appears not to have appreciated the seriousness of what Whitman thought most despicable in the affair, the surreptitious method used in obtaining his evidence. But the same evidence brought to his attention in a less underhanded manner would doubtless have had the same result on Whitman's fortunes, for this political representative of the land of liberty and aspirant for the Vice-Presidency (whom Lincoln refused as a running mate) did not believe in the liberty of literature to deal with matters obnoxious to the moral reactions of the average man. Long afterward, Harlan found that by his action he had decapitated, not Whitman whose good was stronger than his bad, but himself, and is said to have acknowledged his error of judgment. However, pressed for a written statement of his position, he declared that the dismissal, like many others, was dictated by a post-war policy of economy, adding that Whitman's chief, the Hon. William P. Dole, had named Whitman as the clerk most easily to be spared in the Indian Bureau.

Had Harland talked with Whitman, the latter would perhaps have confessed to him that he himself was unsatisfied with some passages in his earlier editions—that he was now eliminating many of these lines and altering others for the new edition, though he would not admit that there had been any evil intent even at the time of writing. Shortly before, Whitman had written O'Connor, "I see now some things in it I should not put in if I were to write now, but yet I shall certainly let them stand, even if but for proofs of phrases passed away." But, with characteristic obstinacy, he would not alter his original plan for putting a man's entire life in a book. The high esteem in which he and "Drum-Taps" were held at the moment, among persons of prominence and sense, indeed only strengthened the proof, which his book sought to make, that good might grow from evil. This optimistic Emersonian doctrine was of more importance than the vicissitudes of his personal life, though the latter might serve to point the moral. Unfortunately, however, he did not make the most of his autobiographical method in setting forth that truth, for he did not always arrange his poems in the order of their composition. Only recently has that been done.

Whitman might have appealed to Lincoln, whom he believed to be favorably impressed by his personal appearance, if not by his poetry. But alas, the war which had slain a million privates, had also taken the Martyr-Chief, despite his charity for all, his malice for none. The ship had ridden out the storm and, with sail and rudder wrecked, was making into a peaceful port—

> The port is near, the bells I hear, the people all exulting,
> While follow eyes the steady keel, the vessel grim and daring;
>> But O heart! heart! heart!
>> O the bleeding drops of red,
>>> Where on the deck my Captain lies,
>>> Fallen cold and dead.

Early on the morning of Saturday, April 15th, news was flashed to New York that Abraham Lincoln had been shot by an assassin. The evil tidings enveloped the city with the swiftness of a storm cloud. Whitman was at home with his mother. Both were stunned, as only those who love deeply and purely can be stunned. The daily routine—the meals prepared, but no mouthful touched by either throughout the day—the extras hungrily scanned in hope of the President's recovery. It was a personal grief to Whitman, who had trusted in the President's purposes and relied on his skill when many did not, finding a certain kindred loneliness with him as a silent but comprehending Great Companion on the Open Road of duty. Returning to Washington, Whitman learned from a friend, Peter Doyle, the whole story of the murder, the latter having seen it from the balcony of the theater. For Whitman, it was throughout life a solemn memorial. At home or at the house of a friend, years afterward, he would lift his glass in silence toward the picture of his dead chief and drink to his memory. Now, however, he must find relief in song, and in doing so composed what Swinburne, a master of melody himself, described as the "most sonorous nocturne ever chanted in the church of the world." "When Lilacs Last in the Dooryard Bloom'd" is just that, national religious music, and no mere occasional poem. Whitman's lines must be read as music is read. Fragmentary quotation here would only do violence to its delicate interwoven *motifs* of lilac scent and singing thrush and symbolical star, to its incremental repetitions, to its haunting, uplifting suggestiveness. Taking what one may look upon as quite accidental experiences, coincident with his personal shock in the loss of Lincoln, Whitman succeeded in weaving them together with an effect of actuality which was not that of mere circumstantial detail but rather that of the national emotion transfiguring for the moment the individual's world with the quality of something universal. Whitman said that never thereafter could he think of the lilac bush without thinking of Lincoln. And never can the reader of this sublimest of our poems.

It belonged as the capstone to his "Drum-Taps"; but the book was already in print. So Whitman stopped its sale, and later added this poem with the stanzaic elegy, "O Captain, My Captain," as a sequel, bound in late copies. The "spirit whose work was done," the spirit of liberty at war, had laid to rest private and chief in the common patriot's grave where malice cannot follow; and Whitman sang for both a song of pride and peace. Moreover he added a note of reconciliation which, had he lived to read it, would have brought tears to the eyes of the man who had spoken the inaugural in March.

Word over all, beautiful as the sky,
Beautiful that war and all its deeds of carnage must in time be utterly
  lost,
That the hands of the sisters Death and Night incessantly wash again,
  and ever again, this soil'd world;
For my enemy is dead, a man as divine as myself is dead,
I look where he lies white-faced and still in the coffin—I draw near,
Bend down and touch lightly with my lips the white face in the coffin.

BOOK VI

ONE INCREASING PURPOSE

HE war was over. The returning private whom Whitman saw was not the forlorn individual of Hamlin Garland's sketch, suddenly stripped of his glamour and glory. He was in serried ranks marching in review down the avenues of Washington. In that sight was a thrill which the individual soldier can never inspire. It seems to promise the perpetuation of a power recently displayed so terribly in battle. And Whitman, whose thought, now that the hospitals were emptying, turned to his favorite dream, sought to catch for future use the full dramatic significance of the moment. He realized that he, at least, would never see another like it.

As your ranks, your immortal ranks, return, return from the battles;
While the muskets of the young men yet lean over their shoulders;
While I look on the bayonets bristling over their shoulders;
While those slanted bayonets, whole forests of them, appearing in the
　distance, approach and pass on, returning homeward,
Moving with steady motion, swaying to and fro, to the right and left,
Evenly, lightly rising and falling, as the steps keep time;
—Spirit of hours I knew, all hectic red one day, but pale as death next
　day;
Touch my mouth, ere you depart—press my lips close!
Leave me your pulses of rage! bequeath them to me! fill me with currents
　convulsive!
Let them scorch and blister out of my chants, when you are gone;
Let them identify you to the future, in these songs.

It was the average man, in the army as out of it, that had inspired him and enlisted his affection. By the end of 1865, however, nearly all the hospitals were gone from within and about Washington, and shoulder straps were less common on the streets. Whitman still devoted his Sunday afternoons to what soldiers remained to be cared for, but he suddenly found his exacting occupation gone. The war had exerted a salutary influence in dissipating, without decreasing, his passion for friends; now he would find it returning upon him—his life-long quest for friend and lover. It would still give him moments of sadness, even of torment; but the war had also weakened his vitality, and with it the strength of all his emotions, and had taught him, moreover, with his increasing years, to express his friendship in a more and more paternal manner. His next intimate friendship will reveal this. But before turning to it, let us see if nothing survives in him of the author of *Efans d'Adam*.

Whitman was markedly reticent about all his more personal affairs, a natural concomitant, perhaps, of the symbolical candor in his verse. Which was cause, which effect, the reader may judge. But though we do not know the subsequent history of his earlier adventure with woman, we do know that in Washington, about this time, he had an unhappy romantic attachment. Whether it began when his inamorata, like other women in the capital, seeing his Jovian form on the street or reading his verse in the parlor, sent him some tender missive, neither history nor tradition can say. We know only that they corresponded, and that one of her letters, betraying her feelings for Whitman, fell into her husband's hands—for, unluckily, she was encumbered with a husband. A rather jealous one at that, it would seem; for he flew into a rage, and abused Walt violently. I am often tempted to think that "To a Certain Civilian" was addressed to him as a parting shot. The lady appears to have been refined and gentle. And when she was touched with pity for Walt, he was ready to marry her—confirmed bachelor though he was—had she been free. The pathetic poem he sent to her, his most ideal love, we know.

Out of the rolling ocean, the crowd, came a drop gently to me,
Whispering, *I love you, before long I die,*
I have traveled a long way, merely to look on you, to touch you.
For I could not die till I once look'd on you,
For I fear'd I might afterward lose you.

(Now we have met, we have look'd, we are safe;
Return in peace to the ocean, my love;
I too am part of that ocean, my love—we are not so much separated;
Behold the great rondure—the cohesion of all, how perfect!
But as for me, for you, the irresistible sea is to separate us,
As for an hour carrying us diverse—yet cannot carry us diverse for ever;
Be not impatient—a little space— Know you, I salute the air, the ocean
    and the land,
Every day at sundown for your dear sake, my love.)

Surely he who could write so tenderly, and with such resignation to the laws of life as we know it here, has learned something by experience in defying the "irresistible sea." His love
was its own excuse for being, yet he recognizes that even love is
not always master of the ironies of one's personal destiny.

The little that we know of this futile connection comes to us
through the memoirs of Mrs. O'Connor. With this family
Whitman continued to be on the best of terms, dining with them
regularly and basking in their unqualified admiration. Whitman
was singularly fortunate, not only in being able to attract people
of intelligence and influence as friends, but, without effort, in
enlisting their services in his behalf and in behalf of the new
American literature of which he looked upon himself as the
founder. When Walt lost his position under Secretary Harlan,
O'Connor was irate as only an Irishman with an education can
be irate—eloquently. Though another clerkship was soon
found for Whitman, this time in Hubley Ashton's own department, the Attorney General's, O'Connor could be satisfied by
nothing less than the publishing of "The Good Gray Poet,"
a pamphlet protesting against Harlan's action with such a flow
of indignation as is not easily matched in the history of polemics.
It is more like oratory, hot with personal feeling, piling up
illustrations with sensational, if not always, enduring effect, and
sparing no epithets in its attempt to heap calumny on Harlan's
devoted head. O'Connor's argument was that Whitman's life
in the hospitals gave the lie to any imputation of bad character

that might be based on his authorship of the "Leaves," and that even if passages in his book, read alone, did prove offensive, the judgment of this book rests with the reader, not with any official inquisitor. At great length he culled passages from the classics to show that a consistent application of Harlan's punitive principles would condemn them all. Essentially it was the argument of Milton's "Areopagitica." Of course, O'Connor did not know all of Whitman's life, nor did he understand all the poetry which was the expression of that life. Whitman himself at this time would hardly have gone quite so far in its defense. Few modern readers would condemn "Leaves of Grass" because of a few blemishes; but this constitutes no reason, in morals or in art, why that which is falsely fragmentary should be defended *per se.* The best service done Whitman's fame by the brilliant effort of his friend, however, was its fixing upon him a fit and enduring sobriquet, "The Good Gray Poet," a title which, it is interesting to note, was supplied by Whitman. To give his panegyric in another form, O'Connor two years later wrote a story, "The Carpenter," in which the Christ-rôle is given to Whitman.

Other friends at this period began to come to Whitman's support, making of his literary fortune a holy cause. John Burroughs was now on intimate terms with this lover of nature who, like himself, had been strongly influenced by Emersonian ideas. Every Sunday Walt had breakfast at the Burroughs home, receiving such a welcome that even his habitual tardiness did not endanger his standing invitation. The "Galaxy" was now opening its pages to Whitman's verse, and prose, and Burroughs printed in it a review of "Drum-Taps." In the next year, 1867, he issued in New York a booklet, "Notes on Walt Whitman as Poet and Person," on which he had been laboring for some time. The special reason for its publication seems to have been a desire to promote the sale of Whitman's new edition of "Leaves of Grass," later issues of which were to include "Drum-Taps" and its "Sequel." Doubtless Burroughs, born to write, was glad to publish his first book. But when, after a long life of authorship in which he had written much about Whitman, he collected his works, he left this one out, probably for the reason that it was not wholly his. He had no information about Whitman that Whitman had not supplied him with, and perhaps half the book, including quotations, was actually written by the poet. The latter's anonymous self-criticisms of his first edition were now reappearing in another form. Whitman was so eager to get his book and his conception of America before the people that, in his eagerness for his own success, which indeed was more the success of his mission than any mere personal profit, he seems to have forgotten something that was due to his young friend and to the reader of the "Notes." Later Burroughs would do a much more ambitious book about his idol, but even there his criticism is fundamentally Whitman's conception of himself rather than the expression of an independent judgment. Whitman was obviously an intellectual and emotional planet big enough to attract lesser minds out of their true orbits. Nor did he see why he should blame himself for doing so. But the book was not an unrelieved eulogy, for all that. As if to confess, in a general way, some of the misdeeds of his private life which were "open to criticism," Whitman has Burroughs to say that in youth he "had sounded all the experiences of life with all their passions, pleasures, and abandonments." O'Connor's panegyric, to have been biographically accurate, should have taken these experiences into consideration as well as those of the Washington hospitals; but perhaps the over-praise in "The Good Gray Poet" was what prompted this guarded confession in the "Notes." For Whitman loved the truth, and, like the rest of us, spoke as much of it as he thought he could afford.

Since we are primarily concerned with seeing Whitman himself as he makes his slow but increasing way through the middle of the nineteenth-century America, it is fortunate that Burroughs, with his keen eye and graphic pen, has caught for us one of those little incidents which, though of constant occurrence with

Whitman, nevertheless reveal the heart of the man as truly as the more theatric gestures of warrior or statesman.

"I give here a glimpse of him on a Navy Yard horse car . . . one summer day at sundown. The car is crowded and suffocatingly hot, with many passengers on the rear platform, and among them a bearded, florid-faced man, elderly, but agile, resting against the dash, by the side of the young conductor, and evidently his intimate friend. The man wears a broad-brim white hat. Among the jam inside near the door, a young English woman, of the working class, with two children, has had trouble all the way with the youngest, a strong, fat, fretful bright babe of fourteen or fifteen months, who bids fair to worry the mother completely out, besides becoming a howling nuisance to everybody. As the car tugs around Capitol Hill the young one is more demoniac than ever, and the flushed and perspiring mother is just ready to burst into tears with weariness and vexation. The car stops at the top of the Hill to let off most of the rear platform passengers, and the white-hatted man reaches inside and gently but firmly disengaging the babe from its stifling place in the mother's arms, takes it in his own, and out in the air. The astonished and excited child, partly in fear, partly in satisfaction at the change, stops its screaming, and as the man adjusts it more securely to his breast, plants its chubby hands against him, and pushing off as far as it can, gives a good long look squarely in his face—then as if satisfied snuggles down with its head on his neck, and in less than a minute is sound and peacefully asleep without another whimper, utterly fagged out. A square or so more and the conductor, who has had an unusually hard and uninterrupted day's work, gets off for his first meal and relief since morning. And now the white-hatted man, holding the slumbering babe also, acts as conductor the rest of the distance, keeping his eye on the passengers inside, who have by this time thinned out greatly. He makes a very good conductor, pulling the bell to stop or go on as needed, and seems to enjoy the occupation. The babe meanwhile rests its fat cheeks close on his neck and gray beard, one of his arms vigilantly surrounding it, while the other signals, from time to time with the strap; and the flushed mother inside has a good half hour to breathe, and cool, and recover herself."

A strange type of bohemian this, who, wherever he went among simple people, made the world his home, and homelike. His own energies were not greatly taxed by the clerical duties whereby he made a comfortable living; but the surplus he gladly spent in easing the burden from weaker and less fortunate folk. It was not, however, with the impersonal philanthropy of the Abolitionist; for as he said, he gave not charity but himself. Few could resist the compliment of his friendship. Least of all the young Irish conductor on this car; he was a friend with a special affinity for Walt. His name was Pete Doyle, who as a Confederate prisoner paroled in Washington, had drifted into the employment of the street car company. He was nineteen when Walt first met him, in 1866. Doyle's account of this first meeting is none the less suggestive for his lack of education.

"The night was very stormy, he had been over to see Burroughs before he came down to take the car—the storm was awful. Walt had his blanket—it was thrown around his shoulders—he seemed like an old sea-captain. He was the only passenger, it was a lonely night, so I thought I would go in and talk with him. Something in me made me do it and something in him drew me that way. He used to say there was something in me had the same effect on him. Anyway, I went into the car. We were familiar at once—I put my hand on his knee—we understood. He did not get out at the end of the trip—in fact, went all the way back with me. I think the year of this was 1866. From that time on we were the biggest sort of friends."

What could be the basis for such an unusual, yet such an enduring, friendship? With Eldridge, or Burroughs, or Ashton, or Thoreau, or Emerson, or Conway, or O'Connor, Whitman might have intellectual comradeship and ideal stimulation.

Many were the feasts of reason at the O'Connor home, among spirits equally matched, possessing a common interest in world literature and affairs. Even Congressman James Garfield, later President, coming up behind Whitman on the street, would salute him with a quotation from his poetry. But Doyle could tell Whitman nothing he did not know, could understand little that he did. Between them there was, to be sure, the attraction felt by personalities fundamentally in tune. But that is much more akin to love than to friendship, and is subject to the vicissitudes of love. For enduring friendship each friend must supply some need of the other, if the feeling is not to pass into indifference or patronage. Yet in the letters which were exchanged between Walt Whitman and Peter Doyle through many years, tokens of a friendship which was not broken till Doyle stood in 1892 at the graveside of his "affectionate father and comrade," is trace of nothing humiliating on the part of either. As for Doyle, the service was companionship in a city of strangers; and more, it was the advice, encouragement, paternal interest of which his not very adventurous spirit stood in need. Whitman took charge of his savings, like a father, advised him concerning his work and advancement, encouraged him to study, gave him relief on days of hard work, and, after working hours, took with him long walks on the beautiful moonlit roads about Washington. When together, they were as careless of the decorous and conventional world about them as two schoolboys. If the fancy struck them, they would purchase a watermelon from a market wagon and sit down on the curb of the avenue to enjoy it, unmindful of the amused smiles of passers-by. Perhaps for Whitman there was in this even a secret enjoyment; for he knew the value of creating a rôle for himself in the public mind as a "people's poet," and took delight in doing what poets who traded in "respectability" did not care or dare to do. For his part, Whitman found in this young friend an audience to his liking.

Sometimes, after Pete had come off duty, they would go to a café and call for their beer; then Whitman would begin a dis-

course on the heavenly bodies.   Presently he would find his companion sound asleep on the table, and like a mother unwilling to
wake her weary infant, Whitman would stand guard over him
till closing time.   Perhaps his vanity was hurt by the discovery
that this man taken at random from the people could not follow
him into his poetic flights, giving small assurance that his verse
would ever be popular with the masses.   But it was also gratifying to be able to talk to his heart's content, like Dr. Johnson,
without having to reply to the sharp questions of an O'Connor
or others trained in the schools.   Chiefly, however, he found in
Doyle some one to love.   The hospitals were closed to him, and
on Doyle he lavished the paternal affection which had given
him so much noble pleasure during the war.   Now and then
there is a momentary outcropping of the old Calamus feeling
that a love so great as his could not be fully returned.   But
Doyle was so obviously wrapped up in his big friend, and so
dependent upon him, that thoughts of jealousy could not last
long.   Nevertheless, though neither of them comprehended the
psychology of their·attachment for each other, Whitman had
learned something through his long experience with such emotions, and at times felt that they should be carefully restrained.
Once, in his private notebooks, he exclaimed: "Depress the
adhesive nature—   It is in excess—making life a torment.   All
this diseased, feverish, disproportionate *adhesiveness.*"   And he
held up to his own emulation the example of the wise man of
Epictetus and the story of Merlin, "Strong & wise & beautiful
at 100 years old."   He was at his best with Doyle when in the
presence of nature.   There he would sing snatches from the
operas, spout heroic speeches from Shakespeare, or indulge in
thinking aloud on some of the many subjects which as verse
were taking shape in his mind.   It was not unlike the outpour-
ings of a precocious, enthusiastic boy.

Yet Whitman was no boy.   He was now approaching the
climax of maturity in his intellect and his art.   For a few years,
as he anticipated, he would cast his longest shadow on the pages

of his books, and then fate would deal with him much as it had dealt with Lincoln.

The years of disillusionment which quickly follow even a successful "idealistic" war are peculiarly trying to the idealist. The illusion of progress has so quickly passed into the reality of stupid reaction wherewith pigmy politicians, no longer led by a great statesman or actuated by the fear and pride of war, seem determined to compensate themselves for the unwonted heroism which the national emergency has called forth. In morale as in materials, war is always a mortgage on the future; and those who lack the imagination to dwell in that future are first to foreclose the mortgage. Nothing could have been more discouraging to Whitman, had he looked to government for the salvation of his country, than the incompetent administration of Andrew Johnson following upon that of Abraham Lincoln. The whole reconstruction policy, which made the worst of a disastrous war, must have depressed him deeply. It was a heated argument on the fitness of the late slaves to receive the ballot which caused a serious break in his friendly relations with O'Connor, the uncompromising Abolitionist. But the philosophy on which Whitman relied in this discouraging period was securely rooted in his faith; it was the philosophy of "Leaves of Grass," to which he now added a new meaning. During the war he had little time for thinking or writing about the future; he was too busy with personal service. But after a relatively fallow period these new experiences demanded expression, this time in prose as well as in verse.

In 1867 and 1868 he had sent to the "Galaxy" essays on "Democracy" and on "Personalism," treating of the paradox of individualism and social unity. By 1870 he issued a pamphlet, "Democratic Vistas," in which the "Galaxy" essays were, none too deftly, incorporated. Whitman had a bad habit of using what he had published for one purpose as a means to the accomplishment of quite a different purpose, and without altering its structure accordingly. This lack of careful revision is more apparent in his prose than his verse, and accounts, in large

MEN OF THE DAY.
No. 18.

FROM

"The Fifth Avenue Journal."

A Mirror of Art, Literature and Society.

CARICATURE OF WHITMAN, 1872

Courtesy of Mr. Alfred F. Goldsmith

measure, for the neglect that has to this day met most of his prose, except the diary notes which could only suffer by any revision. And this is most unfortunate, for, if the reader has but patience to plow through many a turgid mystical passage, he will come, now and then, upon paragraphs of prose as vibrant and as eloquent as anything in his verse. In the whole intention and spirit of the "Vistas," coming in the dark days of American post-bellum literature, one takes the measure of as devout and as knightly a crusader as our literary history has to offer. More, he who is acquainted with what our publishers were then offering and with what was soon to come from the new school of Western writers—Mark Twain, Joaquin Miller, Bret Harte, and the rest—will recognize in Whitman both a prophet and a leader. Lowell's simpler and better known address on "Democracy" in Birmingham came a decade and a half later, yet repeated some of Whitman's arguments.

The triumph of faith over despair which makes the "Vistas" a significant milestone in the growth of Walt Whitman, inviting comparison with Carlyle's indictment of democracy in "Shooting Niagara" (which in part prompted the "Vistas" as a rejoinder), is the more noteworthy in a man who, had he not been a creator, would certainly have been a satirist. We recall the bitter poem "Respondez" in the second edition and Whitman's unqualified denunciation of the political systems just before the Civil War. And here in the "Vistas" reappears that note of America's failure when judged only by her past achievement. Admitting not only the natural advantages and resources of America, but the phenomenal success of her pioneering spirit and inventive genius in all that concerns material civilization, he yet fails to see the type of personality he called for in the "Leaves of Grass."

"Are there, indeed, *men* here worthy the name? Are there athletes? Are there perfect women, to match the generous material luxuriance? Are there crops of fine youths, and majestic old persons? Are there arts worthy freedom and a rich people? Is there a great moral and religious civilization—the only justification of a great material one? Confess that to severe eyes, using the moral microscope on humanity, a sort of dry and flat Sahara appears, these cities, crowded with petty grotesques, malformations, phantoms, playing meaningless antics. Confess that everywhere, in shop, street, church, theater, barroom, official chair, are pervading flippancy and vulgarity, low cunning, infidelity—everywhere the youth puny, impudent, foppish, prematurely ripe—everywhere an abnormal libidinousness, unhealthy forms, male, female, painted, padded, dyed, chignon'd, muddy complexions, bad blood, the capacity for good motherhood deceasing or deceas'd, shallow notions of beauty, with a range of manners, or rather lack of manners, (considering the advantages enjoy'd), probably the meanest to be seen in the world."

Did we not know the depth of Whitman's affection for his country we should be tempted to set down such a description to spleen, or to some morbid projection of his own unhappiness, as similar indictments by foreign visitors, however competent, have commonly been attributed to racial or national jealousy. But this was his deliberate opinion. His was no cheap optimism. One who knows how recently Americans have ceased to suffer from "dyspepsia" as a national disease, to study the physiology and hygiene which Whitman urged, to treat women with the respect due to equals, to look upon art as an essential of life, to become a reading people gradually learning to enjoy more and more substantial diet, can appreciate the Brobdignasian scorn of Whitman for the "plentiful little mannikins" of his day, "skipping around in collars and tail'd coats." Satirical "Main Streets" are still in point, to be sure, and the sudden increase of wealth has thrown the character of the average man into painful contrast with his material possessions; but no one who looks upon the America of 1926 can fail to see much that appeared to Whitman only through the vistas of his imagination.

> "Ah Genoese thy dream! thy dream!
> Centuries after thou art laid in thy grave,
> The shore thou foundest verifies thy dream.

Indeed it was the consciousness of imperfection in the present, both in his environment and in his inner emotional life, that drove him to think of the future, and his dreams naturally bore, in reverse, the stamp of his particular wants. No more the animal exuberance of the First Edition. He has come to knowledge of himself, of his land. He has found it necessary to discipline his personal emotions, even to impose upon himself a penance lest he sacrifice his soul, his self-reliance, by defying the inexorable decrees of his sometimes unhappy fate. And his solace comes, as it did to all the dreaming prophets and Puritans, in visions of a new heaven, on a new earth. This was to be accomplished, he announced, by "a new founded literature, not merely to copy and reflect existing surfaces, or pander to what is called taste—not only to amuse, pass away time, celebrate the beautiful, the refined, the past, or exhibit technical, rhythmic, or grammatical dexterity—but a literature underlying life, religious, consistent with science, handling the elements and forces with competent power, teaching and training men—and, as perhaps the most precious of its results, achieving the entire redemption of woman out of these incredible holds and webs of silliness, millinery, and every kind of dyspeptic depletion—and thus insuring to the States a strong and sweet Female Race, a race of perfect Mothers." There is something a little pathetic in this book. The strong young prophet whose barbaric yawp was to create a new style, a new objective for American writers, looking about after fifteen years of earnest work and confident prophecy, finds little accomplished. He himself is without even a publisher. He begins to realize that, save only Time and a few young champions, he is without allies. A premonition of an early eclipse of his powers steals upon his spirit. He even has doubts whether he has not too hastily ignored the assistance which merely technical art, had he possessed it, might have given him. Style is more important than he had thought, but it is now too late fundamentally to alter his style. So he calls upon others to carry forward the flaming torch which is to light his country toward its destined goal. Government is but machinery. There must be governors, and, in a republic, they must be the average men. Until such is the case, all is experiment. So, like Emerson long before, he calls upon the American scholar, writer, teacher, to "disseminate culture among the masses," the culture of the "manly and courageous instincts, and loving perceptions, and of self-respect." His Calamus idea now becomes, not the mere indulgence in the emotions provoked by individuals as such, but, "running like a half-hid warp through all the myriad audible and visible worldly interests of America, threads of manly friendship, fond and loving, pure and sweet, strong and life-long, carried to a degree hitherto unknown—not only giving tone to individual character, and making it unprecedently emotional, muscular, heroic, and refined, but having the deepest relations to general politics." It is still friendship, but purged of its selfishness, its morbidity, its dross; it is the soul of the body politic. The individualist has been taught to live in a community. It can thus be seen that to Whitman's original idea of heroic, epic autobiography, celebrating the individual not only in himself but as a type of what the race might be, an epic in which the youth and overflowing health of the author by necessity laid most emphasis on the body and what depends on the body, he now adds a new message, the chant of the national soul. It is this which is to guide the new race of bards toward a common unseen, far-off divine event—"the prophetic vision, the joy of being toss'd in the brave turmoil of these times—the promulgation of the path, obedient, lowly, reverent to the voice, the gesture of the god, or holy ghost, which others see not, hear not—with the proud consciousness that amid whatever clouds, seductions, or heart-wearying postponements, we have never deserted, never despair'd, never abandon'd the faith."

And when we turn to read the verse he was writing at this time, we are impressed anew with the fact that we have a different Whitman. Here is no longer the youthful feeling of immortality born of high animal spirits, nor even the agonized realism of the war-time verse; here is the aspiration of the pioneer soul, taught by frustrated human hopes, if not disgust, yet a certain despair of realizing itself through union with another in this life.

What is this separate Nature, so unnatural?
What is this Earth, to our affections? (unloving earth, without a throb
    to answer ours;
Cold earth, the place of graves.)

The mystic survives in him; he makes rendezvous, not with the Great Companions, but with the Comrade perfect. There was in a notebook of 1862–3 a poem of the Calamus type comparing the spider, throwing out experimental anchors of silk, to the individual soldier seeking his proper comrade and lover. But when the poem was perfected in structure and published, among the "Whispers of Heavenly Death," in 1871, it contained but one note—that of religious mysticism, the soul's outreaching for reality.

A noiseless, patient spider,
I mark'd, where, on a little promontory it stood isolated,
Mark'd how to explore the vacant vast surrounding,
It launch'd forth filament, filament, filament, out of itself,
Ever unreeling them, ever tirelessly speeding them.

And you O my soul where you stand,
Surrounded, detached, in measureless oceans of space,
Ceaselessly musing, venturing, throwing, seeking the spheres to connect
    them;
Till the bridge you will need be form'd—till the ductile anchor hold,
Till the gossamer thread you fling catch somewhere, O my Soul.

With that peculiarly realistic mysticism which informs the first edition, he had begun by declaring, like Blake, "Divine am I inside and out; I exist as I am, that is enough." But now his gods are ideals, by so much has his aspiring imagination outrun his personal growth. He sings, not the "average" man, but the "Ideal Man," not life, but the unplumbed vistas of Death, not "Identity" but the "Old Cause" of the amelioration of the race. In "Proud Music of the Storm" he comes very near reaching the climax of his technical skill, with marvelous smoothness interpreting an actual storm, linking its various movements of sound to all the music he had ever heard, and finally realizing that the two have been harmonized—physical phenomenon and poetic memory—by something deeper than either, the Quaker's "inner voice," the poet's "light that never was on sea or land," in which are "Man and Art, with Nature fused again." All the effects of operatic music are made use of in a harmony of sound till then unheard in America.

One main theme in "Democratic Vistas," it will be remembered, was the necessity that America should produce an original literature. In September, 1871, Whitman was "rather staggered" to receive an invitation to deliver a poem at the opening of the annual exhibition of the American Institute, in New York. He accepted. But Whitman could not command his inspiration even so well as Lowell did in his famous *tour de force,* the "Commemoration Ode." Accordingly he fell back upon ideas recently used in the "Vistas." His stock of cardinal ideas was, indeed, small, though he was always keenly interested in new facts. Herein he was somewhat handicapped by the sort of newspaper training which had given bent to his thinking. In working over the "Democratic Vistas" in verse, therefore, he had to force his inspiration, and the result was as sad as the early catalogues had been. Indeed he instinctively fell back on the catalogue method. Perhaps he realized how flat the verse was, and sympathized with the reader to a certain extent by deliberately parodying his own normal style. When the poem was published in a separate booklet, Whitman included a clipping from the Washington *Chronicle* about the occasion. Though unsigned, this was a letter from himself, still under the awkward necessity of being his own anonymous press agent.

"Imagine yourself," he wrote for the friendly *Chronicle,* "inside a huge barn-like edifice of a couple of acres, spanned by immense arches, like the ribs of some leviathan ship (whose skeleton hull inverted the structure might be said to resemble), and this building, crowded & crammed with incipient displays of goods and machinery—every thing that grows & is made—and a thousand men actually engaged at work, in their shirt-sleeves, putting the said goods & machinery in order—all with a noise, movement, & variety as if a good-sized city was in process of being built.   In the middle of this, to an audience of perhaps two or three thousand people, with a fringe on the outside of five or six hundred partially-hushed workmen, carpenters, machinists, & the like, with saws, wrenches, or hammers in their hands, Walt Whitman, last Thursday, gave his already celebrated poem before the American Institute.   His manner was at first sight coldly quiet, but you soon felt a magnetism & felt stirred.   His great figure was clothed in gray, with white vest, no necktie, & his beard was unshorn as ever.   His voice is magnificent, & is to be mentioned with Nature's oceans & the music of forests & hills.   His gestures are few, but significant.   Sometimes he stands with his hands in his breast pockets; once or twice he walked a few steps to & fro.   He did not mind the distant noises & the litter & machinery, but doubtless rather enjoyed them.   He was perfectly self-possessed.   His apostrophe to the Stars and Stripes which floated above him, describing them in far different scenes in battle, was most impassioned.   Also his 'Away with war itself!' & his scornful 'Away with novels, plots, & plays of foreign courts!'   A few allusions of his poem were in playful tone, but the main impression was markedly serious, animated, & earnest.   He was applauded as he advanced to read, besides several times throughout, & at the close.   He did not respond in the usual way by bowing.   All the directors & officers of the Institute crowded around him & heartily thanked him.   He extricated himself, regained his old Panama hat & stick, and, without waiting for the rest of the exercises, made a quiet exit by the steps at the back of the stand.

"The real audience of this chant of peace, invention, & labor, however, was to follow.   Of the New York & Brooklyn evening and morning dailies, twelve out of seventeen published the poem in full the same evening or the next morning."

What a setting for a Whitman poem on American industry.

Who else, except Joaquin Miller, would have been so little disturbed by that setting? How he had watched himself, and the impression he was making! The boy writer for the magazines, adoring the "last of the sacred army" of Revolutionary heroes, now delights in believing himself adored and, not satisfied with the courtesy of the press in giving him ample space, he must describe it for himself. It was the American way, of creating a pose, as though an old Panama hat had more poetic virtue in it than a new one. And yet it is only fair for us to remember that there were many Whitmans. If the poet in him read the poem, the journalist in him wrote up the occasion. It was characteristic of his perennial, if not always endearing, childishness that the two Whitmans were not at enmity with each other.

About the same time Whitman was invited to deliver a poem at the Commencement of Dartmouth College. The invitation seems to have originated with certain students who thought, by inviting a radical poet, to have fun at the expense of the more conservatively orthodox Congregationalists of the faculty. Of this, of course, Whitman was unaware. He took it all as a *bona fide* tribute to his growing fame as a national poet, and conducted himself accordingly. He continued to act that part, as he had long conceived it. The poem, "As a Strong Bird on Pinions Free," monotonously read from type, made no impression on Dartmouth, though Whitman's personal charm insured for him cordial entertainment. But Whitman, who had abandoned his earlier professed attitude of letting his verse make its own way, cheerfully waiting for his recognition, again called upon his press agent, himself, to make the most out of the occasion. Doubtless he wrote nothing he did not believe, and desired perhaps less to push his book than to explain it as he believed others would not or could not; yet his tendency to coin hope into fact, to make use of friendly journals to review himself anonymously, is a little pathetic in its disclosure of his lack of the Olympian patience he wished others to believe his, and in its revelation (doubtless against all his expectation) of a certain tendency to deception. A few passages from this review, which, though sent to the press, seems not to have appeared in print after all, will indicate the discouragement in his soul at his poetic prospect, a discouragement which was most poignant when he assumed his most optimistic pose.

"The late Dartmouth College utterance of the above-named celebrity is again arousing attention to his theory of the poet's art, and its exemplification in his writings. An intellectual career, steadily pressing its way amid strong impediments, through the past sixteen or seventeen years, and evidencing itself during that time in the good-sized volume of poems, 'Leaves of Grass,' and the small prose book, 'Democratic Vistas,' shows no sign of flagging energy in its late effusions, the American Institute poem, the cheering apostrophe to France, or in this College Commencement piece, 'As a Strong Bird, on Pinions Free,' which, with some others, forms the first installment of a new volume just published. . . ."

As the forced emphasis betrays, this flagging imagination is just what these late effusions do show. As if to make up for want of commanding example, Whitman again explains his "theory," which original poets too often confuse with their proper business. He unblushingly announces the immediate growth of his fame, as he had long before told Emerson of the rapid sale of his first edition.

"Expectation is even now more and more stimulated, and already, by a few of the boldest prophets, some very audacious speculations are launched forth. Time only can show if there is indeed anything in them. This Walt Whitman—this queer one whom most of us have watched, with more or less amusement, walking by—this goer and comer, for years, about New York and Washington—good natured with everybody, like some farmer, or mate of some coasting vessel, familiarly accosted by all, hardly any one of us stopping to Mr. him—this man of many characters, among the rest that of volunteer help in the army hospitals and on the field during the whole of the late war, carefully tending all the wounded he could, southern or northern—if it should turn out that in this plain unsuspected old customer, dressed in gray & wearing no neck tie, America and her republican institutions are possessing that *rara avis* a real national poet, chanting, putting in form, in her own proud spirit, first class style, for present & future time, her democratic shapes even as the bards of Judah put in song, for all time to come, the Hebrew spirit, and Homer the war-life of prehistoric Greece, and Shakespeare the feudal shapes of Europe's kings and lords!

"Whether or not the future will justify such extravagant claims of his admirers, only that future itself can show. But Walt Whitman is certainly taking position as an original force and new power in literature."

We are accustomed, of course, to think that such words would sound better in other mouths. In O'Connor's and Burroughs's, for instance. And so they would, and did. And yet the thing which kept Whitman at his poetic task was his frank faith in himself, his genuine admiration for his achievements of poetry and friendship. And it would be unfair not to remember that in him remained, as in most men of genius, some of the engaging naïveté of the boy. We smiled good naturedly at the lad, who, eager to be a man, proudly displays his biceps. But he laughs best who laughs last, and none can deny that, gambling on his own immortality, Whitman has certainly now begun to collect his winnings from that lady of fortune, the Future. But for his confidence, or if one prefer over-confidence, which nevertheless was more in his words than in his inmost heart, American literature would to-day be without its most commanding figure. If any one, the poet must be allowed the defect of his qualities.

But confidence is not creation, and had Whitman not written lines fit to live, we should not to-day be recalling the vagaries of his genius. If the American Institute poem and the Dartmouth Commencement effort, taken with his press descriptions of himself, seem to indicate that he is failing as a poet, we must hasten to place beside "Proud Music of the Storm" a poem which he declared to contain more of his real spiritual autobiography than any other he ever wrote. I refer, of course, to "Passage to India," ostensibly an occasional poem celebrating the almost simultaneous completion of the Suez waterway to the East and the transcontinental railway to the West. These final achievements of man's effort to subdue the earth into a human community through which a single blood could course in the arteries of travel and commerce, were but a material symbol of his own life-long dream of the brotherhood of man. It was more than that; it was the mystic passion for the union of the past and the future in an eternal present. The whole span of evolution was to be glimpsed as easily as the radio encompasses the globe. Passage to India, not for spice and gems, but to the elder land of wisdom and art where are the "towers of fables immortal fashioned from mortal dreams," the perpetual epic of Ulysses. The explorer, scientist, inventor, empire-builder can be justified only by one who will soothe with a hint of eternity the "hearts as of fretted children" which have tormented men since the expulsion from Eden, by one who will at last find a passage to the Land of Heart's Desire.

All affection shall be fully responded to, the secret shall be told,
All these separations and gaps shall be taken up and hook'd and link'd
    together,
The whole earth, this cold, impassive voiceless earth, shall be completely
    justified,
Trinitas divine shall be gloriously accomplish'd by the true son of God,
    the poet,
(He shall indeed pass the straits and conquer the mountains,
He shall double the cape of Good Hope to some purpose,)
Nature and Man shall be disjoin'd and diffused no more,
The true son of God shall absolutely fuse them.

Identifying himself with this true son of God, the poetic soul, he would be off, as in the wondrous days of 1855, with his vision.

O soul, repressless, I with thee and thou with me,
Thy circumnavigation of the world begin,

Of man, the voyage of his mind's return,
To reason's early paradise,
Back, back to wisdom's birth, to innocent intuitions,
Again with fair creation.

O we can wait no longer,
We too take ship O soul,
Joyous we too launch out on trackless seas,
Fearless for unknown shores on waves of ecstasy to sail,
Amid the wafting winds, (thou pressing me to thee, I thee to me, O soul,)
Caroling free, singing our songs of God,
Chanting our chant of pleasant exploration.

But, sailing so far into the past, one at length confronts the future, the infinite.

Sail forth—steer for the deep waters only,
Reckless O soul, exploring, I with thee, and thou with me,
For we are bound where mariner has never yet dared to go,
And we will risk the ship, ourselves and all.

O my brave soul!
O farther farther sail!
O daring joy, but safe! are they not all the seas of God?
O farther, farther, farther sail!

This spirit of spiritual discovery, of absolute faith, links Whitman with the genius of American pioneering history and explains his dauntless confidence in himself and in the average man; it links him moreover with the great lovers, prophets, liberators of mankind. In this poem, and in "The Mystic Trumpeter" and "The Prayer of Columbus" soon afterward to be published, Whitman sings his noblest, his purest note—and his real swan song. For, though he is to live and write for twenty years more, a great affliction will soon touch body and mind; the rest will be late afternoon.

Yet there will be compensations. His leaves of grass grew from hardy, democratic, universal roots; and now those roots begin to spread. Other hands will water them, till they shall have refreshed with their greenness every part where poets dwell. The history of that influence is the story of a book, and requires a book to tell it; we shall limit ourselves to that part of it which will throw light upon what remains to relate of the story of Walt Whitman.

The transplantation of the grass seeds was most natural. Even the first edition had in some cases been sent by American readers, like Emerson and Thoreau, to friends in England. When Moncure Conway went to England he took with him his personal memories, and his great admiration for Whitman, with whom he maintained a correspondence. In 1866 he had written a long and favorable, if somewhat diffident, article on Whitman for the "Fortnightly Review." Shortly afterwards he was laboring, with other enthusiastic young English writers, to bring Whitman to the notice of the English public through reviews and an English edition. As early as 1858 a German-American friend of Whitman, working with him on the Brooklyn *Times,* had attempted to translate Whitman's verse into German, desisting only when he found himself unequal to the task. In 1868 Ferdinand Freiligrath wrote an article and made translations from "Leaves of Grass" in the Augsburg *Allgemeine Zeitung,* praising Whitman as a modern universal poet. Three years later Edward Dowden took the lead among a group of Dublin admirers in advertising the new poet, through an article on "The Poetry of Democracy" in the "Westminster Review," as a few months later Thérese Bentzon was to praise him, with characteristic French discrimination, in the pages of the *Revue des deux Mondes,* and Rudolph Schmidt, in Copenhagen, translating and reviewing. With most of these Whitman was in correspondence, sometimes furnishing himself the material on which their articles were based. But our story is concerned chiefly with the friends he was making in England. He sent an autographed copy of the "Leaves" to Tennyson—the Tennyson whose youthful "Maud" Whitman had anonymously reviewed in contrast to his own just published first edition, much to the disparagement of the former. Tennyson replied kindly, inviting Whitman to visit him on the Isle of Pines. The British poet found in Whitman "a great big something" which he could not define, but doubtless liked him all the more for being so different from himself. So John Addington Symonds, the Oxford esthete whose over-developed scholarship coupled with his frail body and unfortunate emotional organization placed him in urgent need of the cosmic religious life which Whitman could inspire, no less than of the sane and well rounded life in the presence of nature which Whitman taught. Concluding a beautiful and penetrating study of Whitman, published a year after the latter's death, Symonds testified to what Whitman's verse had done for him personally. "He taught me to comprehend the harmony between the democratic spirit, science, and that larger religion to which the modern world is being led by the conception of human brotherhood, and by the spirituality inherent in any really scientific view of the universe. He gave body, concrete vitality, to the religious creed which I had been already forming for myself upon the study of Goethe, Greek and Roman Stoics, Giordano Bruno, and the founders of the evolutionary doctrine. He inspired me with faith, and made me feel that optimism was not unreasonable. This gave me great cheer in those evil years of enforced idleness and intellectual torpor which my health imposed upon me. Moreover, he helped to free me from many conceits and pettinesses to which academic culture is liable. He opened my eyes to the beauty, goodness and greatness which may be found in all worthy human beings, the humblest and the highest. He made me respect personality more than attainments or position in the world. Through him I stripped my soul of social prejudices." This obviously is a religious result, and in so far justifies Whitman in his repeated assertion that "Leaves of Grass" is primarily a religious deliverance. Yet there was, mixed with it, a strange and pathetic element, which, when understood, helps to account for this widely read scholar's devotion to a single book, and demonstrates likewise, an element in Whitman not wholly religious. The tragic peculiarities of Symonds's emotional nature are well known. It was doubtless these peculiarities which led him to his masterful studies in Greek and Renaissance literature. And his book on Whitman, taken with his letters to his American idol, indicate that it was the Calamus poems which meant most to him. For in these poems he thought he recognized a kindred but more heroic spirit, and in them he glimpsed a possible spiritual sublimation of emotional tendencies which to his highly civilized intelligence were, when observed in themselves, obnoxious. When much later he suggested this interpretation to Whitman, the latter was at first evasive, and finally defiant, denying any such fundamental kinship in their natures and even going so far as to make a confession—itself of necessity painful—to his younger disciple. This, he doubtless thought, would prove the denial. The confession was nothing less than that, though unmarried, he was the father of children, from whom he had been separated by considerations of their interest and fortune. The heat which Whitman displayed in discussing the questions of Symonds betrays a buried fear which he had thought the experiences of the war had killed outright, and betrays also the fact that he had perhaps cultivated a profound ignorance of his own psychological make-up. His moods he would study and express, with little reserve; but analyze them he could not, nor did he encourage others to do so. That might have inhibited the expression which gave him his chief relief. Indeed the questions of Symonds should have been put before the publication of the 1860 edition. Whitman's post-war determination to emphasize the spiritual elements of life, as we have seen, shows how definitely he had himself turned his back on the less wholesome elements in some of the Calamus poems. But the law of compensation makes no allowance for the young poet's lack of circumspection, rendering the dross of his lines as long a literary life as his more satisfying sentiments.

Another who was introduced to Whitman in the 1860's was Swinburne. Acutely sensitive to the feelings on the part of many Victorians that England was decadent, and himself singing in

rapid alliterative lines which but half concealed the despair in
the heart of the poet, Swinburne at first was shocked into hope
by Whitman's youthful confidence, notwithstanding his artistic
deficiencies. In "Songs before Sunrise" he published his tribute,
"To Walt Whitman in America."

> Send but a song oversea for us,
>   Heart of their hearts who are free,
> Heart of their singer, to be for us
>   More than our singing can be;
> Ours, in the tempest at error,
> With no light but the twilight of terror;
>   Send us a song oversea!
>
> Sweet-smelling of pine leaves and grasses,
>   And blown as a tree through and through
> With the winds of the keen mountain-passes,
>   And tender as sun-smitten dew;
> Sharp-tongued as the winter that shakes
> The wastes of your limitless lakes,
>   Wide-eyed as the sea-line's blue.

It was comforting to Whitman, who had in a way not only turned
his back on the technical masters of poetry but had even defied
them, to receive such praise from one of these masters. He
could not know, of course, that Swinburne would later recant
to the extent of publishing in the "Fortnightly" a severe criticism
of Whitman's art and philosophy. By that time, however,
Whitman would not need the endorsement of a Swinburne, and
could dismiss the incident with the amused and quite impersonal
remark, "Ain't he the damnedest simulacrum?"

The artist William Bell Scott, who had first shown the
"Leaves of Grass" to Swinburne, also introduced it to William
Rossetti. Like Symonds, Rossetti was repelled by Whitman's
occasional want of taste, and knew, what Hotten, the publisher,
was to tell him, that it would be legally impossible to reprint
the "Leaves" in England without some form of suppression for

these frank passages. Disliking expurgation as a form of poetic mutilation, he nevertheless desired England to know Whitman, and therefore determined to bring out a volume of selections from which would be omitted entirely "any poem, though otherwise fine and unobjectionable, which contains any of his extreme crudities of expression in the way of indecency." This was in 1867. When advised of the project, Whitman was no more willing to authorize an expurgated edition in England than in America; he would have considered that not only weak and unmanly, but untrue to himself and to his mission. He did not object, however, to Rossetti's editing a volume of selections on his own responsibility, and in this his native stubbornness was yielding to wise advice. It was, to be sure, not adopting the course advised by Emerson seven years before, but it was going half way. Whitman's very appreciable following in England from that day to this can largely be attributed to the good sense of his tactful English editor. Squeamish American readers— which term in Whitman's day included most American readers —had no similar opportunity to approach Whitman through his best work alone. It so happened, also, that the Rossetti selection was the medium of bringing our poet yet another rare tribute, different from any yet.

Two years after his volume was published, Rossetti received, one day in June, a letter from his friend Mrs. Anne Gilchrist, the gifted widow of Blake's biographer, and the friend of Tennyson and, later, of the Carlyles. "I was calling on Madox Brown a fortnight ago," she said, "and he put in my hands your edition of Walt Whitman's poems. I shall not cease to thank him for that. Since I have had it, I can read no other book: it holds me entirely spell-bound, and I go through it again and again with deepening delight and wonder." Rossetti was delighted, and lost no time in making reply. "Your letter has given me keen pleasure this morning. That glorious man Whitman will one day be known as one of the greatest sons of Earth, a few steps below Shakespeare on the throne of immortality.

What a tearing-away of the obscuring veil of use and wont from the visage of man and of life! I am doing myself the pleasure of at once ordering a copy of the 'Selections' for you, which you will be so kind as to accept. Genuine—i. e., *enthusiastic*—appreciators are not so common, and must be cultivated when they appear. . . . Anybody who values Whitman as you do ought to read the whole of him." With remarkable enthusiasm Mrs. Gilchrist sat down the same day again to write to Rossetti. "There is nothing in him that I shall ever let go my hold of. For me the reading of his poems is truly a new birth of the soul. I shall quite fearlessly accept your kind offer of the loan of a complete edition, certain that great and divinely beautiful nature has not, could not infuse any poison into the wine he has poured out for us. And as for what you specially allude to, who so well able to bear it—I will say, to judge wisely of it—as one who, having been a happy wife and mother, has learned to accept all things with tenderness, to feel a sacredness in all? Perhaps Walt Whitman has forgotten—or, through some theory in his head, has overridden—the truth that our instincts are beautiful facts of nature, as well as our bodies; and that we have a strong instinct of silence about some things."

Bringing to her reading of Whitman a faith, like his own, that the new science would, when approached in a religious spirit, open new opportunities for the poet to link reality with the soul, and with Blake's mystical treatment of good and evil fresh in her mind, she was prepared to read the deleted poems by "the light that glows out of the rest of the volume." Madame Blanc would have considered equally just that criticism which would read the rest of the book in their light. But Mrs. Gilchrist was not a critic; she was an accepter, a devotee. There is a certain possessive quality, a personal element, in a woman's acceptance. To be sure, the mysticism of Whitman stimulated and satisfied her mind. "If the man of science is happy about the atoms," she wrote Rossetti, "if he is not balked or baffled by apparent decay or destruction, but can see far enough into the dimness to know that not only is each atom imperishable, but that its

ANNE GILCHRIST

endowments, characteristics, affinities, electric and other attractions and repulsions—however suspended, hid, dormant, masked, when it enters into new combinations—remain unchanged, be it for thousands of years, and, when it is again set free, manifest themselves in the old way, shall not the poet be happy about the vital whole? shall the highest force, the vital, that controls and compels into complete subservience for its own purposes the rest, be the only one that is destructible? and the love and thought that endow the whole be less enduring than the gravitating, chemical, electric powers that endow its atoms?" But she is not lost in the abstractions of her thought. Her emotions are still more powerful. She adds, "But identity is the essence of love and thought—I still I, you still you." And she is moved by her emotional stress, as if a pent-up force were suddenly released, to have the temerity to read Whitman's book not only as an open letter to a friendly world, but as a personal advertisement for a special love.

> I loved a certain person ardently, and my love was not returned.
> Yet out of that I have written these songs,

Whitman had written; and Mrs. Gilchrist, denied by fate the high companionship and intimacy for which she knew herself exceptionally fitted, cast off discretion and allowed herself to believe that fate had been reserving her, not only to appreciate the purity of intent which actuated the author of "Leaves of Grass," but to be the mate of the man who had so strangely identified himself with that book. A proper delicacy restrained the impulse to write Whitman at once, telling him that his messenger dove had sighted land in England. But she did write all she dared to Rossetti, who quoted therefrom to O'Connor. When the letter was shown to Whitman, he was doubly elated. "I am deeply touched by these sympathies and convictions, coming from a woman and from England," he wrote Rossetti, "and I am sure if the (anonymous) lady knew how much comfort it has been to me to get them, she would not only pardon you for transmitting them but approve that action. I realize indeed of this smiling and emphatic *well done* from the heart and conscience of a true wife and mother, and one, too, whose sense of the poetic, as I glean from your letter, after flowing through the heart and conscience, must also move through and satisfy science as much as the esthetic, that I had hitherto received no eulogium so magnificent." Truly he had not; for his American admirers knew the man as well as the book—in some cases knew the book chiefly through the man—whereas Mrs. Gilchrist, with only the book before her, had gone farther than they. O'Connor had apologized for Whitman; Mrs. Gilchrist praised him, as only a woman can praise the man she loves. Whitman, never quite at his ease about the "Children of Adam" poems, thought that such an effect upon such a woman settled the matter for all time. They would do as he had intended them to do. It was characteristic of his type of mind that he should himself have read into these poems, not merely the youthful impulses out of which they were born, but the religious aspirations which succeeded. But he was somewhat hasty in concluding that Mrs. Gilchrist's eulogy was conclusive, or her case typical. Naturally prejudiced by his long-deferred hope, he cannot be blamed for seeing in her the type of perfect reader he was writing for. He could not know how charged with personal meaning were her words about his frankness of expression: "Now none need turn away their thoughts with pain or shame; though only lovers and poets may say what they will,—the lover to his own, the poet to all, because all are in a sense his own." So, little suspecting what would come of it, Whitman sent to the anonymous lady, by Rossetti, a photograph of himself, and even suggested that his letter be given her if she wanted it. She dared to hope that the missive was in some way personal, and gladly consented to work over her letter to Rossetti into an article to be published in America. And that article was intended as a love letter. Whitman was staggered at the warmth of its praise, being, as he said, unused to it; but engrossed in its bearing on his poetic career, he did not yet suspect that in it a lady was taking her only opportunity to let him know that through his book she had

fallen in love with him—at least, with her image of him. "A
Woman's Estimate of Walt Whitman" appeared in the Boston
"Radical" for May, 1870. But the hoped-for advances from
Whitman did not come, and the English lady, pining for some
one to love and finding none so close to her ideal as Whitman,
poured out her soul to his portrait for more than a year. At
length, able to stand this ingrowing passion no longer, she convinced herself that she should write to him frankly concerning
her history and her feeling toward him. If we may forget
that she herself, though not without struggle, was doing violence to one of the instincts which are beautiful facts of nature,
we can perceive in this letter the very sublimity of love. Alas
for her, it is an instinct in man to be shy when woman grows
forward, however sincerely she may do it; and by this time
Whitman knew perfectly well the difference between the fair
creatures of his imagination and the women whom he loved.
He had just sworn off, in his private notebooks, from his futile
"pursuit" of some inamorata which he recognized as undigni-
fied in him; and he was not likely to invite disaster again. We
may not here quote her whole letter, that were to wrest it from
its appropriate setting; but a single passage will indicate that
she was proposing marriage to Whitman.

"In May, 1869, came the voice over the Atlantic to me—O,
the voice of my Mate: it must be so—my love rises up out of
the very depths of the grief and tramples upon despair. I can
wait—any time, a lifetime, many lifetimes—I can suffer, I can
dare, I can learn, grow, toil, but nothing in life or death can tear
out of my heart the passionate belief that one day I shall hear
that voice say to me, 'My Mate. The one I so much want.
Bride, Wife, indissoluble eternal!' It is not happiness I plead
with God for—it is the very life of my Soul, my love is its life.
Dear Walt. It is a sweet & precious thing, this love; it clings
so close, so close to the Soul and Body, all so tenderly dear, so
beautiful, so sacred; it yearns with such passion to soothe and
comfort & fill thee with sweet tender joy; it aspires as grandly
as gloriously as thy own soul. Strong to soar—soft and tender

to nestle and caress.   If God were to say to me, 'See—he that you love you shall not be given to in this life—he is going to set sail on the unknown sea—will you go with him?' never yet has bride sprung into her husband's arms with the joy with which I would take thy hand and spring from the shore."

It seems heartless to analyze so beautiful an avowal.   But to do so will explain the sequel as nothing else can.   It requires little experience in the self-deceptions of the hungry human heart to perceive that Mrs. Gilchrist is really writing her letter to herself, seeking by unqualified avowal to convince herself of the reality of that which, during the year of silence, must often have presented itself to her judgment as an illusion.   She says she can wait, but the letter shows that she cannot; she says it is a mating of souls she craves, but she proposes marriage.   She was in love, no doubt, and had all the symptoms of a first love in evidence; but with whom?   Not the real Walt Whitman, of course, for him she had never seen.   And if she found in his "Leaves of Grass" more vital suggestions of a personality than she had discovered in any other book, yet even there she distorted the real man by idealizing the very passages which, to prevent idolization and parasitic adulation, Whitman had courageously inserted.

Nearly two months passed, and no answer.   The suspense was excruciating, for she was too intelligent not to know that she had risked much.   She would write again.   Could he have failed to receive her letter?   Could that missive have fallen into other hands?   Would he not at least let her know that he had heard from her, and thus spare her "the needless suffering of uncertainty"?   Did he resent advances from her?   He was himself making the advances, she tried to persuade herself.   "It is not true that thou hast not sought or loved me.   For when I read the divine poems I feel all folded round in thy love: I feel often as if thou wast pleading so passionately for the love of the woman that can understand thee—that I know not how to bear the yearning tenderness that fills my breast."

If never before, Whitman must now have realized the dangers

that lie in attempting to confuse the man and the writer as he had done. Her reasoning, though specious enough in itself, was an *argumentum ad hominem* so far as he was concerned. Coming to see that Mrs. Gilchrist was a lover, rather than a disinterested admirer of his book, Whitman considered how best to prevent her from wounding herself with her passion. He had himself suffered too much from unreturned affection not to be gentle with such a noble, if deluded, soul. And just as in his dirge on Lincoln he had found death to be cool and enfolding, so he knew that on earth death's shadow, silence, may be the gentlest of answers, silence which can be interpreted by each according to his peculiar needs. But it was now obvious that silence would not be taken as an answer. So he wrote a brief reply, so carefully worded and proportioned, so delicate in its necessary refusal, that it was among the masterpieces of his spirit. It could have been written only by one who could meet Cardinal Newman's definition of a gentleman as one who never willingly gives pain.

> "Washington, D. C.
> "November 3, 1871.

"I have been waiting quite a while for time and the right mood, to answer your letter in a spirit as serious as its own, and in the same unmitigated trust and affection. But more daily work than ever has fallen to me to do the present season, and though I am well and contented, my best moods seem to shun me. I wish to give to it a day, a sort of Sabbath, or holy day, apart to itself, under serene and propitious influences, confident that I could then write you a letter which would do you good, and me too. But I must at least show without further delay that I am not insensible to your love. I too send you my love. And do you feel no disappointment because I now write so briefly. My book is my best letter, my response, my truest explanation of all. In it I have put my body and spirit. You understand this better and fuller and clearer than any one else. And I too fully and clearly understand the loving letter it has evoked. Enough that there surely exists so beautiful and a delicate relation, accepted by both of us with joy."

Never was the *double entendre* used with more kindness. The lady has betrayed herself. The gentleman will afford her an easy retreat by putting an obviously false construction on her words. She has cited his book as a love-letter; very well, then let it remain his love-letter. Subtlety was a weapon Whitman had used for a long while; for did he not at times have to play hide and seek with his own deepest desires?

But even on the receipt of this letter Mrs. Gilchrist will not face the truth. She reasons that Whitman has never received her letter, or he would have answered a plain proposal plainly. And yet she has been rebuffed, and she knows it. She takes counsel of hope. "I can wait," she says. "I can grow great & beautiful through sorrow & suffering, working, struggling, yearning, loving so, all alone, as I have now done nearly three years—it will be three in May, since I first read the book, first knew what the word *love* meant." To fill in the waiting period, she gossips about her interests, or his; she cannot bear the idea of breaking off the correspondence. Whitman replies infrequently, and then taking care to express as much interest in her children as in herself. About this time came Tennyson's invitation to visit him, and Whitman mentions it, with the suggestion that another inducement to his accepting would be the opportunity to see her and her children. "But it is a dream only," he adds, and except for a gossipy letter or two the next month, Whitman writes no more for nearly a year. But Mrs. Gilchrist's love proves greater than her pride, and she continues to write. "Shall you never find it in your heart to say a kind word to me again? or a word of some sort?" But she had an enemy she knew not of. That very month Whitman was stricken with paralysis.

The reader will remember that in 1864, after a year and a half of hospital visiting, Whitman broke down. He regained his robustness of spirit, but never was quite the physically perfect

Washington City, U.S.
November 3, 1871.

Dear friend,

I have been waiting quite a long while for time & the right mood to answer your letter in a spirit as serious as its own, & in the same unmitigated trust & affection. But more daily work than ever has fallen upon me to do the current season. & though I am well & contented, my best moods seem to shun me. I wished to give to it a day, a sort of Sabbath or holy day apart to itself, under serene & propitious influences —

confident that I could then write you a letter which would do you good, & me too. But I must at least show, without further delay, that I am not insensible to your love. I too send you my love. And do you feel no disappointment because I now write but briefly. My book is my best letter, my response, my truest explanation of all. In it I have put my body & spirit. You understand this better & fuller & clearer than any one else.

And I too fully &
clearly understand
the loving & womanly
letter it has evoked.
Enough that there
surely exists between
us so beautiful &
delicate a relation,
accepted by both of
us with joy.
                Walt Whitman

man again. After a time he began to suffer from spells of dizziness. He had to wear glasses for reading. The last letter he had sent Mrs. Gilchrist was from Brooklyn, where he spent two months in the spring of 1872, trying to shake off, without the assistance of doctors (whom his long immunity had caused him to distrust), the recurring spells which told him that all was not well within. Again, in the middle of that summer, he went home to rest. The final blow came in January. Some years later he told a friend how it had happened.

"On the night of the 22d of February, 1873, I was in the Treasury building in Washington; outside it was raining, sleeting, and quite cold and dark. The office was comfortable, and I had a good fire. I was lazily reading Bulwer's 'What Will He Do With It?' But I did not feel well, and put aside the book several times. I remained at the office until pretty late. My lodging-room was about a hundred yards down the street. At last I got up to go home. At the door of the Treasury one of the friendly group of guards asked me what ailed me, and said I looked quite ill. He proposed to let a man take his place while he would convey me home. I said, No, I can go well enough. He again said he would go with me, but I again declined. Then he went down the steps and stood at the door with his lantern until I reached the house where I lived. I walked up to my room and went to bed and to sleep—woke up about three or four o'clock and found that I could not move my left arm or leg—did not feel particularly uneasy about it—was in no pain and even did not seem to be very ill—thought it would pass off—went to sleep again and slept till daylight. Then, however, I found that I could not get up—could not move. After several hours, some friends came in, and they immediately sent for a doctor—fortunately a very good one, Dr. W. B. Drinkard. He looked very grave—thought my condition markedly serious. I did not think so: I supposed the attack would pass off soon—but it did not."

Three months before, Whitman's mother, now approaching eighty, had failed in health and had been taken to Camden, New

Jersey, to spend her few remaining days with George, who was engaged in business there. Whitman knew that he must con-. ceal from his mother the serious nature of his illness, lest he aggravate her own. The same tenderness which had enforced his silence towards Mrs. Gilchrist expressed itself in a forced cheerfulness in the letters he wrote every day or two from his sick bed to his mother.

"Dearest Mother, I wrote you Sunday enclosing the $20, which I suppose you rec'd all safe.

"I am still anchored here in my bed—I am sitting up now on the side—Mrs. O'Connor has just been to see me—I was glad to see her—I am still improving, but slowly—the doctor did not come yesterday, which I suppose is a good sign—I expect him this afternoon or evening—he evidently thinks I am on the gain—Pete has just come in, & will take this to the p.o. for me—Love to you dear mother, & to all."

But fate, having dealt largely with Whitman, seemed now determined to break him, body and spirit. Jeff's wife, Martha, to whom Walt was devoted, was dying of consumption in St. Louis. The end came but a few weeks after his stroke. His reason told him, and he comforted his mother, that she was better off; but his heart would be appeased no more easily than Mrs. Gilchrist's. "Poor Martha—the thoughts of her still come up in my mind, as I sit here a great deal of the time alone— Poor Jeff, & poor children too——."

But as the early spring of the South began to make glad the earth with bird and leaf, Whitman gradually grew able to shuffle along to a street car for a ride, or to the office to read and write letters, though he could not take up his regular tasks. His mother, however, rapidly failed, till Walt grew alarmed.

"Dear mother, I feel very anxious about you—it is very distressing to have the nervous system affected, it always makes one feel so discouraged, that is the worst of it— Mother I am afraid you are more unwell than you say—I think about it night & day—the enclosed letter came to me yesterday—Jeff sent it to me, by mistake (may-be one for me has gone to you)—

I got another letter from Jeff today—all are well— Jeff too is anxious about you— Mother try to write a line soon after you get this— I am writing this in the office— Mother I shall come on."

A few days later, the last of May, he hastened by train to her bedside. He looked for the last time into eyes which had found more deep and abiding affection in his own than ever had any one else. When she died, he had less to live for. Two years later, preparing for publication a collection of his miscellaneous prose writings, the thought of her was more real to him than his new book. "I occupy myself, arranging these pages for publication, still enveloped in thoughts of the death two years since of my dear Mother, the most perfect and magnetic character, the rarest combination of practical, moral and spiritual, and the least selfish, of all and any I have ever known—and by me O so much the most deeply loved."

Her death was necessary for Whitman fully to realize how great had been Mrs. Whitman's influence on him. In the many letters he wrote to her during his war-time ministrations, describing each wounded boy as though they had a common motherly interest in him, it is easy to see that Whitman and his mother were comrades. He approximated her own kindness and comprehension, her own unselfish bestowal of herself on others. But when she died, he realized what she had been to him in the days when his own emotional life had been less self-contained, his self-reliance less sure. His early egotism was a subconscious protection against a sense of inferiority. At that time, though sympathizing with him without comprehension, she had been essential to his happiness and his peace. The contrast which her Dutch wholesomeness presented to the rather ineffectual, if not morbid, spirit of her husband— if one may judge from their records and portraits—must have given her added influence in shaping the ideals of Walt. And if he found in his physical make-up, not only her physique but a certain softness, a certain intuitiveness, a certain passive content with the senses that was in her, it is not strange that he should have loved her by far the most. And this attachment was the more powerful for not being a thing of the mind. He has repeatedly referred to her as a "perfect mother," but there is little evidence, other than his testimony, that she was a remarkable woman. For instance, she was unable to spell or punctuate the simplest letter, unable to discuss books or art in any way. This was a decided disadvantage for the young self-made poet. But does he deplore it? Not at all, he glorifes in it, and thinks of her as one of the "powerful uneducated persons" who were to be the backbone of his ideal democracy. So close was the emotional connection between them that he is content to describe her in general terms that mean so much to him but little to the reader. We have to thank Mrs. Whitman for much that is characteristic in her son, much that is noble; but for much also that is unpolished and inarticulate. Franklin's father, though an uneducated middle-class candle-maker, was able to guide his son, by sheer common sense and knowledge of the world, toward that career which so adequately expressed his talents. But Mrs. Whitman, in somewhat the same situation, could but encourage her son to follow whatever inward light was in him. Had she been a woman of information and intelligence, we might have had something not only more perfect in "Leaves of Grass," but something more perfectly suited to the needs of America. Nevertheless, in his purely personal relationship to his mother, Whitman, from first to last, displayed a filial devotion which is more beautiful than any book he could have written; and we are content to let the man take precedence over his art.

The sun has yet a long journey to the horizon, but unmistakably it is now descending. The great hours of Whitman's labor and love have come and gone. No more will the weak and wounded lean upon his body for strength. The time has come for him to be old—at fifty-four. Nor from that "wounded brain" will his fancy again set sail for the daring passage to India. He may now read with understanding a poem by his first "master," written a few years before.

It is time to be old,
To take in sail:—
The god of bounds,
Who sets to seas a shore,
Came to me in his fatal rounds,
And said, "No more!
No farther shoot
Thy broad ambitious branches, and thy root.
Fancy departs: no more invent;
Contract thy firmament
To compass of a tent."

BOOK VII

THE LONG AFTERNOON

IKE other original poetic geniuses, Whitman had achieved his best effects by expressing through the talents of maturity the spirit of youth. But to the modern mind, such a genius is limited in its influence by reason of its apparent uniqueness. We are disposed to demand that a leader show himself of like passions with other men, tempted by like trials and confronted by like problems. Whitman's comparative freedom from responsibility, and his truly marvelous health, while they seemed adequate cause for his optimism and buoyant courage, detracted somewhat from his influence as an exemplar. But now, like Job, he is to be subjected to what was, for him, the greatest of trials. The loss of his position in the Attorney-General's Department, which occurred when after eighteen months of illness there was no indication of his recovery, was not taken much to heart. "Beyond the independence of a little sum laid aside for burial-money, and of a few clapboards around and shingles overhead on a lot of American soil owned, and the easy dollars that supply the year's plain clothing and meals," he had declared in beginning his poetic mission, the great poet need have no financial care. And this much, for the time at least, he had. But a greater trial would be in his illness; not the unaccustomed pain, though the power to suffer gracefully is hard to acquire in age, but the limitation such illness would place on his mixing with the people who most inspired him, and on basking in the smile of nature, quite as essential to his spirit as food was to his body. The illness would go deeper even than that, for it would cause lassitude, distress in the brain, all but robbing him of his creative power. Perhaps now he would never be able to complete his poetic design, or even to bring together his fugitive writings so as clearly to indicate it. To detail the events of nine-

teen years of this invalidism would be as unnecessary as it were tedious, yet we cannot complete our picture of Whitman without showing how he stood this trial.

For eleven years Whitman was forced to make his home with George, in Camden. He was not looked upon as a dependent, and he was treated with fraternal kindness. George's wife, an excellent woman, was as considerate of his welfare as his own sisters could have been. Nevertheless, it was necessity rather than choice which stranded the old rover in such quiet and unfrequented waters. Making for the seacoast, on his doctor's orders, he had found himself too weak to get there. Whitman was, of course, in no position to say so, but in George he saw that American bourgeoisie against which, despite his championship of the "average man," his poetry was aimed, and despite his glorification of the heroic qualities which that "average man" had displayed in the war—none more than George Whitman. But men like George were unable to pioneer for a better world, unable even to protect the liberty already gained, since to their unimaginative minds liberty meant little more than comfortable convention. "George believes in pipes, not in poems," he said, adding that none of his immediate family ever knew what he was really up to in his poetry. Very different this from the conversations with Burroughs and O'Connor and his newspaper friends in Washington, and sadly different his present room, that in which his mother had died, from the exhilarating walks along the Potomac in the mystical moonlight. But, dragging his paralyzed left leg along with his cane, and followed by his dog—apparently the first pet he has ever had or needed—he would make his way to the street car. It was a shabby substitute for the Broadway stages, or even for the Washington cars where he had been saluted daily by persons of importance. But he had not lost his faculty for making friends, and soon he had installed himself as a patron deity on the driver's platform; or he would ply back and forth on the ferries to Philadelphia. He would sometimes kill an afternoon hour in the Mercantile Library, and he gradually found his way to the printing offices.

There, as he grew stronger, he would set up the rare poems he composed, or the more numerous prose pieces, reminiscent of the last thrilling years of his life, and send them off to be printed in the "Graphic" or elsewhere. A few months after the death of his mother, George moved into a more spacious house that he had built on Stevens Street (for George was prospering in business, and had the ideals of the man who prospers). Here Whitman installed himself on the top floor, where was plenty of sunshine. But he was lonely, and to ease his loneliness he wrote letters to Pete Doyle. For a time he was able to believe that his malady would pass. Nothing in his life had as yet taught him that disease could conquer the constitution which he believed invulnerable. He was prejudiced against medicine; but it is doubtful whether medicine could have cured him. At length he seems to have given up hope. The prose sketches of Washington were without traces of despondency, were as vivid and as suggestive as ever, yet he felt it time to sing a song of farewell ere his muse, his "Fancy," should depart. For the very reason that he had chosen to think little about his income, he was the more depressed when it stopped altogether. He might write Doyle, week after week, that he would yet resume their free comradeship together, but the dismissal from his clerkship was a stubborn fact. And at the same time, his agents in New York began to swindle him of his small profits on the sale of his books.

In the summer of 1872 he was invited to recite a commencement poem at Tufts College, in Massachusetts. For this occasion he wrote the "Song of the Universal," though he was unable to make the journey to Massachusetts to read the poem in person. "By common consent," he wrote a few years later, "there is nothing better for man or woman than a perfect and noble life, morally without flaw, happily balanced in activity, physically sound and pure, giving its due proportion, and no more, to the sympathetic, the human emotional element—a life, in these, unhasting, unresting, untiring to the end. And yet there is another shape of personality dearer far to the artist-sense, (which likes the play of strongest lights and shades), where the perfect character, the good, the heroic, although never attain'd, is never lost sight of, but through failures, sorrows, temporary downfalls, is return'd to again and again, and while often violated, is passionately adhered to as long as mind, muscles, voice, obey the power we call volition. This sort of personality we see more or less in Burns, Byron, Schiller, and George Sand." And of course he meant, in Walt Whitman, and the America of which he was the rightful poet. So he would sing, in simple, lyric lines, the song of faith, of amelioration.

I.

Come, said the Muse,
Sing me a song no poet yet has chanted,
Sing me the Universal.

In this broad Earth of ours,
Amid the measureless grossness and the slag,
Enclosed and safe within its central heart,
Nestles the seed Perfection.

By every life a share; or more or less,
None born but it is born,—conceal'd or unconceal'd the seed is waiting.

2.

Lo! keen-eyed, towering Science,
As from tall peaks the Modern overlooking,
Successive, absolute fiats issuing.

Yet again, lo! the Soul, above all science;
For it, has History gather'd like a husk around the globe;
For it, the entire star-myriads roll through the sky.

In spiral routes, by long detours,
(As a much-tacking ship upon the sea,)

For it, the partial to the permanent flowing,
For it, the Real to the Ideal tends.

For it, the mystic evolution;
Not the right only justified,—what we call evil also justified.

Forth from their masks, no matter what,
From the huge festering trunk—from craft and guile and tears,
Health to emerge, and joy—joy universal.

Out of the bulk, the morbid and the shallow,
Out of the bad majority—the varied countless frauds of men and States,
Electric, antiseptic yet—cleaving, suffusing all,
Only the Good is universal.

3.

Over the mountain growths, disease and sorrow,
An uncaught bird is ever hovering, hovering,
High in the purer, happier air.

From imperfection's murkiest cloud,
Darts always forth one ray of perfect light,
One flash of Heaven's glory.

To fashion's, custom's discord,
To the mad Babel-din, the deafening orgies,
Soothing each lull, a strain is heard, just heard,
From some far shore, the final chorus sounding.

4.

O the blest eyes! the happy hearts!
That see—that know the guiding thread so fine,
Along the mighty labyrinth!

5.

And thou, America!
For the Scheme's culmination—its Thought and its Reality,
For these, (not for thyself,) Thou hast arrived.
Thou too surroundest all,

Embracing, carrying, welcoming all, Thou too, by pathways broad and
new,
To the Ideal tendest.

The measur'd faiths of other lands—the grandeurs of the past,
Are not for Thee—but grandeurs of Thine own;
Deific faiths and amplitudes, absorbing, comprehending all,
All eligible to all.

All, all for immortality!
Love, like the light, silently wrapping all!
Nature's amelioration blessing all!
The blossoms, fruits of ages,—orchards divine and certain;
Forms, objects, growths, humanities, to Spiritual Images ripening.

6.

Give me, O God, to sing that thought!
Give me—give him or her I love, this quenchless faith
In Thy ensemble. Whatever else withheld, withhold not from us,
Belief in plan of Thee enclosed in Time and Space;
Health, peace, salvation universal.

Is it a dream?
Nay, but the lack of it the dream,
And, failing it, life's lore and wealth a dream,
And all the world a dream.

About this time he wrote for "Harper's" the "Song of
the Redwood Tree," making still more personal his valedictory.

Farewell my brethren,
Farewell O earth and sky, farewell ye neighboring waters,
My time has ended, my term has come.

With appropriate symbolism, the mighty poet, about to fall
and "leave a lonesome place against the sky," identifies himself with the "mighty tree its death-chant chanting," and shares
a dignity with the woods and waves.

Nor yield we mournfully majestic brothers,
We who have grandly fill'd our time;

With Nature's calm content, with tacit huge delight,
We welcome what we fought for through the past,
And leave the field for them.
For them predicted long,
For a superber race, they too to grandly fill their time,
For them we abdicate, in them ourselves ye forest kings!

And then, retiring to his closet, he addresses his last great song
to his God.   Again symbolism, modest and sincere.   It is the
prayer of Columbus he sings, and has a right to sing.   The
theme had engaged the attention of American writers from the
first, who with Columbiads, sonnets on Columbus, narratives of
his voyages and what not had thought to pay him a compliment
from the world he had discovered.   But the bow of Ulysses will
bend only in the hands of Ulysses.   Poets and professional writers, borrowing the very verse forms they employed, and discovering no new world for themselves, could not hope to do justice
to a theme so sublime.   But with the unconscious assurance of
great power, Whitman sings the song of Columbus, and of all
great pioneers.   When Anne Gilchrist received a copy of the
poem, she wrote him a hasty note, the more eloquent for its brevity.

"March 9th, 1874.

"With full heart, with eyes wet with tears of joy & I know not
what other deep emotion—pain of yearning pity blent with sense
of grandeur—dearest Friend, have I read and reread the great,
sacred Poem just come to me.   O august Columbus! whose sorrows, sufferings, struggles are more to be envied than any triumph of conquering warrior—as I see him in your poem his figure merges into yours, brother of Columbus.   Completer of his
work, discoverer of the spiritual, the ideal America—you too
have sailed over stormy seas to your goal—surrounded with
mocking disbelievers—you too have paid the price of health—
our Columbus.

"Your accents pierce me through and through."

"Your loving Annie."

A batter'd, wreck'd old man,
Thrown on this savage shore, far, far from home,
Pent by the sea and dark rebellious brows, twelve dreary months,
Sore, stiff with many toils, sicken'd and nigh to death,
I take my way along the island's edge,
Venting a heavy heart.

I am too full of woe!
Haply I may not live another day;
I cannot rest O God, I cannot eat or drink or sleep,
Till I put forth myself, my prayer, once more to Thee,
Breathe, bathe myself once more in Thee, commune with Thee,
Report myself once more to Thee.

     . . . .

All my emprises have been fill'd with Thee,
My speculations, plans, begun and carried on in thought of Thee,
Sailing the deep or journeying the land for Thee;
Intentions, purports, aspirations mine, leaving results to Thee.

O I am sure they really came from Thee,
The urge, the ardor, the unconquerable will,
The potent, felt, interior command, stronger than words,
A message from the Heavens whispering to me even in sleep,
These sped me on.

     . . . .

One effort more, my altar this bleak sand;
That Thou O God my life hast lighted,
With ray of light, steady, ineffable, vouchsafed of Thee,
Light rare untellable, lighting the very light,
Beyond all signs, descriptions, languages;
For that O God, be it my latest word, here on my knees,
Old, poor, and paralyzed, I thank Thee.

     . . . .

My hands, my limbs grow nerveless,
My brain feels rack'd, bewilder'd,
Let the old timbers part, I will not part,
I will cling fast to Thee, O God, though the waves buffet me,
Thee, Thee at least I know.

Were this the story of a demi-god, as some have told it, and not that of a very human man, the end should come at this point. It invites apotheosis. But with the passing of this gloomy year, and the next, passed also the worst of his present illness. He wrote little to Mrs. Gilchrist, though she continued to write. With characteristic assurance that her affection was returned in kind, she seems to have taken his present of a ring as a sort of betrothal, and writes now as an intimate. Were she not kept in England by the necessity of caring for her own invalid mother and her children, she would have come to America at once on hearing of Walt's illness, that she might care for him. Besides she hoped that her children might grow up in the America which she had idealized from his poetic descriptions. But if he did not write, he did send her newspapers and magazines. On these she begged him to underscore the word "London" in the address whenever he was improving in health, so hungry was her heart for grounds of hope. He seldom did. And when, conversing with Moncure Conway in December, 1875, she learned from the latter, who had recently visited Whitman, that the poet had given up all hope of recovery, she did her best to nurse his discouraged spirit, unwilling to be cheated, even by Death himself, of that brief human happiness she had for six years thought hers by right. "Those words [of Mr. Conway] were like a sharp knife plunged into me—they choked me with bitter tears. Don't give up that hope for the sake of those that so tenderly, passionately, love you—would give their lives with joy for you. O cling to life with a resolute hold, my beloved, to bless us with your presence [—] unspeakably dear, beneficent presence—me to taste of it before so very long now—thirsting, pining, loving me."

Just how much Whitman may have been stimulated by this appeal to his hope and his pity, we do not know; but a few months later he had taken a new lease on life, his malady yielding in a measure to a different regimen. By the middle of 1876 Whitman was able to betake himself to Whitehorse, a hamlet ten or twelve miles from Camden, toward the sea. Here he boarded with a farmer, named Stafford, at various times during the ensuing summers. The family was fond of Whitman, and while they did not understand his poetry, seemed to understand the man, and his needs. By day or night, the broken poet was allowed to consort with Nature, as he would. Not far from the house ran Timber Creek, protected by woodland, where Whitman varied his sun baths with baths in the mud of a marl pit. Far from cruel eyes, the din of contending critics, the noisy activity of the city, he here lay down in confidence on the breast of Nature, and she crooned and soothed him back to partial health. And as if determined to wrest some poetic advantage even from his convalescence, Whitman became sensitive, as never before, to the intimate, friendly spirit of a Nature which had always been to him a trifle august. His habit of recording his impressions again asserts itself. Let us take from his cheerful diary a few specimen days.

"After you have exhausted what there is in business, politics, conviviality, love, and so on—have found that none of these finally satisfy, or permanently wear—what remains? Nature remains; to bring out from their torpid recesses, the affinities of a man or woman with the open air, the trees, fields, the changes of seasons—the sun by day, and the stars of heaven by night. We will begin from these convictions. Literature flies so high and is so hotly spiced, that our notes may seem hardly more than breaths of common air, or draughts of water to drink. But that is part of our lesson.

"Dear, soothing, healthy, restoration-hours—after three confining years of paralysis—after the long strain of the war, and its wounds and death."

"Away then to loosen, to unstring the divine bow, so tense, so long. Away, from curtain, carpet, sofa, book—from 'society' —from city house, street, and modern improvements and luxuries—away to the primitive winding, aforementioned wooded creek, with its untrimm'd bushes and turfy banks—away from ligatures, tight boots, buttons, and the whole cast-iron civilized life—from entourage of artificial store, machine, studio, office, parlor—from tailordom and fashion's clothes—from any clothes, perhaps, for the nonce, the summer heats advancing, there in those watery, shaded solitudes. Away, thou soul, (let me pick thee out singly, reader dear, and talk in perfect freedom, negligently, confidentially,) for one day and night at least, returning to the naked source-life of us all—to the breast of the great silent savage all-acceptive Mother. Alas! how many of us are so sodden—how many of us have wander'd so far away, that return is almost impossible."

He sits up through the night, listening to the flight of migrating birds, not, like Audubon, to estimate their number, but to pick out the familiar voices of his unseen friends. By day he strolls down to his tryst at the creek, drinking in health and joy through every sense and pore, as in his youth.

"The wild cherry and pear-blows—the wild violets, their blue eyes looking up and saluting my feet, as I saunter the wood-edge —the rosy blush of budding apple-trees—the light-clear emerald hue of the wheat-fields—the darker green of the rye—a warm elasticity pervading the air—the cedar-bushes profusely deck'd with their little brown apples—the summer fully awakening— the convocation of black birds, garrulous flocks of them, gathering on some tree, and making the hour and place noisy as I sit near."

"Nature marches in procession, in sections, like the corps of an army. All have done much for me, and still do. But for the last two days it has been the great wild bee, the humble-bee, or 'bumble,' as the children call him. As I walk, or hobble, from the farm-house down to the creek, I traverse the before-mentioned lane, fenced by old rails, with many splits, splinters, breaks, holes, &c., the choice habitat of those crooning, hairy insects. Up and down and by and between these rails, they swarm and dart and fly in countless myriads. As I wend slowly along, I am often accompanied with a moving cloud of them. They play a leading part in my morning, midday or sunset rambles, and often dominate the landscape in a way I never before thought of—fill the long lane, not by scores or hundreds only, but by thousands. Large and vivacious and swift, with wonderful momentum and a loud swelling, perpetual hum, varied now and then by something almost like a shriek, they dart to and fro, in rapid flashes, chasing each other, and (little things as they are,) conveying to me a new and pronounc'd sense of strength, beauty, vitality and movement. . . .

"As I write, I am seated under a big wild-cherry tree—the warm day temper'd by partial clouds and a fresh breeze, neither too heavy nor light—and here I sit long and long, envelop'd in the deep musical drone of these bees, flitting, balancing, darting to and fro about me by hundreds—big fellows with light yellow jackets, great glistening swelling bodies, stumpy heads and gauzy wings—humming their perpetual rich mellow boom. (Is there not a hint in it for a musical composition, of which it should be the back-ground? some bumble-bee symphony?)"

That peculiarly American insect—"hot midsummer's petted crone"—which so pleased Emerson with its epicurean philosophy, seems, not only in a passage like this, written with Thoreau's accuracy and far more than Thoreau's sympathy, but also in much of his early poetry to create the background of his own musical composition. Now an evening piece:

"And still the clear notes of the quail—the quiver of leaf-shadows over the paper as I write—the sky aloft, with white clouds, and the sun well declining to the west—the swift darting of many sand-swallows coming and going, their holes in a neighboring marl-bank—the odor of the cedar and oak, so palpable, as evening approaches—perfume, color, the bronze-and-gold of nearly ripen'd wheat—clover fields, with honey scent—the well-up maize, with long and rustling leaves—the great patches of thriving potatoes, dusky green, fleck'd all over with white blossoms—the old, warty, venerable oak above me—and ever, mix'd with the dual notes of the quail, the soughing of the wind through some near-by pines.

"As I rise for return, I linger long to a delicious song-epilogue (is it the hermit-thrush?) from some bushy recess off there in the swamp, repeated leisurely and pensively over and over again. This, to the circle-gambols of the swallows flying by dozens in concentric rings in the last rays of sunset, like flashes of some airy wheel."

Or take something more mystical, more pantheistic:

"But now pleasantly imprison'd here under the big oak—the rain dripping, and the sky cover'd with leaden clouds—nothing but the pond on one side, and the other a spread of grass, spotted with the milky blossoms of the wild carrot—the sound of an axe wielded at some distant wood-pile—yet in this dull scene, (as most folks would call it,) why am I so (almost) happy here and alone? Why would any intrusion, even from people I like, spoil the charm? But am I alone? Doubtless there comes a time—perhaps it has come to me—when one feels through his whole being, and pronouncedly the emotional part, that identity between himself subjectively and Nature objectively which Schelling and Fichte are so fond of pressing. How it is I know not, but I often realize a presence here—in clear moods I am certain of it, and neither chemistry nor reasoning nor esthetics will give the least explanation. All the past two summers it has been strengthening and nourishing my sick body and soul, as never before. Thanks, invisible physician, for thy silent delicious medicine, thy day and night, thy water and thy airs, the banks, the grass, the trees, and e'en the weeds."

That was a mood which Wordsworth could have understood, or the Greek poets. To get it would be worth having been "suckled in a creed outworn"; only Whitman found it perfectly consonant with the most modern creeds. "I had a sort of dream-trance the other day, in which I saw my favorite trees step out and promenade up, down and around, very curiously— with a whisper from one, leaning down as he pass'd me, *We do all this on the present occasion, exceptionally, just for you.*" Few poets go farther in recalling to us the vanishing perceptions of childhood.

These leaves torn from "Specimen Days" not only indicate
the method of Whitman's restoration and the source of his
sweetness of spirit, but they reveal, too, how much his prose
has improved by contact with his increasingly meticulous verse.
A final passage will record his reaction to the more majestic aspects of nature, and show how, like a musician rather than a
painter, he transferred the mood of the sea to his written page.

"One bright December mid-day lately I spent down on the
New Jersey sea-shore, reaching it by a little more than an hour's
railroad trip over the old Camden and Atlantic. I had started
betimes, fortified by nice strong coffee, and a good breakfast
(cook'd by the hands I love, my dear sister Lou's—how much
better it makes the victuals taste, and then assimilate, strengthen
you, perhaps makes the whole day comfortable afterwards).
Five or six miles at the last, our track enter'd a broad region of
salt grass meadows, intersected by lagoons, and cut up everywhere by watery runs. The sedgy perfume, delightful to my
nostrils, reminded me of 'the mash' and south bay of my native
island. I could have journey'd contentedly till night through
these flat and odorous sea-prairies. . . . After dinner (as there
were nearly two hours to spare) I walked off in another direction, (hardly met or saw a person,) and taking possession
of what appear'd to have been the reception-room of an old
bath-house range, had a broad expanse of view all to myself—
quaint, refreshing, unimpeded—a dry area of sedge and Indian
grass immediately before and around me—space, simple, un-
ornamented space. Distant vessels, and the far-off, just visible
trailing smoke of an inward bound steamer; more plainly, ships,
brigs, schooners, in sight, most of them with every sail set to the
firm and steady wind.

"The attractions, fascinations there are in sea and shore!
How one dwells on their simplicity, even vacuity! What is it in
us, arous'd by those indirections and directions? That spread
of waves and gray-white beach, salt, monotonous, senseless—such
an entire absence of art, books, talk, elegance—so indescribably
comforting, even this winter day—grim, yet so delicate-looking,

so spiritual—striking emotional, impalpable depths, subtler than
all the poems, paintings, music, I have ever read, seen, heard.
(Yet let me be fair, perhaps it is because I have read those
poems and heard that music.)

"Even as a boy, I had the fancy, the wish, to write a piece,
perhaps a poem, about the sea-shore—that suggesting, dividing
line, contact, junction, the solid marrying the liquid—that curious, lurking something, (as doubtless every objective form finally
becomes to the subjective spirit,) which means far more than its
mere first sight, grand as that is—blending the real and ideal,
and each made portion of the other.   Hours, days, in my Long
Island youth and early manhood, I haunted the shores of Rock-
away or Coney island, or away east to the Hamptons or Montauk.   Once, at the latter place, (by the old lighthouse, nothing
but sea-tossings in sight in every direction as far as the eye could
reach), I remember well, I felt that I must one day write a
book expressing this liquid, mystic theme.   Afterward, I recol-
lect, how it came to me that instead of any lyrical or epical or literary attempt, the sea-shore should be an invisible *influence,* a
pervading gauge and tally for me, in my composition.   (Let me
give a hint here to young writers.   I am not sure but I have un-
wittingly follow'd out the same rule with other powers besides
sea and shores—avoiding them, in the way of any dead set at
poetizing them, as too big for formal handling—quite satisfied
if I could indirectly show that we have met and fused, even if
only once, but enough—that we have really absorb'd each other
and understand each other.)"

The year 1876 was being celebrated, especially at Philadelphia, as the centennial of the signing of the Declaration of Independence, from which Whitman had, in his third edition, affected
to date all things American.   Sidney Lanier was to write his
"Psalm of the West" as a cantata for the opening of the exposition.   Whitman felt that he himself was the man who should
have done that, if only he had been in his prime.   But at least
he would bring out a new and handsome edition.   It would be

a birthday gift to his country—and might bring in some sorely needed revenue. It was to be in two volumes, this "Author's Edition," in half leather, with photographs of the poet and his autograph in each set. The first volume, a reprint of the 1871 edition, which had not sold, was called "Leaves of Grass." The other volume, "Two Rivulets," contained both prose and poetry, incorporating "Democratic Vistas," "As a Strong Bird on Pinions Free," and "Passage to India," and publishing for the first time in collected form, the "Memoranda during the War" which he had projected in 1863, a group of "Centennial Songs" (in which the American Institute Poem was rededicated to the Philadelphia Exposition), and other fugitive prose and poetry written since his last volume. The title was meant to suggest, not so much the blending of prose and verse, as two themes; first, speculations on political and literary conditions in America, and second, a realistic and imaginative treatment of death and immortality. It was not a symmetrical book; but at least it brought together, as best the author could in his illness, the writings which he thought would endure.

Somewhat to his surprise, the book sold, fairly well in America, much more rapidly in England. This foreign success was due partly to the active solicitation of Rossetti and Mrs. Gilchrist, partly to an international squabble concerning the new edition and especially concerning the alleged neglect of Whitman by American publishers and critics. We have seen that from the first Whitman found it hard to bear with equanimity his lack of popularity in America. This is sufficiently revealed in his willingness to write or to influence reviews of his work. But the impatience of his friends was greater than his own. And now that he was marooned in Camden, and in need of cash, it was natural, though hardly heroic, for him to let this feeling grow. He was naïve enough not to trace it logically to his physical and financial debâcle. In January, 1876, appeared an article in the *West Jersey Press* which the student of Whitman will recognize as inspired, if not actually written, by him. It complained of the neglect of his books. "They had been met,

and are met to-day, with the determined denial, disgust and scorn
of orthodox American authors, publishers and editors, and, in a
pecuniary and worldly sense, have certainly wrecked the life of
their author. . . . But the poet himself is more resolute and
persevering than ever." The article was quoted in the London
"Athenæum," and provoked Robert Buchanan, in the London
Daily News, to excoriate Americans on this neglect. Such was
the beginning of a wrangle which occupied the British and
American press for some weeks. Bayard Taylor and George
William Curtis protested that Whitman had the same opportunity that other writers had in getting his work published, and
that his "neglect" had been shared by many of our great
authors. It was possible for him to have no regular publisher,
they said, or to have poems returned by editors, without the necessity of assuming that any conspiracy existed to suppress him.
Burroughs went to the defense of Buchanan and Whitman; and
even Alfred Austin, who saw little in Whitman's verse form
but highly respected the man for his war service, wrote to the
press in his favor. All of this was publicity, though certainly
not of a sort that Whitman could have calculated on, or desired.
The real returns came more privately. Rossetti wrote to Whitman to get the facts, asking how his British friends might aid
him. In part, this was Whitman's reply:

"I am jogging along still about the same in physical condition
—still certainly no worse, and I sometimes lately suspect rather
better, or at any rate more adjusted to the situation. Even begin to think of making some move, some change of base, &c.:
the doctors have been advising it for over two years, but I
haven't felt to do it yet. My paralysis does not lift—I cannot
walk any distance—I still have this baffling, obstinate, apparently
chronic affection of the stomachic apparatus and liver: yet I get
out of doors a little every day—write and read in moderation—
appetite sufficiently good—(eat only plain food, but always did
that)—digestion tolerable—spirits unflagging. . . .

"My dear friend, your offers of help, and those of my other
British friends, I think I fully appreciate, in the right spirit,

welcome and acceptive—leaving the matter altogether in your and their hands, and to your and their convenience, discretion, leisure, and nicety. Though poor now, even to penury, I have not so far been deprived of any physical thing I need or wish whatever, and I feel confident I shall not in the future. During my employment of seven years or more in Washington after the war (1865–'72) I regularly saved part of my wages: and, though the sum has now become about exhausted by my expenses of the last three years, there are already beginning at present welcome dribbles hitherward from the sales of my new edition, which I job and sell, myself, (all through this illness, my book-agents for three years in New York successively, badly cheated me,) and shall continue to dispose of my books myself. And *that* is the way I should prefer to glean my support. In that way I cheerfully accept all the aid my friends find it convenient to proffer."

Rossetti and Mrs. Gilchrist bestirred themselves to get subscribers, once they had Whitman's permission to do so. The response was immediate, and cheered Whitman in his hour of gloom, not only with the inflow of money enough to serve him for some years, but with the proof that he had made a strong impression in England. Among those who subscribed, some sending two or three times the high price asked for the books, were the Rossettis, Mrs. Gilchrist, Lord Houghton, Edward Dowden, Edward Carpenter, Tennyson, Ruskin, Gosse, T. W. Rolleston, George Saintsbury, Moncure Conway, J. H. McCarthy, Madox Brown, G. H. Lewes, and E. J. A. Balfour.

But while Mrs. Gilchrist was giving this testimonial of her loyalty and her desire to be of real service, her mind was chiefly engrossed with a plan to come to America, where she seems to have counted on finding a lover if not a husband—aged and broken in health, to be sure, but yet a fulfillment of her now familiar dream.

This Whitman did not desire, either on her account or on his. He must have disliked being forced into a position from which he could not retreat. He must now have regretted his efforts to be kind, to break to her gently the fact that his heart was not at her disposal, perhaps not at his own. In the very letter in which he advised her of having sent her a set of the Centennial Edition, he insisted, in italics: "My dearest friend, *I do not approve your American trans-settlement. I see so many things here you have no idea of—the social, and almost every other kind of crudeness, meagreness, here (at least in appearance). Don't do anything towards it nor resolve in it nor make any move at all in it without further advice from me. If I should get well enough to voyage, we will talk about it yet in London.*"

Anything at all to stop her; even the polite fiction about his going to London. Anything, that is, short of wounding her with the plain fact that she could not expect to find in him what her imagination had put there. But it would not work. What was crudeness to one who was in love? And what even his express command—when she was in love, not with him, but with her dream? Her mother had died the year before, and her eldest son, Percy, was shortly to have a home of his own. Beatrice, her other daughter, could complete her medical education in Philadelphia, which she could not do in London, and the trip would be good for her young artist son, Herbert. And so, packing up her household goods as if she meant to spend the rest of her days in America, she took ship and arrived in Philadelphia in September, 1876.

The story of their meeting would be illuminating, but neither Whitman nor Mrs. Gilchrist has left any record of it. He being the man he was, and she being a woman, this meeting must have defined and clarified their relationship better than letters, or even spoken words, could ever do. Did Whitman cross to Philadelphia to meet the ship on which she had sailed? Or did she have to pay the first visit, like a pilgrim, instead of receiving it like a lover courted? We do not know, but may be permitted to guess he chose the latter alternative. Whitman, if not uneasy about the meeting, was at least a little on the defensive. He preferred to let the whole journey seem a pilgrimage. That part he could act, without risk to his independence and with the least possible danger of wounding a woman who had cast such a tribute at his feet. Were this the story of Anne Gilchrist, imagination would insist on picturing the hopes and fears that must have warred for the mastery in her breast as she approached the hour of which, for seven years, she had dreamed, the hour which would either give to airy nothings a local habitation or else show them to be what they were. But ours is the story of the invalid poet pursued. Fortunately for him, the very ambiguity in his book which precipitated this anomalous situation made it possible for him to extricate himself. He had but to continue to act the part of a poet, and after a few painful moments, all would be well. Provided only she should not have the power of fascinating him as she had hypnotized herself. Even there, Whitman was fortified; he had learned the limitations of personal fascination, and he had known enough beautiful women to be able to see at once that Mrs. Gilchrist's charm was more of the mind and soul than of the face or figure. She herself seemed to realize this, and to put her best foot foremost. Nevertheless there was something sublime in her foolish courage. And it is necessary for the reader to know only that the bearing of both parties in this unrecorded meeting was such as to substitute a lofty yet intimate friendship for a romance which fate had not decreed. During the residence of the Gilchrists in Philadelphia Whitman was a regular, a constant, visitor, sometimes occupying for weeks the room set apart for him in their house on Twenty-second Street. Once, at least, Whitman took all the Gilchrists to the theater, to see Joaquin Miller's new play, "The Danites." Under the careful tutoring of Anne Gilchrist, and by reason of his own benignant charm, Whitman was accepted by the son and daughter as cordially as by the mother. Grace, he declared to a friend, was his favorite in the household. Other guests were invited, and the Gilchrist home took on something of the character of a modest salon. Lofty discussions of literature, of science, or history and art were for persons as old as Mrs. Gilchrist and Whitman, appropriate substitutes for the scenes of endearment on which she had dwelt in fond anticipation.   It is to Whitman's credit that, in a situation like this, he could have inspired the lady to feel, not the fury of a woman scorned, but such admiration as she expressed soon after her first meeting with Whitman in a letter she wrote to William Rossetti.

"I need not tell you that our greatest pleasure is the society of Mr. Whitman, who fully realizes the ideal I had formed from his poems, and brings such an atmosphere of cordiality and geniality with him as is indescribable.   He is really making slow, but, I trust, steady progress toward recovery, having been much cheered (and no doubt that acted favorably upon his health) by the sympathy manifested toward him in England and the pleasure of finding so many buyers of his poems there."

Mrs. Gilchrist remained in Philadelphia more than a year, before going to Boston, Concord and New York, to meet the literary society which dominated, as yet, American letters. After knowing Whitman in person for a year, she wrote Rossetti:

"We are having delightful evenings this winter; how often do I wish you could make one in the circle around our tea table where sits on my right hand every evening but Sunday Walt Whitman.   He has made great progress in health and recovered powers of getting about during the year we have been here: nevertheless the lameness—the dragging instead of lifting the left leg continues; and this together with his white hair and beard give him a look of age curiously contradicted by his face, which has not only the ruddy freshness but the full, rounded contours of youth, nowhere drawn or wrinkled or sunk; it is a face as indicative of serenity and goodness and of mental and bodily health as the brow is of intellectual power.   But I notice he occasionally speaks of himself as having a 'wounded brain,' and of being still quite altered from his former self."

At forty he had described himself as "a child, very old"; and now at fifty-six he might even the score by affirming that he was an old man, yet very young.

That Whitman was really improving in health is indicated by his ability to travel. John Burroughs, who had, since Whitman knew him in Washington, built a home at Esopus on the Hudson, met Whitman at Mrs. Gilchrist's one day in February, and accompanied him to New York. There he was the guest of Mr. J. H. Johnston and his wife, Alma Calder Johnston, both of whom loved him as a man and adored him as a poet. To spend a month in such a home was as beneficial to him as the Timber Creek loafing had been. He moved slowly along Broadway, taking the salutes of such stage drivers as remembered him, and occasionally climbing to the box for a ride; he renewed his acquaintance with the ferry pilots and deck hands; he visited the many spots dear to him by association in the days of his vigorous youth. He even submitted to a degree of lionizing, showing himself at the receptions which Johnstons held in his honor, and attending formal soirées at the Portfolio and Palette Clubs. He was invited to join the Authors Club, and though declining, was grateful for the honor. The Whitman who was so uncomfortable in evening clothes in New Orleans could now enjoy the poet's privilege—as he understood it—of dressing in strong contrast to the élite of New York society, wearing his loose sack suit of English gray, his spotless white shirt, collar open at the neck, with no necktie.

A little later in the year it began to be clear that Mrs. Gilchrist was but the first of a long line of pilgrims who were to make their way to Camden, from England and from various parts of America, to pay their homage to the poet and, returning, to champion him and his cause. Edward Carpenter came in May—Edward Carpenter whose "Towards Democracy" was to reflect, not the genius, but at least something of the spirit and method of "Leaves of Grass." Long afterwards Carpenter described this meeting with Whitman.

"Meanwhile in that first ten minutes I was becoming conscious of an impression which subsequently grew even more marked—the impression, namely, of immense vista or background in his personality. If I had thought before (and I do not know that I had) that Whitman was eccentric, unbalanced, violent, my first interview certainly produced quite a contrary effect. No one could be more considerate, I may almost say courteous; no one could have more simplicity of manner and freedom from egotistical wrigglings; and I never yet met any one who gave me more the impression of *knowing what he was doing* than he did. Yet away and beyond all this I was aware of a certain radiant power in him, a large benign effluence and inclusiveness, as of the sun, which filled the place where he was —yet with something of reserve and sadness in it too, and a sense of remoteness and inaccessibility."

In the autumn appeared a pilgrim from Canada who was to be still more closely identified with Whitman's life and fame. This was Dr. Richard Maurice Bucke, of London, who had for years been reading Whitman's poetry. At first he had been puzzled and even antagonized by the strange verse, like Mrs. Johnston, who tells of having flung the book more than once to the top shelf of the book-case with the determination to read it no more. But there was something in it which lured them both back, and made them eager to meet the author, in the hope of finding in his personality that which could only be suggested by his gnomic words. And both were won, when they had seen him. In the case of Dr. Bucke, this was not due to any explanation Whitman chose to make of himself—why should a man have to explain himself? Indeed the poet spoke perhaps a scant hundred words. Yet Dr. Bucke was "almost amazed by the beauty and majesty of his person and the gracious air of purity" that surrounded him. He was himself a remarkable man, and something of a mystic. He was at the time the head of an Insane Asylum in London, and rated a good alienist. But though the meeting with Whitman seemed in every way commonplace and ordinary, it was the occasion of a mystical experience, which he described as comparable only to the "slight intoxication of champagne, or to falling in love." "It seemed to me at that time certain that he was either actually a god or in some sense clearly and entirely præter-human." It colored Bucke's whole life, and made him Whitman's friend, host, biographer and literary executor. Indeed it led him to write a book, "Cosmic Consciousness," setting forth the opinion that those who could share the state of mind he discovered in Whitman were harbingers of a new stage of evolution. In all of this one will detect a certain ignorance of the history of religious experience, and many personal limitations and predilections. Yet it is perhaps the most striking illustration of the power that Whitman sometimes had of revealing to others their own latent mystical faculties.

The next year Whitman spent a month again with his friends, the Johnstons, who now lived opposite Central Park. The impulse to go to New York this time was due to his seeing in the paper an announcement of the death of his old friend, William Cullen Bryant. In maintaining the sacerdotal dignity of the bards they had much in common, and in their absorption in nature, their tendency to view mankind *en masse*. Whitman's fondness for individuals, however, gave him a greater range in poetizing, a greater warmth and human cheer. He belonged, also, as truly to the nineteenth century as Bryant belonged, by temperament and training, to the eighteenth.

From New York Whitman ventured on up the Hudson to enjoy a pleasant week with Burroughs. Returning, he loafed again in New York, meeting more of the young literati, and coming to see that, after all, he was not unknown, or unhonored, in his own country, his publishing failures to the contrary notwithstanding.

The next year, 1879, he repeated his New York visit, this time the excuse being an invitation to deliver a lecture on the anniversary of Lincoln's assassination. Whitman had never failed to remember the day, but now he saw in its return an opportunity to add to his income by lecturing. He attempted to tell nothing new, nor even to display any oratorical powers— indeed he sat as he read from a manuscript; yet the result of this trial lecture in an incommodious hall was such as to revive his old plan of lecturing regularly instead of depending on his pen.

The Lincoln lecture was delivered each year for thirteen years, often taking the form of a benefit for the lecturer. Especially was this the case in 1886 and 1887, when, in Philadelphia and in New York, he realized six or seven hundred dollars from each reading. In the latter case Andrew Carnegie sent a check for $350 for his box in the Madison Square Theater. Mark Twain was there, and St. Gaudens, Edmund Clarence Stedman, John Hay, General Sherman, and even James Russell Lowell, with whom he had had, temperamentally, so little in common. It was a tribute from his friends; and he was not more touched by the hotel reception which followed than he was by the appearance of Stedman's little daughter on the stage, presenting him a bouquet with the words "Mr. Whitman, here are some lilacs that in our dooryard bloom'd." As the old poet kissed her, the audience applauded.

But to return to 1879: Whitman's steady regaining of his strength is apparent in the fact that this year he took a long journey to Colorado, with some railroad friends, and the next year a still longer trip to visit Dr. Bucke in Canada, and with him to explore the grandeurs of the Saguenay. The western trip was uneventful, except for the fact that it gave him his first sight of really grand mountains, between which and his own poems he fancied a genuine resemblance. In St. Louis he stopped with Jeff for a few months, doubtless recalling how much water had flowed down the Mississippi since his 1848 journey to New Orleans with his brother. The West was rapidly fulfilling the dream of his youth, reënforcing his cheerful faith in the future.

And yet, when he went to deliver his Lincoln lecture in Boston the next year, he was forced to admit that the East was just as progressive, and in many ways retaining the preëminence of its early history. The city of Boston, for instance, was not the city he had seen in 1860. "Old Boston with its zigzag streets and multitudinous angles, (crush up a sheet of letter-paper in your hand, throw it down, stamp it flat, and that is a map of old Boston)—new Boston with its miles upon miles of large and costly houses—Beacon street, Commonwealth avenue, and a hundred others." It was the Boston about which Howells was beginning to write with such pleasant clarity—the Howells who as a young man had been charmed by Whitman's cordial handclasp in the old days at Pfaff's on Broadway. During his visit, Whitman returned a visit Longfellow had paid the invalid in Camden three years before. Though in youth he had shared the fondness of the sentimental 1840's for Longfellow, when he set out on his own poetic mission he had striven to combat the Longfellow tradition as something too imitative for America. Now, having outgrown some of his self-consciousness, he puts himself on record as including Longfellow among the "mighty four who stamp this first American century with its birthmarks of poetic literature"—Emerson first, then Longfellow, Bryant and Whittier. Longfellow he now praises "for rich color, graceful forms and incidents—all that makes life beautiful and love refined—competing with the singers of Europe on their own ground, and, with one exception, better and finer works than that of any of them."

Apparently for the first time, he saw the pictures of Millet, at the home of Mr. Quincy Shaw, and recognized at once in them the expression of a kindred spirit, a method similar to his own.

This visit probably had some connection with a letter which the poet received from a leading Boston publisher, J. R. Osgood, a few months later, proposing to bring out a new and complete "Leaves of Grass." The reader will recall that Whitman had never had but one regular publisher, the unlucky firm of Thayer and Eldridge, whose business was ruined by the Civil War. To one who had been complaining for years of his neglect at the hands of editors and publishers, such a proposal, particularly when it came from Boston, must have taken him somewhat aback. Feeling that there might be some reservation in the mind of the publisher, Whitman replied that he would be glad to have his book published—was in fact, preparing a new, one-volume edition of his poems at the moment—but that he would countenance no expurgations or omissions.   Thereupon the publisher asked to see the manuscript, which, with many minor alterations, and rearrangements, was sent, and accepted.   Later in the year Whitman returned to Boston to see the book through the press with the same affectionate particularity that had marked its every edition.

In Boston, Whitman spent much time under the elms of the Common, recalling the very words of the conversation with Emerson concerning the "Children of Adam" poems when he was preparing the 1860 edition.   He perhaps had a premonition that he had not heard the last of those poems.   And he had not.   But at the time his mind was at peace, and his hopes high. Selling books from his room in Camden was poor business, at best; but a publisher like Osgood would not have taken the book unless he was sure of making money thereby, for himself and for the author.

During his stay, Whitman found time to run out to Concord, for a short visit with his friend F. B. Sanborn.   A private reception was held for him, which the Emersons attended.

"Never had I a better piece of luck befall me," he wrote in his diary, "a long and blessed evening with Emerson, in a way I couldn't have wish'd better or different.   For nearly two hours he had been placidly sitting where I could see his face in the best light, near me.   Mrs. S.'s back-parlor well fill'd with people, neighbors, many fresh and charming faces, women, mostly young, but some old.   My friend A. B. Alcott and his daughter Louisa were there early.   A good deal of talk, the subject Henry Thoreau—some new glints of his life and fortunes, with letters to and from him—one of the best by Margaret Fuller, others by Horace Greeley, Channing, &c.—one from Thoreau himself, most quaint and interesting.   (No doubt I seem'd very stupid to the roomful of company, taking hardly any part in the conversation; but I had 'my own pail to milk in,' as the Swiss proverb puts it.)   My seat and the relative arrangement were such that, without being rude, or anything of the kind, I could just look squarely at E., which I did a good part of the two hours. On entering, he had spoken very briefly and politely to several of the company, then settled himself in his chair, a trifle push'd back, and, though a listener and apparently an alert one, remain'd silent through the whole talk and discussion. A lady friend quietly took a seat next him, to give special attention. A good color in his face, eyes clear, with the well-known expression of sweetness, and the old clear-peering aspect quite the same."

Better still was the next day, when Emerson had Whitman and the Sanborns to dinner, with other guests. Whitman looked upon this as symbolical of Emerson's unaltering approval of his work, as well as of himself, an interpretation which shows that even yet he was not quite indifferent to what the one-time "master" thought of him, or the value to himself, as advertising, of Emerson's endorsement.

In another day he visited the Manse, the battle-ground marked by French's "Minute Man," and Sleepy Hollow. "I got out [of the buggy] and went up of course on foot, and stood a long while and pondered" beside the near-together graves of Hawthorne and Thoreau. Thence to Walden Pond for another meditative hour, in which the poet carried his stone to add to the cairn which marks the spot of the hermit hut of Thoreau. It was like taking a farewell of many old friends, this Boston-Concord trip; and within the year both Emerson and Longfellow were to precede him to that life beyond concerning which his poems were more and more being composed.

True to expectations, the new edition began with a brisk sale. By March some two thousand copies had been sold; Whitman's royalties, had they been paid, would have amounted to about $500. But in May broke a storm which he may have feared, though he could not have foreseen it. The book had come to the notice of the Society for the Suppression of Vice—for Massachusetts had then as now its Comstockian agency for dealing with such matters. This society complained to State

Attorney-General Marston, and he instructed the Boston District Attorney, Oliver Stevens, to take action, more or less as a matter of routine. Stevens advised Osgood that the new book was subject to prosecution as falling "within the provisions of the Public Statutes respecting obscene literature," and stating that if it were not suppressed by the publisher action would have to be taken in the courts. Osgood, fearing the effect of such a prosecution on the reputation of his firm, asked Whitman if he were willing to cancel the passages alluded to. Again the poet was faced with the dilemma Emerson had presented two decades before. He realized that this might be his last book, and the solid gains he had so slowly effected with his poetic crusade were dear to the old and enfeebled man. Moreover, he stood in need of the royalties that were already mounting. Doubtless his experience with a world which loves nothing so much as compromise had taught him to respect worldly prudence and expediency a little more than he had in his inspired, self-confident youth. Perhaps he thought it a pity that he might not put himself on record entire without being forced in candor to hint experiences which were not to his credit. However, it was too late to live his life over, or to change the confessional character of his book. With all his faults, had he not learned more of life by living than the stoic and ascetic Emerson had discovered through contemplation? Nevertheless, he wrote Osgood that he would cancel some ten lines and half a dozen words and phrases, as in fact he had already done in earlier editions. But Stevens itemized more than eighty lines as the minimum of expurgation which would satisfy the law. This was too much mutilation for Whitman, whose book, it must be remembered, was his other self, and he rejected the proposition. He would not, as a compromise, even consent to eliminate the two poems "A Woman Waits for Me" and "To a Common Prostitute." There were other poems which, in expression, were more offensive to popular taste, but these two were, as we have seen, too personal for him to destroy them without qualms. The outcome of the matter was that, without hard feeling on the part of Whitman or his publisher, the plates were turned over to the poet in lieu of royalties. With them Whitman at once issued a small edition himself, and then found in Rees Welsh and Company, of Philadelphia, a publisher who was eager to stand a prosecution for the advertising value it would have. No legal action ensued, however, and even in Boston the Postmaster received from Washington orders to revoke his order including "Leaves of Grass" from the mails. This was due to the effective protest of Whitman's friend Talcott Williams, a young journalist of Philadelphia. Yet the sales were better than ever, an edition of three thousand being sold in one day. The affair was the occasion of a partial reconciliation with O'Connor, who attacked Marston, Stevens and Osgood without mercy in the press, as he had attacked Harlan seventeen years before.

O'Connor's "The Good Gray Poet" again appeared in print, with a lengthy supplement, in a biography of Whitman published the next year, from the pen of Dr. Bucke. This latter disciple worshiped his hero with such abandon, like Burroughs praising "Leaves of Grass" as the "bible of democracy," that Whitman had to urge him to tone down many passages, and to include criticisms of an adverse nature in order to give it an air of fairness. As in the case of Burroughs's "Notes," Whitman had a hand in the manuscript himself, writing many pages and sometimes altering the shading of others. In sending the manuscript back to Bucke, he wrote, "The character you give me is not a true one in the main—I am by no means that benevolent, equable, good happy creature you portray, but let that pass—I have left it as you wrote." * Nevertheless the book is full of information, documents, testimonials which have ever since been of great value to biographers. Like the new edition of the "Leaves" it was more or less what Whitman would have the world think of him.

But Dr. Bucke's book announced his greatness in too posi-

---

* Quoted, without the cancellations, from the draft which Whitman retained.

tive a fashion to stimulate the demand for his "Leaves" or the "Specimen Days," also recently issued by David McKay, successor to Rees Welsh. As his health improved and as he won the public endorsement of more and more prominent Americans, he was able to sell prose articles and poems to the magazines, at good prices. For a time, in 1888, he was paid one hundred dollars a month for regular brief contributions to the New York *Herald,* later collected in "November Boughs." He continued his annual lectures on Lincoln which, though never popularly attended, were always the occasion of generous subscription from wealthy friends who wished thus to aid him. In 1885, at the suggestion of Mary Davis, his housekeeper (of whom we shall speak presently), Thomas Donaldson, a Philadelphia friend, invited such admirers of the poet as W. D. O'Connor, Horace Howard Furness, Talcott Williams, Charles Dudley Warner, Oliver Wendell Holmes, Richard Watson Gilder, Edwin Booth, and Mark Twain to subscribe ten dollars each for the purchase of a horse and buggy, now that Whitman was no longer able to get about on foot. A year or so later an attempt was made to obtain for Whitman an invalid pension from the Government, on the basis of his war service. The bill was favorably reported, but Whitman declined to approve the measure, declaring he had not served for pay. In 1887 his friends in Boston, at the suggestion of William Sloane Kennedy, sent him eight hundred dollars for the purpose of building him a cottage at Timber Creek. He was too feeble to make use of the gift in that way, however, and it was by agreement put to other uses. Still nearer the end of his life, Robert Ingersoll, being asked for a contribution for Whitman's nursing expenses, offered to deliver a benefit lecture—on "Liberty in Literature"—in Philadelphia. With the assistance of J. H. Johnston in making the arrangements, he did this, handing Whitman the proceeds, eight hundred sixtynine dollars. English friends were equally liberal. Even the newspapers were solicitous, the New York *Tribune* taking up a subscription for flowers to cheer his sickroom. But for all this, there was a time when Whitman was in dire poverty.

George Whitman, prospering in business, determined to retire to the country, and in 1884 he built a commodious house at Burlington, New Jersey, designing a special room for Walt. But Whitman was sure that he was coming into his own as a poet, and wished to remain in town where he might keep in touch with people and affairs, and where he might continue to receive the many pilgrims who made Camden their Mecca. Even the offer to build him a separate shanty at Burlington, where he might continue his life-long habits of irregularity without too great inconvenience to the household, did not persuade him. Moreover he had saved the profits of his Rees Welsh edition to buy a house of his own. Before he could do this his brother removed to the new house, and Whitman took a room in Camden. For some years, before he had a publisher, he had been a familiar figure in Camden and Philadelphia, moving slowly along with a basket filled with his books on his arm, selling them as he could. The sight was in itself enough to provoke pity. And pity it did incite in the breast of a certain Mrs. Mary Davis, whose occupation in life seemed to be that of pitying and caring for others. From her rented house not far from Stevens Street she had often seen Whitman pass, though she had never met him. One frosty morning in the following winter, however, Whitman came to her door, in need. She welcomed him to her neat and cheerful kitchen, laid breakfast before him and, charmed by his enthusiastic, hopeful child's heart, as she was touched by his need of a woman's care, she invited him to return. This he did, and gradually she took a more personal interest in him, mending his clothes, listening to his dreams of better days to come, nourishing him with excellent cooking. About this time Whitman bought for $1750 a little old two-story house in Mickle Street, Number 328 then, a Whitman museum at No. 330 now. Mr. George W. Childs, the Philadelphia philanthropist, lent him the five hundred dollars he needed to close this purchase. But when he moved in, it was to a bare hermitage indeed. A bed, a goods box to write on, a table on which stood an oil stove to warm his milk—that was all. Even heat was wanting. Quite impossible, such independence. And yet his first experiment, that of boarding with the former tenants in return for rent, was, because of incompatibility, still more impossible. But Whitman, the poetic pioneer, had the spirit and the training of the conquerors of the frontier. He would invite a visitor, no matter who, to dine with him in this scene of poverty, with no more apology than Francis Marion made for his diet of roasted potatoes. He was an old man, however, and ill, and such an abode obviously could not serve for long. Moreover, there was Mrs. Davis, paying rent and well supplied with furniture. Why not strike a bargain with her, by which she should share his house, and in return equip it with her furniture and board him? She would not listen to such a proposal when it was made, but Whitman, like most sentimentalists, had an eye to his own advantage in worldly matters, and he had persistency. And, though he may not have known it, Mrs. Davis had had no training in protecting herself from the demands of those who saw the tenderness of her heart. Moreover, though she knew nothing about Whitman's poetry, nor could, she was, like stronger men and women than she, attracted by the man himself. The young sea-captain she had secretly married had been drowned on his first voyage thereafter, the secrecy of their union preventing Mrs. Davis even from claiming his property, though other small legacies had given her enough to live on. Some years later Whitman gave her a ring, in token of his appreciation of her goodness to him. Did she place upon this a construction similar to that which had misled Mrs. Gilchrist? Those who do themselves injustice in too much Martha-like serving of others not infrequently find compensating desires gradually but unconsciously controlling their will; did Mrs. Davis, after tending Whitman faithfully as a wife could have done, and without a wife's standing or prerogatives, live in hope that he would finally marry her so as to leave her the property which began to increase toward his death? We do not know. But we do know that she felt that she was bearing more than her share of the expenses and the work of the household; and we know that, when Whitman's final will left her but five hundred dollars out of some six thousand in the bequest, not counting his title to the house, she sued the estate for five thousand more. That she had some law and some justice on her side is sufficiently indicated by the jury's award of five hundred dollars.

But that is to state the facts of the case too barely. We do not know the terms of the agreement except in a general way. We do not know, except from Mrs. Davis, that Whitman promised to share with her any increase in fortune he might have. We do know that she took him to care for when he was in great distress and that she cared for him, voluntarily, at the cost of her strength, her property, and her own prospects. With a certain dislike of financial responsibility, and a certain child-like willingness to accept services or gifts without inquiring whether the service he himself had rendered the world would benefit the particular donors, Whitman combined also a marked Dutch thriftiness which naturally increased with age. Not that he was penurious chiefly for himself. Every other month he paid the expenses of his imbecile brother Eddie, and he sent frequent sums to his sister in Vermont. Nevertheless only a sense of business responsibility can save from disaster such arrangements as his with Mrs. Davis. Furthermore, there are indications that Mrs. Davis's emotions, not to say her affections, were involved, which made it harder for both—either to continue or to break the arrangement when it appeared that they did not understand it in the same way. Whitman was, at first, looked upon in Camden by certain classes of the population as such a disreputable character, at least as the author of such an impossible book, that the village mind built up a kind of legend about him. It mattered little that he was on friendly terms with all classes of people. The children, for instance, would play on his cellar door under his window, in hope of catching the pennies which occasionally would drop therefrom. So Mrs. Davis was in a measure ostracized by their unconventional, though perfectly proper, arrangement. Naturally she subconsciously demanded compensation for that. One could wish that Whitman, who was generally so sensitive to the feelings of others, had taken the devotion of this woman less as a matter of course. He was appreciative, but a little aloof. Gradually he looked upon her as a "housekeeper and friend," but the friend only increased the value of the capable housekeeper. Or did Whitman use this method of protecting both his independence and Mrs. Davis's feelings? He was, after all, something of a bohemian in his habits. His own family had never been able to make him regular in his hours, his meals, his plans. It was too much to hope that a woman who did not control his heart, and was unable to enter into his intellectual life, would do so. But the difficulty of the whole matter lay in the fact that while Whitman's increasing fame brought him more money, more visitors and a greater sense of his importance, it brought Mrs. Davis more work, less authority in the house, and increased levies on her financial resources—for Whitman did not often' defray the increased expenses due to his many guests. Given the two characters, injustice of a sort was certain to follow from such a bargain; and yet, given the two characters as they were in that cheerless winter of 1884, that bargain was itself inevitable. The most serious weakness of Whitman's stoical philosophy lay in the fact that with him inevitability ended the matter. The irony of the story is appreciated only when it is known how many other homes were open, or had been open to Whitman. Shortly after the war a wealthy bachelor in New York had asked Whitman to share his apartments; a Philadelphia friend opened his home to him in these later years; Burroughs begged him to retire to Esopus at his expense; and the Johnstons, in New York, seeing him in his poverty in Mickle Street, urged him to live with them, where he could be cared for properly. And yet, with all the realistic details which Elizabeth Keller has so graphically pictured, and all the pathos, the last seven years of Whitman's life were perhaps the most picturesque, as if his nature had at once bared itself of superfluities the better to reveal its fundamental qualities, and at the same time had irresistibly called to its own. The very disorder in which he reigned was but a projection of one side of his mind, an old-age replica of the newspaper offices in which he had spent his youth.

The house was on a mean street, not far from the ferry, the railway depot, and the street car line, so that there was much noise; worse still, a guano factory nearby contaminated the air with its odors. Of none of these things, however, did Whitman complain. In his back yard was a grape vine, a pear tree, and the lilacs which he loved. Before his window stood a single shade tree under which he would sit on summer evenings. With Mrs. Davis's furniture and the accumulation of his own belongings, the house was crowded. Until too ill to descend the stairs, Whitman received callers in the front room on the first floor which was cluttered with unsold copies of early editions of his books. Dining-room and kitchen were one, but crowded only as a ship's cabin is crowded, neatly. His bed-room was upstairs, at the front, a large room, where, between two north windows, the poet would sit in an immense cane-seated chair draped with a wolfskin. On one side of the room stood an immense wooden bed, none too comfortable, and opposite it a sheet-iron stove. An ancient trunk and sundry boxes hoarded the manuscripts which are to-day so useful in tracing his literary history, as well as many personal relics—for while Whitman might give away such things, he could not destroy them. Everywhere else, as visitors have testified, was a litter of books, newspapers, manuscripts, printer's proofs, on the chairs, on the table, overflowing the waste-baskets, covering the floor and even spreading out under the wash-stand and the bed. From this litter, Whitman seemed to be able to fish out with his cane almost anything that was wanted. The mantle was equally crowded with photographs of his friends, while paintings of his father and his mother, and another of the Indian chief Osceola, partly hid the cheap and ugly wall-paper. Here ruled Walt Whitman, until his last days never suffering the profanation of the broom. He had kept his independence when he had forsworn marriage in youth; now he was the victim of it.

He had been in the little house about a year when news came

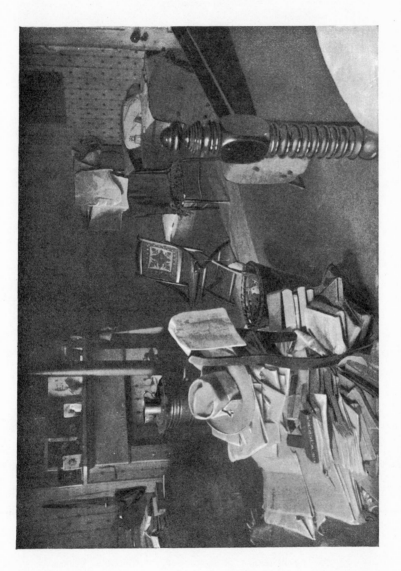

INTERIOR OF WHITMAN'S HOME IN MICKLE STREET, CAMDEN

Courtesy of Mr. Milton I. D. Einstein

of the death of Mrs. Gilchrist. Their correspondence since her return to England showed how constant was their friendship, how high their regard for each other. Whitman's last letter to her she never received, it being mailed eight days after her death; but to her son he wrote, on receipt of the shocking news:

"I have received your letter. Nothing now remains but a sweet and rich memory—none more beautiful all time, all life, all the earth—I cannot write anything of a letter to-day. I must sit alone and think."

But a little later he wrote the poem "Going Somewhere" as a memorial to her. The theme was immortality, concerning which he was thinking more and more. To Ingersoll, the agnostic, he said, concerning the after-life, "Well, Robert, I don't know —for anybody but *myself*. But for *myself*—I am as certain of it as I am that we are all here!" Through mystical ecstasy, he had sought union with the cosmos itself; and now he felt that he could perish no more than the Deity of whom he knew himself a part. Only a year or so before, at Cape May, he had written a poem as·suggestive of this union as any he had ever penned.

With husky-haughty lips, O sea!
Where day and night I wend thy surf-beat shore,
Imaging to myself thy varied strange suggestions,
(I see and plainly list thy talk and conference here,)
Thy troops of white-maned racers racing to the goal,
Thy ample, smiling face, dash'd with the sparkling dimples of the sun,
Thy brooding scowls and murk—thy unloos'd hurricanes,
Thy unsubduedness, caprices, wilfulness;
Great as thou art above the rest, thy many tears—a lack from all eternity
    in thy content,
(Nought but the greatest struggles, wrongs, defeats, could make thee
    greatest—no less could make thee,)
Thy lonely state—something thou ever seek'st and seek'st, yet never
    gain'st,
Surely some right withheld—some voice, in huge monotonous rage, of
    freedom-lover pent,

Some vast heart, like a planet's chain'd and chafing in those breakers,
By lengthen'd swell, and spasm, and panting breath,
And rhythmic rasping of thy sands and waves,
And serpent hiss, and savage peals of laughter,
And undertones of distant lion roar,
(Sounding, appealing to the sky's deaf ear—but now, rapport for once,
A phantom in the night thy confidant for once,)
The first and last confession of the globe,
Outsurging, muttering from thy soul's abysms,
The tale of cosmic elemental passion,
Thou tellest to a kindred soul.

It is no marvel that one who could feel such a kinship with Nature should be able to remind other men and women of their deeper selves. In his last years Whitman was to have not only the readers for whom he had waited so long, but personal friends who honored themselves in easing his last years and in cheering a home which otherwise must have been a prison. Burroughs and Bucke and Johnston and Rossetti remained faithful to him. To their ranks were added many younger men, in Boston, in Philadelphia, in England. At Bolton, England, was a group whose chief tie was a devotion to Whitman and his writings. In Philadelphia was Thomas B. Harned, a prosperous lawyer and a lover of literature, who not only entertained Whitman at his home when the latter was able to make the journey, but supplied him with delicacies and gave him professional assistance when needed. Talcott Williams and Francis Howard Williams, a poet and journalist, did much for Whitman through the local press. Horace Traubel, the most active of them all, had known Whitman ever since the days when as a boy he had lingered at the doorstep of the Stevens Street house to discuss with him the books he had been reading, impressed from the first less by his prophetic rôle than by his human attractiveness, "a large man, of generous nature, magnetic beyond speech." When Whitman moved to his "shack," as he called it, and before he had a housekeeper, Traubel would go by after office hours to assist him in preparing his meals, or to run on errands to the

printer. Only Boswell has shown such devotion, and Boswell's
devotion was not so practical or so independent. To one who
had given so long a proof of affection to the poet and his poetry
Whitman gratefuly entrusted many manuscripts, documents, con-
fidences. With Dr. Bucke and Harned, Traubel was to be Whitman's literary executor, and Whitman received the ardent young
disciple evening after evening for years, knowing that he would
make notes of their discussions, for use in a voluminous diary to
be published when the poet was gone. The subjects of these
conversations are too varied to be adequately gone into here.
They reveal nothing new in Whitman's character, of course, and
the light they shed on his influence belongs in a volume to which
I have referred as needing yet to be written, tracing that influence
in full. A list of others who came to Mickle Street and went
away happy, often to set down their impression of one of the
most striking men America has ever produced, is such as few
poets can match. Thomas Eakins, Herbert Gilchrist and Alexander came to paint him, as Waters and Charles Hine had done
before; Sidney Morse was busy for weeks in his back yard making a bust. Edmund Gosse and Bram Stoker, Ernest Rhys and
Justin McCarthy, Dr. Johnston of the Bolton group and Oscar
Wilde, Joaquin Miller and Sir Edwin Arnold all paid their respects. Sir Edwin surprised Whitman by offering to quote from
memory any one of Whitman's poems which the latter would
select. These names must suggest the quality of his influence
on those who had opportunity to judge of the man as well as of
his work. Not all thought that the work did complete justice
to the man; few thought the man inferior to what he had written.

In June, 1888, Whitman one day sent Mrs. Davis to summon
his horse and buggy from the livery stable, and after a long
drive, turned to the river to watch the setting sun. Lost in rev-
ery, he remained motionless till thoroughly chilled by the damps
of evening. This was the beginning of a new paralytic shock,
rendering him for the time speechless and putting an end to his
rides altogether. A wheel chair was substituted, but it was also

necessary for him to have a nurse, a man, to push it, and to care for him at home. Without consulting Whitman, Traubel and Harned organized a group of Whitman's admirers who regularly contributed to a fund for the expenses of this nurse, not desisting when his expected death was delayed four years. A will was made, as in Washington; but Whitman had both the determination to live and remarkable physical stamina. In that same year, indeed, he succeeded, with Traubel's assistance, in bringing out "November Boughs," a collection of prose and poetry which had already appeared in print. The next year saw a new edition of the "Leaves," with some alterations, the "November Boughs" poems appearing now as "Sands at Seventy," and with a preface-like essay, "A Backward Glance O'er Travell'd Roads," second in importance only to the preface to the First Edition.

On Christmas, 1890, in the evening, Whitman was visited by Thomas Donaldson. The poet spoke of the way he had spent the afternoon—in selecting a site for his tomb, the owners of Harleigh Cemetery having offered to present him with one.

"Well, cheerful occupation, eh?" replied Donaldson.

"Yes, yes," said Walt, "still we must get ready. But I am not going to die yet awhile," he added with a twinkle in his eye, "only getting the case ready for this old hulk. I am offered any location I like. I have picked out a bit of a hill, with a southern exposure, among the trees. I like to be with the trees. . . . Yes, I think I have selected a comfortable grave."

The tomb, though simple, was to be impressive as well as "comfortable." And Whitman was to have use for it as soon as it was completed. It was to be a family vault, to which the bodies of his parents and his brothers (Jeff had died a month before) were to be removed. It was massive granite, unhewn, blending into the side of the hill. But it was far more expensive than Whitman had been led to believe, and even the $2500 which he finally paid, plus a considerable sum which Harned quietly added, represented a reduction from the exorbitant demands whereby the unscrupulous builder sought to impose on the some-times simple old man. By a singular coincidence, the same charge of egotism which was provoked by his first edition was raised against his saving money, at times sorely needed, for this tomb. Even Mary Davis, who was willing to serve and to wait while he lived, and who seemed more broken-hearted than even his relatives when he died, thought that this money might with more justice have been willed to her. To her Whitman the poet meant little, and his significance to later generations still less.

In April of the next year Whitman was able to be wheeled over to Philadelphia to deliver his last tribute to Lincoln, though not without a great exertion. On his birthday his friends, feeling that it would be impossible for him to have a dinner at Reisser's Restaurant as on the previous year, brought in a caterer and made room for a banquet in his own home. The next day Whitman wrote Dr. John Johnston the following letter with the request that it be reproduced in facsimile and forwarded to those who had sent felicitations on his birthday the evening before.

"Well, here I am launched on my 73d year. We had our birth anniversary spree last even'g. Ab't 40 people—choice friends mostly—twelve or so women. Tennyson sent a short and sweet letter over his own sign manual. Y'r cable was rec'd & read. Lots of bits of speeches with gems in them. We had a capital supper, (or dinner,)—chicken soup, salmon, roast lamb, &c., &c., &c. I had been under a horrible spell f'm 5 to 6, but Warry got me dress'd & down—(like carrying down a great log)—& Traubel had all ready for me a big goblet of first-rate iced champagne—I suppose I swigged it off at once. I certainly welcom'd them all forthwith & at once felt if I was to go down I would not fail without a desperate struggle. Must have drunk near two bottles of champagne the even'g. So I added (I felt to) a few words of honor & reverence for our Emerson, Bryant, Longfellow dead—and then for Whittier & Tennyson, the boss of us all (specifying all)——not four minutes altogether —then held out with them *for three hours,* talking lots, lots impromptu. Dr. B. is here. Horace T. is married. Fine sunny noon."

In December he was bedfast, with pneumonia. Dr. Bucke came down from London and arranged for a trained nurse to care for the patient. The physicians who attended him, at various times, Drs. Longacre, Osler, and McAlester, not to mention Dr. Bucke, never presented bills for their services. Though Whitman was suffering from pneumonia, pleurisy, tuberculosis and other ailments, he did not die at once, as even the physicians expected. But he knew that he would not get well. In fact, he had known for a year that his end, and the end of his singing, was approaching. In March he had brought out a little book, to say farewell to his Muse. It was without any fire of inspiration, but showed him unflinching in his desire and determination to put his entire life into his book. And now, incorporating these old-age poems in a second annex, he would bring out a final edition of the "Leaves of Grass." Traubel had to superintend much of the work. Even so, it appeared that the book would have to be posthumously published. But the printer was urged to rush the binding of a limited number of copies, that the dying poet might send them as a farewell gift to his many friends. The "deathbed edition" this was called. As the end drew near, he felt neither fear nor reluctance to go. Nor did he even lose his quiet sense of humor. "Well, doctors, what is the verdict?" he would ask, adding by way of explanation for the question, "It would be a satisfaction to know how the cat is going to jump." On March 26th he passed away, to join his Fancy.

Good-bye my Fancy!
Farewell dear mate, dear love!
I'm going away, I know not where,
Or to what fortune, or whether I may ever see you again,
So Good-bye my Fancy.
Now for my last—let me look back a moment;
The slower fainter ticking of the clock is in me,
Exit, nightfall, and soon the heart-thud stopping.

Long have we lived, joy'd, caress'd together;
Delightful!—now separation—Good-bye my Fancy.

Yet let me not be too hasty,

Long indeed have we lived, slept, filter'd, become really blended into one;

Then if we die together, (yes, we'll remain one,)

If we go anywhere we'll go together to meet what happens,

May-be we'll be better off and blither, and learn something,

May-be it is yourself now really ushering me to the true songs, (who knows?)

May-be it is you the mortal knob really undoing, turning—so now finally,

Good-bye—and hail! my Fancy.

LIST OF WHITMAN'S MORE IMPORTANT VOLUMES

1855   Leaves of Grass, Brooklyn. First Edition.
1856   Leaves of Grass, Brooklyn.
1860   Leaves of Grass, Boston.
1865   Walt Whitman's Drum-Taps, New York.
1867   Leaves of Grass, New York.
1871   Leaves of Grass, Washington.
1871   After All Not To Create Only, Boston.
1871   Democratic Vistas, Washington.
1871   Passage to India, Washington.
1872   As a Strong Bird on Pinions Free and Other Poems, Washington.
1875   Memoranda During the War, Camden, N. J.
1876   Leaves of Grass, Camden, N. J.
1876   Two Rivulets, Camden, N. J.
1881–2   Leaves of Grass, Boston.
1881   Leaves of Grass, London.
1881   Leaves of Grass, London.
1882   Leaves of Grass, Philadelphia.
1882–3   Specimen Days and Collect, Philadelphia.
1884   Leaves of Grass, Glasgow.
1887   Specimen Days in America, London.
1888   November Boughs, Philadelphia.
1888   Democratic Vistas, and Other Papers, London.
1888   Complete Poems and Prose of Walt Whitman, 1855–1888, Camden, N. J.
1889   Leaves of Grass, Camden, N. J.
1891–2   Leaves of Grass, Philadelphia.
1891   Good-Bye, My Fancy, Philadelphia.
1892   Complete Prose Works, Philadelphia.
1897   Leaves of Grass, Boston.
1897   Calamus, Boston.
1898   Complete Prose Works, Boston.
1898   The Wound Dresser, Boston.
1899   Notes and Fragments, London (Canada).

1900 Leaves of Grass, Philadelphia.

1902 The Complete Writings of Walt Whitman, ten vols., New York and London.

1904 An American Primer, Boston.

1904 Walt Whitman's Diary in Canada, Boston.

1908 Leaves of Grass, New York.

1908 Complete Prose Works, New York.

1913 Criticism: An Essay, Newark, N. J.

1914 Leaves of Grass, New York.

1914 Leaves of Grass, New York.

1917 Leaves of Grass, Garden City, N. Y.

1919 Leaves of Grass, Portland, Me. Facsimile First Edition.

1920 The Gathering of the Forces, 2 vols., New York and London.

1921 The Uncollected Poetry and Prose of Walt Whitman, 2 vols., Garden City and Toronto.

1924 Leaves of Grass, Garden City. Inclusive Edition.

1926 Leaves of Grass; Abridged Edition with Prose Selections, Garden City, N. Y.

INDEX

INDEX